THE UNDEAD MOTHER

Psychoanalytic explorations of masculinity, femininity, and matricide

BY

Christina Wieland

KARNAC

LONDON   **NEW YORK**

First published in 2000 by
Rebus Press

Reprinted 2002 by
H. Karnac (Books) Ltd.
6 Pembroke Buildings
London NW10 6RE

Chapter 9 of this book first appeared as 'Beauty and the Beast: the father's unconscious and the riddle of femininity', in *The British Journal of Psychotherapy,* Vol. 8, No. 2.
Chapter 10 was first published as 'The good-enough mother and the use of the object in women', in *Winnicott Studies,* no. 9

ISBN: 1 85575 913 6

www.karnacbooks.com

Printed and bound by Antony Rowe Ltd, Eastbourne

To my parents

And what is now becoming apparent in the most everyday things and in the whole of our society and our culture is that, at a primal level, they function on the basis of matricide.

—Luce Irigaray, 'The Bodily Encounter with the Mother' (Irigaray 1991: 36)

ACKNOWLEDGMENTS

Many thanks to Karl Figlio, who read and commented on the manuscript of this book, over many years, and whose insightful and encouraging comments made this book possible; to Duncan Barford, my editor, for his constructive criticism, and for his detailed and thorough editing of the manuscript; to Kirsty Hall, my publisher, for her courteous and unobtrusive help; to my family, for their support and patience during the long period of gestation; to my students and trainees, for all the helpful discussions I have had with them; and to all my patients.

A NOTE ON TEXTS

Quotations and references to Freud are given according to the *Standard Edition of the Complete Psychological Works of Sigmund Freud*. 24 Vols. Translated and edited by James Strachey in collaboration with Anna Freud, assisted by Alix Strachey and Alan Tyson. London: The Hogarth Press and the Institute of Psycho-Analysis; New York: Norton, 1953-1974.

CONTENTS

Introduction

Look there! See him! See him at last!
Watch every doorway, lest the murderer
Steal away and escape unpunished!
Once again he has found protection;
Closely clinging to the immortal
Goddess's image, that he offers
His life for trial, for the dead of his land.

No hope can rescue him.
A mother's blood once spilt
None can restore again. (Aeschylus 1986: 15)

This is a book about matricide, about matricide and separation from the mother, about matricide and gender, matricide and destructiveness. It began as an exploration of femininity but, as it became apparent to me that femininity can only be understood in relation to masculinity, an exploration into masculinity became necessary. This led me to look in detail at Freud's theory of the development of masculinity through the castration complex and the dissolution of the Oedipus complex, and to his theory of femininity as a deviation from this basic model. Thus the starting point of this book is classical Freudian theory seen and re-interpreted through myths, novels, fairy tales and clinical material. The understanding which emerges (always within Western culture) is of a masculine psychic structure that is founded on a psychic murder, the murder of the early mother, and the subsequent elevation of the father to custodian of the psyche. The feminine psyche emerges as a response to this masculine terror of the mother.

The complementarity of masculinity and femininity are taken for granted in this study. In other words, I see masculinity and femininity as constructed within the mind, as complementary opposites, and as mutual projections and phantasies which define themselves in relation to one another. Consequently, an understanding of masculinity is essential to an understanding of femininity. Nowhere is this clearer than in the father-daughter relationship which shapes the feminine unconscious. The formation of femininity within this relationship I view as the daughter's response to the father's masculine unconscious. As I see it, a collusion with masculine phantasies and anxieties is essential to the formation of femininity.

I believe that the strength of Freud's theory of gender identity is its portrayal of masculinity and femininity as mutual projection systems which adhere to the dichotomy between that which is 'intact' and that which is 'castrated': the boy's castration anxiety is projected onto the girl, who accepts it in exchange for love. This is my interpretation of Freud's description of the change of object—from mother to father—in women. How this relates to what I have called 'the murder of the mother' is the main theme of this book.

As I see it, the development of gender identity entails—basically—firstly a struggle to position oneself in relation to the mother, and—secondly—a struggle to position oneself in relation to the opposite sex. At the very heart of the development of gender identity lies the issue of separation from mother, in which father plays a crucial part. Separation from mother is the most fundamental problem of human development. Whether it is achieved, to what degree it is achieved, and the way in which it is achieved are important issues, not only in relation to the development of gender identity, but also in respect to the development of the individual as a whole. Indeed, the very constitution of the binary opposition 'masculine/feminine', within the psyche, begins with the boy's attempt to define himself as *different from* mother—that is, his attempt to *dis-identify* from mother (Greenson 1993). Dis-identification is part of the process of separation. It is the argument of this book that the boy's dis-identification and separation from mother is not a smooth and easy process but a violent affair that resembles matricide. The prototype of this is to be found in the Greek myth of the murder of Clytemnestra in *The Oresteia* (Aeschylus 1986). The Oresteian myth occupies a central place among the Greek myths and, together with the Oedipus myth, constitutes a complete psychological account of the development of the Greek masculine and modern Western unconscious.

For Julia Kristeva matricide and separation from mother are synonymous. In *Black Sun* she writes:

> For man and for woman the loss of the mother is a bio-logical and psychic necessity, the first step on the way to becoming autonomous. Matricide is our vital necessity, the sine-qua-non condition of our individuation... The lesser or greater violence of matricidal drive, depending on individuals and the milieus's tolerance, entails, when it is hindered, its inversion on the self; the maternal object having been introjected, the depressive or melancholic putting to death of the self is what follows, instead of mat-ricide. (Kristeva 1989: 27-8)

Kristeva assumes here that the only way a child can separate from mother is in a radical, violent and total manner which resembles a murder. The alternative, Kristeva says, is the black sun of depression and melancholia. Although I do not agree with Kristeva that this is the only means by which separation from mother can be achieved, I think, nevertheless, that this is the way Western culture has followed—a way which leads to an individual becoming fatally divided against himself and per-petually in terror of the powerful maternal 'murdered' object. This divided Western psyche has been described by Freud in his model of the unconscious and of the repression barrier. It is a model that describes an individual cut off from his roots and his origin—the model of an alienated individual. It is a psyche dominated by the super-ego whose task is to oversee the main-tenance of the repression barrier and, in so doing, to protect the psyche from persecution by the 'murdered' maternal object. This model is more suited—as Freud eventually found out—to describe the male rather than the female psyche. In this sense, matricide is a masculine rather than a feminine solution (although, as this book argues, woman uses man's matricidal psyche to achieve a species of separation from mother). That murder cannot lead to separation is obvious, since murder ties the murderer irrevocably to his victim. More than love or hate, it creates a persecutory *present* object, rather than an absent one. This possesses a hallucinatory, psychotic quality which must be thwarted if the murderer is to remain sane. The super-ego undertakes precisely this role, becoming the custodian of the psyche, yet at the same time imposing its own persecutory presence on the psyche.

I think that Freud came close to seeing the pathological nature of a whole culture whose individuals were characterised by a rigid repression barrier maintained by the operation of a harsh super-ego. His analysis of the super-ego in *Civilization and its Discontents* (1930) reveals the deathly quality of this agency, which has become—as he put it in a previous paper—'a pure culture of the death instinct' (Freud 1923b: 53). Although he sees the difficulty of speaking about a cultural or 'communal neurosis', he nevertheless thinks that this is not an entirely implausible approach. He writes:

> I would not say that an attempt of this kind to carry psychoanalysis over to the cultural community was absurd or doomed to be fruitless. But we should have to be very cautious and not forget that, after all, we are only dealing with analogies and that it is dangerous, not only with men but also with concepts, to tear them from the sphere in which they have originated and been evolved. Moreover, the diagnosis of communal neuroses is faced with special difficulty. In an individual neurosis we take as our starting point the contrast that distinguishes the patient from his environment, which is assumed to be 'normal'. For a group all of whose members are affected by one and the same disorder no such background could exist; it would have to be found elsewhere. And as regards the therapeutic application of our knowledge, what would be the use of the most correct analysis of social neuroses, since no one possesses authority to impose such therapy upon a group? But in spite of all these difficulties, we may expect that one day someone will venture to embark upon a pathology of cultural communities. (Freud 1930: 144)

The second half of the twentieth century has seen a spate of social and cultural psychoanalytic criticism. The catastrophic events of two world wars combined with the equally catastrophic influence Western culture has had on the ecology of the planet as a whole, have made this cultural 'self-analysis' both possible and necessary. This book concentrates on the psychic structure of the Western psyche, with special emphasis on gender and on matricide as a structural definition of gender.

But what has Freud's model to do with the contemporary Western individual and why is a book like this relevant today? After all, the changes that are taking place today seem to have created an individual that is, in some way, and quite deliberately, the inverse of the Freudian individual. The possession of woman—wife or daughter—by the father is a thing of the past. Far from having a rigid family structure we seem to be witnessing the gradual disappearance not only of paternal authority but of any definite family structure. Where the Freudian individual had a strong and rigid super-ego, the contemporary individual seems to lack a super-ego altogether. Whereas the Freudian individual was characterised by a rigid repression barrier, was self-possessed and self-controlled and had a persecutory sense of guilt, the contemporary individual seems to lack self-control, embraces the pleasure principle, and questions all boundaries and all limitations imposed by gender, age, or the human condition in general. So why is a book that takes Freud's theory of the dissolution of the Oedipus complex as its starting point relevant at all? My answer to this question is rather simple. I think that what we are experiencing today is not only progress and liberation from repressive paternal/male authority but also—and in a way that throws us into confusion and a state of terror—a 'return of the repressed'. An understanding of the dynamics of this repressed world is therefore absolutely necessary if we are to avoid a repetition of the past.

This book argues that matricide has been the Western, culturally sanctioned means by which separation from mother has been achieved. However—I shall argue—this does not lead to a genuine separation from mother or to the establishment of a parental couple within the psyche, but to a rigidly divided psyche where persecution reigns. The price of this has proved very high—for the individual, for the culture, and especially for women. As a new century begins, we take stock of the unprecedented destructiveness unleashed on the planet and on fellow human beings by the West. As the paternal super-ego is slowly eroded we are left with the ghosts and the furies, searching for a new way ahead.

Chapter 1

Clytemnestra and Count Dracula

Yet each man kills the thing he loves,
By each let this be heard,
Some do it with a bitter look,
Some with a flattering word.
The coward does it with a kiss,
The brave man with a sword! (Oscar Wilde 1949)

Mark the truth of what I say
The mother is not the true parent of the child
Which is called hers. She is a nurse who tends the growth
Of young seed planted by his true parent, the male.
So, if Fate spares the child, she keeps it, as one might
Keep for some friend a growing plant. And of this truth,
That father without mother may beget, we have
Present, as proof, the daughter of Olympian Zeus :
One never nursed in the dark cradle of the womb;
Yet such a being no god will beget again. (Aeschylus 1986:
169-170)

He is experimenting and doing it well; and if it had not
been that we have crossed his path he would be yet—he
may be yet if we fail—that father or furtherer of a new
order of beings, whose road must lead through Death, not
Life. (Bram Stoker 1983: 389)

Few deaths have been mourned with greater intensity or a
greater exhibition of public grief than that of Diana, Princess of
Wales.
Britain and the world was taken by surprise as the queues of
mourners grew longer, and the number of visitors mounted into
millions. As the sea of flowers which flooded the area transformed Kensington Palace into a shrine and the visitors into pil-

grims, there was no doubt in anyone's mind that something extraordinary was taking place.

This was, undoubtedly, an exhibition of mass hysteria, feeding on itself and perpetuated through the media. Yet the grief was genuine, and the sadness that gripped even extremely rational individuals was extraordinary. This public exhibition of mourning and guilt, this insistence that 'we are all guilty' for Diana's death exposed two deficits in contemporary Western culture which have been extremely influential in forming its character: its lack of a female ideal and its inability to mourn. The two, I maintain, are not unrelated.

A state of mourning is something that the late twentieth century has been uniquely unable to achieve. A culture based on the interchangeability of products and people, a throw-away culture, is not conducive to mourning. The few voices of dissent are easily drowned by the torrent of products designed to satisfy the voracious appetite for more, newer and slicker goods, technological miracles, or human 'images'. Inanimate objects have replaced human ideals. A culture of 'virtual reality' which finds it difficult to distinguish between the living and the inanimate has been created—a culture of the undead. This culture is grounded not in human relationships, but in the destruction of them.

I think that the mourning for Diana, brief as it was, has, nevertheless, exposed the deep yearning for something very fundamental which is missing in Western culture, the lack of which is transforming life into virtual reality. Although the public has pretty quickly returned to its usual greediness to see and hear and possess more and more of Diana, and although the demand for a part of her life and soul seems as insatiable as ever, this brief and intense interval of mourning and guilt cannot be easily written off. I think that this brief interval of grief and mourning revealed the intense yearning for a representation of a female ideal, as well as guilt for the denigration or killing of this ideal. In the absence of a female ideal an 'icon' comes to fill the gap. With her death the cult of Diana moved, I think, from an icon to an ideal, but then back again to an icon.

The female ideal belongs to that area of the psyche which also pertains to the mother-child relationship. The fundamental attacks made by Western culture upon this area are revealed in the deep unreality which is slowly tightening its grip on the Western individual. Within this relationship lie our origins as human individuals—not simply our origins as biological beings. An attack on this relationship, then, is an attack on our humanity, in all its aspects.

In this respect Christianity presented an interesting compromise to the dilemma which confronts us, by attempting to represent the mother-child relationship *alongside* our incarnated and relationship-based humanity. It also lay tremendous importance on mourning. These aspects of Christianity are in stark opposition to classical Greek philosophy and its split between mind and body, first introduced by Plato. This split, however, eventually prevailed in Christianity as well, which remained largely unaffected by the full significance of Christ's incarnation. Neither did the endless representations of Madonna and child influence the dominant creed that both child and mother ultimately belong to father.

The yearning for a female ideal, the mourning of Diana, was one way in which the Western individual attempted to escape the vampirism that has gripped Western culture as a whole. Yet, inevitably, the vampirism has returned with a vengeance, as more and more books, tapes and photographs of Diana are greedily consumed by the very same people who demonstrated real remorse for her death and shed genuine tears as they mourned.

What I call the 'culture of un-death' is portrayed by the fascination of the twentieth century with non-human, semi-human, or humanoid creatures which defy the laws of nature, the laws of birth and death. Two figures in particular, both creations of nineteenth century literature, have seized the imagination of the twentieth Century: Dr. Frankenstein's monster and Count Dracula. Side by side they represent the hidden terror of a culture based on science and rationality which denies its origins in the flesh.

These two figures continue to fascinate, especially through their numerous cinematic versions and their derivatives, haunting us like waking nightmares. The man-made monster and the undead, blood-sucking vampire are at once terrible and uncanny, yet also strangely familiar.

In his essay 'The "Uncanny"' (1919a) Freud analyses the German word *'unheimlich'* (translated into English as 'uncanny') which has its root in *'Heim'*—or 'home'. Freud concludes, therefore, that the uncanny is something which is, in fact, very familiar, but from which we are separated, or which we have split off or repressed. He includes—among many other examples of uncanny phenomena—the fear of death, of the dead, and of spirits, and maintains that all these fears are due to the survival of the old belief that the 'dead man becomes the enemy of his survivor and seeks to carry him off to share his new life with him' (Freud 1919a: 242). With Kleinian theory in mind, I would add that the uncanny is also something we once treasured, and then attacked and destroyed, and from which we are now in terror of retaliation, despite its familiarity to us. In its most negative, terrifying form the uncanny has more in common with Fairbairn's notion of the release or return of the bad object (Fairbairn 1943), as witnessed in cases of demoniacal possession.

In *Dracula* the unholy triad of death, sexuality, and oral greed, reveals its origins in the passions of childhood. It is not difficult to recognise here an early, persecutory, desired and devouring mother—a fascinating and dreaded figure who undermines our efforts to live as ordinary decent human beings who do not need to feed on human blood, yet a figure of whom we cannot rid ourselves, because she is so much part of ourselves, a creation of our fears and greedy loves, the projection of our frustrated, murderous impulses.

We might say that in the vampire a separation between self and object has not been securely established, and a confusion of the two continues. Psychoanalysis teaches us that only through mourning can such a separation take place—a mourning which is a necessary part of the development of the individual. Mourning for the lost object establishes both separateness and reality, and ensures the introjection of the object into the self so that the object becomes assimilated into and enriches the self. In contrast, an unmourned object remains unassimilated and is experienced as a persecutor. I would add that an unmourned object is experienced not only as a dead object, but as a *murdered* object. This is due to the way in which a traumatic event experienced passively is transformed by the subject into an event *caused by* the subject—or, in Freud's words, by 'repeating... passive experiences in an active form' (Freud 1931: 236).

Freud's ideas on mourning were based on a model in which an object could only be given up if in some sense it became part of the subject's self (Freud 1917, 1923b). The processes by which this was brought about Freud described as 'internalisation' and 'identification'. Freud saw separation from the object, loss of the object, and internalisation of the object as inextricably linked. The development of the ego and of the self therefore depends upon the object, but is not confused with it. In this, the quality of the relationship to the object and—therefore—the quality of the identification is crucial.

Melanie Klein developed the theme of identification further. Whereas Freud stressed *introjection* in relation to identification, Klein stressed *projection*. By shifting the emphasis from introjection to projection she introduced the concept of 'projective identification'—a process whereby the subject projects part of himself *into* an object, with the intention of either taking over the object or getting rid of unwanted parts of the self. In this way the subject becomes inextricably tied to the object, with the result that he himself feels depleted and empty. With this concept Klein opened up the understanding of a range of phenomena in which confusion between self and object occurs.

In a masterful paper entitled 'On Identification' (1955) she analyses a novel by a French writer, Julian Green, entitled *If I Were You*. In this story a young man, Fabian Especel, discontented with himself and his lot, enters into a pact with the Devil who gives him a secret formula with a magical power which enables him to enter into other people's bodies and become them. Fabian goes through several transformations becoming, successively, 'Fabian-Pujars', 'Fabian-Esmerard', 'Fabian-Fruges' and—finally—'Fabian-Camille', by entering the bodies of these people and taking over their personalities. With each transformation Fabian becomes more and more alienated from himself, and feels more and more confused about who he is. He also feels a strong resentment towards the person into whom he has transformed himself. Eventually, however, he begins to remember vaguely who he is and attempts to return home, where the body of Fabian himself lies unconscious, looked after by his mother. As he approaches the house—as Fabian-Camille—and walks up the stairs, Fabian gets restless, wakes up and goes to the door. Fabian-Camille calls out his name, whispers the secret formula to him through the keyhole, and goes away. Fabian is found by his mother lying unconscious by the door. He attempts to remember what happened over the last three days during which—ostensibly—he lay unconscious, but he fails. A change in his formerly discontented personality is brought about—however—by the way in which he suddenly gains access to his love for his mother. As Klein puts it:

> With his mother sitting by his bedside he is overcome by the longing to be loved by her and to be able to express his love for her. He wishes to touch her hand, to throw himself into her arms, but feels that she would not respond. In spite of this he realises that if his love for her had been stronger she would have loved him more. The intense affection which he experiences towards her extends suddenly to the whole of humanity and he feels overflowing with an unaccountable happiness. His mother suggests that he should pray, but he can only recall the words 'Our Father'. Then he is again overcome by his mysterious happiness, and dies. (Klein 1955: 151)

Disowning parts of the self, and projecting parts of the self into other people, is the main mechanism of projective identification. The consequences can vary, ranging from persecutory feelings, to feelings of alienation, emptiness, unreality, deadness, narcissistic omnipotence, denial of separateness, or denial of envy. The confusion between self and other, or between subject and object, can be seen as an attack on the self, or as an attack on the object, or as an attack on the *relationship* between them. It is no coincidence that the end of Fabian's colonisation of other people implies a return to his relationship with an external object—his mother—and an evocation of his good, internal father. His re-discovery of his mother as an external object puts an end to the endless projection of parts of himself, and the confusion between himself and other people.

It seems that, for Fabian, separation between subject and object had not taken place, and that the ability to mourn the loss of the object had not developed. If integration of the self and separation from the object have not occurred, then any relationship between subject and object takes the form of a projective identification, of a mutual devouring or a take-over of the object.

The twentieth century has been replete with uncanny, fictional figures that 'invade' or 'take over' human beings in just this way, threatening our survival and 'humanity'. The vampire, the alien, the zombie are all creatures that proliferate themselves by contamination—that is, the person attacked is not killed but is instead transformed into 'one of them'. The victim becomes a new aggressor as his humanity disappears. In all these phantasies we can trace the work of projective identification. An object is attacked and—as an 'object'—it is eradicated. Instead, it becomes part of the self, part of the same.

Count Dracula, more than any other figure of this type, operates through a kind of physical contact which is a parody of love and sexuality, and which creates a chain of contamination and addiction. In his blood-thirsty greediness he displays similarities with other persecutory figures from antiquity, which seek revenge at all costs. Dracula is not unlike the Furies who persecuted Orestes after the murder of his mother Clytemnestra. This provides us with a clue to the ghostly quality of Dracula, and the fascination he has exerted on millions of people. It is as if a murder has taken place, a psychic murder for which no mourning has been possible. A murder, unlike a death, cannot be mourned, for the good self that *could* mourn is lost together with the dead object. The corpse, buried or unburied, rises again and again just at the moment when the perpetrator thinks he has got rid of it, reminding him that it is part of himself. A process of continuous projective identification is established between the murderer and his victim, whereby confusion and persecution follow each other.

To reiterate, what I am suggesting here is that an unmourned lost object reappears not just as a dead object, but as a *murdered* object. To understand this more fully, one must also comprehend the reason for the inability to mourn. The inability to mourn inevitably reveals—I believe—immense ambivalence and hostility towards the object. These feelings are experienced as attacking and murderous towards the object, and thus prevent separation from it.

This inability of the perpetrator to rid himself of his victim, and the transformation of the victim into a new aggressor, is not unlike Fairbairn's view that the individual is devoted to the bad objects in his psyche. In relation to this Fairbairn writes:

> At this point it is worth considering whence bad objects derive their power over the individual. If the child's objects are bad, how does he ever come to internalise them? Why does he not simply reject them as he might reject 'bad' cornflour pudding or 'bad' castor oil? As a matter of fact, the child usually experiences some considerable difficulty in rejecting castor oil, as some of us may know from personal experience. He would reject it if he could; but he is allowed no opportunity to do so. The same applies to his bad objects. However much he may want to reject them, he cannot get away from them. They force themselves upon him; …the child not only internalises his bad objects because they force themselves upon him and he seeks to control them, but also, and above all, because he *needs* them… It is above all the need of the child for his parents, however bad they may appear to him, that compels him to internalise bad objects, and it is because this need remains attached to them in the unconscious that he cannot bring himself to part with

them. It is also his need for them that confers upon them their actual power over him. (Fairbairn 1943: 67-8)

When Fairbairn describes the endopsychic world as one in which parts of the self and parts of a bad object are linked inextricably together, to me he is describing a situation of projective identification as an intrapsychic situation. Fairbairn sees this endopsychic situation arising from the internalisation of the bad object—the bad aspects of the mother, the frustrating or absent mother. It is because the child wants to preserve the external mother as good that the bad mother is split off and internalised.

Although Fairbairn, like Freud, stresses introjection rather than projection, what is introjected—however—is a 'bad' object which is *part of the projection* of the child's own frustration, greed and aggression. In this sense projective and introjective identification work simultaneously, as—indeed—is confirmed in the imagery of Count Dracula.

Fairbairn's re-interpretation of Freud's paper 'A Seventeenth-Century Demonological Neurosis' (1923a) is especially interesting for the way it reveals an attachment to a bad (I would say 'murdered') object, which in turn exposes the process of projective identification at work. Freud's original paper concerns Christoph Haizmann, an artist who—as Fairbairn puts it—'made a pact with the Devil while in a melancholic state precipitated by the death of his father' (Fairbairn 1943: 71). Fairbairn agrees with Freud that the Devil is nobody else but the artist's dead father. What Fairbairn also observes here, however, is the attachment to this bad father/Devil and Haizmann's unwillingness to let go of him.[1]

This addiction—or, as Fairbairn calls it, 'devotion'—to a bad object reveals, I think, the work of projective identification with an internal figure. What interests me here, however, is the way Fairbairn interprets the 'cure' of Christoph Haizmann. He writes :

It is interesting to note too that Christoph's symptoms were only relieved when he invoked the aid of a good object and was rewarded by a return of the unholy pact, which he received, torn to pieces, from the hands of the Blessed Virgin in the chapel of Mariazell. He did not achieve freedom from relapses, however, until he had been received into a religious brotherhood and had thus replaced his pact with the Devil by solemn vows to the service of God. This was presumably a triumph of the moral defence. (Fairbairn 1943: 71)

For Fairbairn, the 'moral defence' is the super-ego whose role he envisages as the defence of the individual against his bad objects. He distinguishes between two kinds of badness, 'conditional' and 'unconditional'. 'It is preferable', Fairbairn writes, 'to be conditionally bad than unconditionally bad' (Fairbairn 1943: 66). In this sense, a melancholic who clings to the accusations of the super-ego is actually defending himself against a much more psychotic attack from the bad, primitive objects in his unconscious. In other words, a paternal super-ego—or a paternal idealised imago, because I think we must differentiate between the two—can also be defending against a maternal primitive bad object.

If we now turn to the work of Wilfred Bion, we can see that—in some ways—he views the bad object in a highly similar manner to Fairbairn, as an 'absent' object. For Bion, two alternative routes open up as a result of the absence of an object: either the no-object becomes a *bad present object*; or it becomes a *thought*. In other words, Bion suggests that absence is a concept which is incomprehensible to the mind. Consequently the lost object becomes either a bad present object, or a thought which *represents* the object. The difference between these two routes is of tremendous importance for the development of the individual. The second leads to the development of thinking and emotional integration. The first leads to an arrest of development, and to endless projective identification

For Bion the main factor here is toleration of frustration. If evasion of frustration predominates, then no thinking will take the place of the absent object. Instead a bad object is introjected. The bad object is synonymous with what Bion called 'beta elements', which cannot be 'digested' by the mind and therefore cannot be used for thinking. Instead, they can only be endlessly re-projected. Bion saw in this splitting and projection the roots of fragmentation and psychosis, as well as of less disturbed phenomena.

However, Bion also viewed projective identification as a basic tool of communication between mother and baby. In his paper 'Attacks on Linking' he writes :

> I shall suppose that there is a normal degree of projective identification, without defining the limits within which normality lies, and that associated with introjective identification this is the foundation on which normal development rests. (Bion 1967: 103)

In this *normal* type of projective identification the baby projects unmanageable feelings into the mother, thus evoking certain feelings in her. The mother, under optimal conditions, processes these feelings and gives them back to the baby in a form he can digest and use:

> Normal development follows if the relationship between infant and breast permits the infant to project a feeling, say, that it is dying into the mother and to reintroject it after its sojourn in the breast has made it tolerable to the infant psyche. If the projection is not accepted by the mother the infant feels that its feeling that it is dying is stripped of such meaning as it has. It therefore reintrojects, not a fear of dying made tolerable but a nameless dread. (Bion 1967: 116)

Nameless dread can be considered a bad object which cannot be assimilated into the psyche, and thus which has to be projected and re-projected. At the other end of the spectrum, if mother gives back to the baby an understanding of its feelings, this experience of being understood can be stored and can lead to the creation of what Bion called 'alpha function', which leads to the development of thinking. This interaction between 'container and contained'—as he eventually called it—is the fundamental process through which we develop both emotionally and intellectually. The inextricable link between emotional and intellectual development is one of the most important contributions made by psychoanalysis. It not only allows us to understand human development but—as I shall argue in more detail—it also allows us to examine the consequences of a culture which has attempted to separate the two and which, in a similar way, has also attempted to separate mother from father and mother from child, in order to create the illusion of an autonomous, 'separate' individual.

What Bion stresses, then, is not the subject, or the object, but the *relationship* between them. In this dynamic link between subject and object lies life, creativity, and the ability to learn from experience and from other people. Bion does not refer directly to 'mourning', but to the emergence of thought out of the lost/absent object. This points, I think, to something akin to mourning—a realisation, a thought, that the object is not there. This realisation of an absent object is different from both hallucination and omnipotent thinking, in which there is an overt denial of loss.

* * *

I shall now attempt to pull together some of the threads we have gathered so far.

A traumatic loss is one in which the experience of helplessness invades the individual and outstrips his ability to assimilate it or to transform it into a 'thought' or a symbol. Instead the lost object is transformed into a *bad present object*, with which the individual is projectively identified. Consequently, the bad present object is experienced both as part of the self and as a foreign body. The present bad object has to be murdered, annihilated, or endlessly projected—yet, in each of these 'solutions' the object refuses to die because it is never mourned. Additionally, if the object is never mourned then the subject cannot acquire a capacity for mourning, or for thinking. An endless vicious circle develops, in which projective identification becomes the dominant mode of operating.

My main interest in all this is in the traumatic manner in which the loss of the Oedipal object—mainly the mother—takes place, and how this particular trauma, which Freud delineated in his paper 'The Dissolution of the Oedipus Complex' (1924), establishes a bad 'murdered' object in the place of the lost object. The boy feels that he must attack this bad object again and again, in an attempt to rid himself of it. This projectively identified, bad/murdered object leads to fears of invasion, contamination, pollution, asphyxiation, and other primitive persecutory fears, or—sometimes—to a deadening of all life and all relationships. Ways in which the bad object may take over part—or the whole—of the psyche vary. This may entail an identification with the dead object, according to the model of Count Dracula, in an oral, addictive solution to the problem. A psychopathic solution is another alternative, perhaps according to the model of a Hitler, a Stalin, or a serial killer. Yet another means is the immersion of oneself in a world of inanimate objects, manufactured goods, and machines of all kinds which cannot be loved or killed.

The myths of Orestes and Oedipus are founding myths which portray the development of the Western masculine unconscious. The dilemma expressed in these myths demands one of two outcomes: either matricide or parricide. It is as if separation from the parents cannot be conceived other than in terms of a psychic murder—either the murder of the mother or the father. The two myths make it obvious that the murder of the mother is the culturally sanctioned solution. For instance, Oedipus' murder of his father is followed by personal and social catastrophe. The murder of Clytemnestra—on the other hand—is ordered and sanctioned by the Gods, and exonerated by the Athenian court. *The Oresteia* ends with the creation of a new social and psychic equilibrium, arrived at via matricide and the paternal super-ego.

It is important to appreciate the exact nature of this new equilibrium; it entails not only the murder of the mother, but also—more importantly—the exoneration of Orestes by the paternal gods. This intervention of the father is very important, because it leads at the same time to the formation of the super-ego and of masculinity.

Although this book is about both female and male development, I have concentrated on the male child in Western culture because there is no feminine solution within Western culture which is not simply a mirror-image of the male. Freud's account of feminine development is, I think, the woman's/daughter's acceptance of the male's horrific projections upon her of a persecutory mother figure, and her attempts to pacify these projections by accepting—as Freud put it—her 'castration'. This is not a sacrifice on her part, however, because it suits her own hate and fear of her mother, and her own desperate attempts to separate from her. Nevertheless, this 'masculine' solution can never be completed in women because, as Freud pointed out, woman remains split between attachment to mother and father, and also between identification with mother and father. In other words, both the phantasy of matricide and the solution to it (that is, the super-ego) are primarily masculine formations to which woman responds by embracing a passive/melancholic identity in which she attacks the very object with which she identifies—her mother.

In *The Oresteia* this 'masculine' solution is adhered to by Electra and by Athene, who both maintain a paternal identification and uphold the murder of the mother. This paternal identification helps woman to separate from mother, but at the expense of a good relationship to the maternal object. There are other, alternative solutions which the woman sometimes adopts, but these involve a denial of the father, or a total submission to him and a denial of mother. (These will be explored in Chapter 6.)

The Oresteia represents the 'hidden version' of the Oedipus complex and its dissolution. The Western psyche, following in the footsteps of Orestes' murder of his mother, and the espousal of a paternal super-ego defence, has merely tolerated the co-existence of a female goddess. This maternal good object—in the person of the Virgin—has proved essential to maintaining a balance in the masculine psyche. However, the female goddess is allowed to exist on condition that she inhabits a lower level of divinity, and is stripped of her sexual and generative power. With the advent of Protestantism, and the consequent death of Mary, this precarious balance has been seriously disturbed, opening the gates for yet more persecution within the psyche.

Although the 'emancipation of woman' has been a particularly Western phenomenon, it has been achieved only on condition that the woman accepts the 'murder of the mother' and joins in a masculine culture. This 'emancipation' of woman in Western culture, then, should not obscure the fact that it is the 'masculine' psyche—based on the murder of the mother—which prevails in both men and women, and which is manifested in the strong anti-life trend evident in Western culture. Again, then, we are confronted with the unique fascination that Count Dracula exerts on this avowedly rational and scientific culture, as if he were a reminder of the ways in which we attempt to create an alternative world which 'does not lead through life'—in the words of the quotation at the head of this chapter—'but through death'. This world which 'does not lead through life' is a manufactured, undead world where omnipotence reigns unfettered.

The loss of paternal authority and the decline of the super-ego, which have become progressively more manifest during the twentieth century, have opened the gates for the return of the bad object. Fascism has been one way in which Western culture attempted to regain paternal authority. Colonialism was another, projected form. As the last vestiges of fascism and colonialism are dying out in Europe, technology is posing itself as the solution to all problems—the new, caring parent; the new, amoral super-ego which provides all the answers through the construction of virtual reality, free from the traditional constraints of biological necessity and our rootedness in parental relationships. However, the destruction of the parents and of the super-ego signals new terrors, leaving us—as we have seen—at the mercy of the aliens, the vampires, and the man-made monsters. Unlike Orestes we have no gods—maternal or paternal—who might provide us with the solution.

The mourning of Diana was an attempt (doomed from the beginning, but nevertheless an attempt) to regain a good maternal object, not through the paternal super-ego, but through mourning the loss of the good object and the loss of goodness. It was an attempt to see ourselves as we are; to see that, as a culture, we are busy killing the things we love. It is significant, however, that in spite of the rhetoric concerning Diana as a mother, nobody would, by any stretch of imagination, see her as the good, devoted mother. Instead she represents the tormented, confused and unmothered Western woman who—nevertheless—is required to become a mother herself. This was always part of the immense fascination Diana herself exerted upon women.

As the twentieth century draws to a close we look back in terror at the unprecedented destructiveness that Western culture has unleashed on the planet and on fellow human beings. The murder of the mother, leading to the murder of the parents, has left us wandering in a man-made world of manufactured and dead objects, a world where birth and death are denied. Virtual reality is winning. We live in a world that looks increasingly alien, increasingly devoid of meaningful relationships, and increasingly pre-occupied with the inanimate.

Chapter 2

Matricide and the Oedipus Complex

In Plato's *Symposium*, Aristophanes describes the emergence of humankind, and of sexual difference and sexuality as part of the same process:

> First of all, you must learn the constitution of man and the modifications which it has undergone, for originally it was different from what it is now... each human being was a rounded whole, with double back and flanks forming a complete circle; it had four hands and an equal number of legs, and two identically similar faces upon a circular neck, with one head common to both faces, which were turned in opposite directions. It had four ears and two organs of generation and everything else to correspond. These people could walk upright like us in either direction, backwards or forwards, but when they wanted to run quickly they used all their eight limbs, and turned rapidly over in a circle, like tumblers who perform a cartwheel and return to the upright position... Their strength and vigour made them very formidable, and their pride was overweening; they attacked the gods, and Homer's story of Ephialtes and Otus attempting to climb up to heaven and set upon the gods is related also to these beings. (Plato 1951: 60)

The power of these first undivided creatures, Aristophanes tells us, challenged the gods who were at a loss as to what to do with them—whether to extinguish them by lightning or to let them continue with their insolence. Eventually they hit upon the idea to divide them into two and thus end their wickedness.

> 'I will cut each one of them in two', Zeus says, 'in this way they will be weaker, and at the same time more profitable to us by being more numerous. They shall walk upright

upon two legs. If there is any sign of wantonness in them
after that... I shall bisect them again, and they shall walk
on one leg...' As he bisected each, he bade Apollo turn
round the face and the half-neck attached to it towards the
cut side, so that the victim, having evidence of bisection
before his eyes, might behave better in the future. He also
bade him to heal the wounds. (Plato 1951: 61)

As the human beings were cut into two, each half yearned for
its other half. When the two halves found one another they
embraced and would not let go, so that they neglected to take
care of themselves and were in danger of dying of hunger. In
fact many perished in this way until Zeus took pity on them and
hit upon the idea of moving their genitals to the front.
Consequently, he made possible reproduction by sexual intercourse.

In this humorous and profound account of the origins of
human beings, which Plato places in the mouth of Aristophanes,
narcissistic injury is linked to the separation of the sexes and
becomes tantamount to being human. In the same way, firstly
the process of birth and—later—the discovery of separateness
and sexual difference create a wound in infantile omnipotence
which never quite heals. Human beings yearn for their original
wholeness, by seeking out the complementary other. As
Aristophanes puts it, in language which thoroughly de-idealis-
es the human condition:

Each one of us then is the mere broken tally of a man, the
result of a bisection which has reduced us to a condition
like that of a flat fish, and each of us is perpetually in
search of his corresponding tally. (Plato 1951: 62)

This state of 'being only half'—Aristophanes appears to be
suggesting—is what is experienced after the discovery of sexual difference. From then onwards human individuals may
attempt to defend themselves against this knowledge but, when
this becomes untenable, they experience a deep yearning for an
other who will complement them. This human condition of

woundedness psychoanalysis has named 'castration'. With this concept Freud brought together narcissistic injury, loss, and sexuality, but in a specifically masculine language.

What Aristophanes' account of the human condition leaves out, however, is the endless manoeuvres that human beings employ in order to *avoid* the knowledge of their wounded state and the pain which the experience of separateness and difference induces in them. Psychoanalysis has taken on the task of exploring and studying these manoeuvres which themselves constitute part of human development and the human condition.

* * *

The separation of baby and placenta is the first wounding and puncture of omnipotence—a kind of fall from grace. The second is the separation from the breast, which heralds a state of mourning, and which is brought to an end by the adoption of an identificatory relation to the mother, marking the beginning of what Klein called the 'femininity-phase' (Klein 1928). The discovery of sexual difference is the next trauma against which the child will try to defend itself. This is the last in a series of separations which rob the child of its wholeness, and leaves it with the feeling of being only half—'a mere broken tally of a man'.

Aristophanes' myth, with its mixture of the burlesque and the profound, reveals the undignified situation in which grandiosity and the loss of omnipotence lands the individual, and the state of helplessness that results. However, this helplessness and state of loss can be regarded as the first step towards individual and sexual maturity.

Aristophanes' account of the separation of the sexes, however, leaves out something very fundamental: the mother. This may not be a coincidence, but rather an inevitable 'symptom' of what I have chosen to explore in this book: the way in which the sexual difference between mother and son leads to masculine defences that result in a split in the psyche, which in turn determines the relation between the sexes.

We could argue that the myth of the separation of the two sexes in Aristophanes follows the lines of Freud's argument: that the first condition of human beings is one of bisexuality and of primary narcissism, and that the separation between the sexes encounters tremendous internal hurdles which have to be overcome. In this the father—Zeus, in this instance—is necessary both for limiting the child's omnipotence and for assisting in his or her struggle towards the recognition of sexual difference. For Freud the main dynamic is the castration complex, whereas for Aristophanes it is divine intervention. However, in both cases, the father—human or divine—is a castrator.

Thinking from an object relations perspective, Melanie Klein regarded the identification with mother as the first significant internal event in human development. For Klein there is a 'femininity-phase' which is characterised by the child's (boy or girl) first identification with mother (Klein 1928: 189). This first identification is accompanied by intense feelings of envy and rivalry. It takes place during the anal phase and is linked, on the one hand, to the epistemophilic instinct and, on the other hand, to the sadism which accompanies the anal phase. This sadism, in turn, is related to the infant's desire to take possession of the mother's body. In 'Early Stages of the Oedipus Complex' (1928) Klein writes:

> The child is still dominated by the anal-sadistic libido-position which impels him to wish to *appropriate* the contents of the womb. He thus begins to be curious about what it contains, what it is like, etc. So the epistemophelic instinct and the desire to take possession come quite early to be most intimately connected with one another... This significant connection ushers in a phase of development in both sexes which is of vital importance, hitherto not sufficiently recognised. It consists of a very early identification with the mother. (Klein 1928: 188-9)

She expands on this as follows:

As in the castration complex of girls, so in the femininity complex of the male, there is the frustrated desire for a special organ. The tendencies to steal and destroy are concerned with the organs of conception, pregnancy and parturition, which the boy assumes to exist in the mother, and further with the vagina and the breasts, the fountain of milk, which are coveted as organs of receptivity and bounty... (Klein 1928: 190)

In a subsequent paper, she describes the boy's phantasised attacks on the mother's body:

...his attacks also represent, among other things, his earliest situations of rivalry with her, and thus form the basis of the boy's femininity-phase. (Klein 1932a: 241)

All these feelings are terrifying for the boy, but also for the girl since she too passes through a similar phase of competition with mother. These terrifying feelings, which entail the risk of retaliation from mother, help to introduce the father as a person towards whom rivalry and envy will be directed. Identification with father, rivalry against him and envy of his penis, may save the child from a retaliatory mother, but implies its own dangers of paternal retaliation and castration.

Evidently, then, Klein—like Freud—regards envy, rivalry, and wishes to appropriate the other as part of the discovery of sexual difference. However, unlike Freud, she views envy of mother and early identification with her as the most fundamental aspect of development for both girls and boys, occurring long before the classical Oedipus complex.

From this point of view, what Aristophanes posits as the pre-genital condition can be seen as a defensive manoeuvre geared towards denial of separateness, envy and sex-difference. Such an undivided creature, who could have a penis, a vagina *and* a womb, would be truly omnipotent, challenging the gods and creating havoc. This would not be a question of 'bisexuality', but of a denial of difference and a clinging onto omnipotence. Indeed, in this image of an undivided creature there is not only a denial of sex-difference but also a denial of the parents; these creatures challenge the gods, Plato tells us, and are very insolent. Since they have no needs and have no dependency upon anyone, the undivided humans can afford to ignore both parents and gods.

Freud described human development in relation to the Oedipus complex. The Oedipus complex is important because it is the locus at which infantile omnipotence comes face to face with the reality of the child's helplessness. Therefore the way the Oedipus complex is resolved—or fails to be resolved—is crucial for the future development of narcissism, and for the negotiation of omnipotence and ambivalence, as well as for ego development and gender identity. As I see it, Western culture fails, on the whole, to facilitate the individual's resolution of the Oedipus complex, relying instead on something akin to psychical matricide, rather than a genuine resolution. To examine how the Oedipus complex is negotiated in the Western psyche I shall now introduce another myth, the murder of Clytemnestra. Its main themes are the murder of the mother, and the idealisation of the father and of the super-ego.

* * *

Clytemnestra's murder is recounted in the second part of Aeschylus' trilogy *The Oresteia* and constitutes, I think, a central myth portraying the genesis of a new type of patriarchy, in which the internal world is created 'in the name of the father'.

The first part of *The Oresteia* begins with the triumphant return of Agamemnon, the commander of the Greek fleet that fought in Troy for ten years. The war has ended with a Greek victory, albeit due to Odysseus' deception using the Trojan horse. Thus a heroic war has ended with a mean act of deception and an abuse of trust. Furthermore, the war had begun with Iphigenia's sacrifice to the gods by Agamemnon, her father, in exchange for favourable winds that would take the Greek fleet to Troy.

There is a history of murder, deception, treason and even cannibalism in the house of the Atreides. Agamemnon is the son of Atreus, and inherited the throne of Argos due to his father's murderous and deceitful acts. Atreus and his brother, Thyestes, quarrelled over which of them should succeed to the throne. Atreus, in order to disqualify Thyestes, invited his brother to dinner and, after murdering Thyestes' children, fed them to their unwitting father. After this horrific act Thyestes went into exile, taking with him his sole surviving son, Aegisthus.

However, this hideous crime continues to haunt the house of Atreides, because—during Agamemnon's absence—Clytemnestra has taken Aegisthus as her lover, and he continues to seek revenge against Agamemnon for the crimes of Atreus against Thyestes. Clytemnestra, for her part, is seeking revenge for the sacrifice of her daughter Iphigenia and for Agamemnon's affair with Cassandra, whom he has brought back from Troy as his mistress. In addition, Clytemnestra is simply unwilling to give up the freedom to which she has grown accustomed during Agamemnon's ten years of absence.

With this as his background, Aeschylus has created a drama of revenge, persecution, and attempts at reparation which portrays the establishment of a new order, a new justice, a new patriarchy, and a new balance of power between mother and father, boy and girl. However, this new internal and external order is clearly based on the murder of Clytemnestra, the powerful mother.

Clytemnestra is a proud and fierce woman who cannot bear to see her ten years of independence squashed by the return of Agamemnon, the arrogant and vulgar hero of Troy. On his arrival she treats him to a hero's welcome and then, the same evening, together with Aegisthus, they murder him. The first part of *The Oresteia* ends with an unrepentant and triumphant Clytemnestra and a joyful Aegisthus.

In the second part Orestes, Agamemnon's son—who has grown up in exile since his father's death—returns to Argos to avenge the murder of his father. With his sister Electra's support, and under the guidance and orders of Apollo, he kills—almost against his will—his mother and Aegisthus.

Orestes, like Hamlet, is portrayed as a noble, disinherited prince caught in a corrupt and murderous parental feud. He wants to avenge his father and to gain his father's inheritance, yet the idea of killing his own mother fills him with horror. There is a moment when, confronted by his mother, he hesitates. He turns to his friend Pylades:

> ORESTES: Pylades, what shall I do? To kill a mother is ter-
>   rible. Shall I show mercy?
> PYLADES: Where then are Apollo's words? His Pythian
>   oracles? What becomes of men's sworn words?
>   Make all men living your enemies, but not the gods.
>   (Aeschylus 1986: 136)

Here Pylades reminds Orestes of Apollo, the divine authori-ty, the guiding paternal god, who has ordered Orestes to kill his mother. Orestes is caught between the two parents—two inter-nal objects at war with each other—and has to decide to whom he will be loyal and with whom he will identify.

> CLYTEMNESTRA: Beware the hounding Furies of a
>   mother's curse.
> ORESTES: How shall I escape my father's curse if I relent?
>   (Aeschylus 1986: 137)

Orestes follows the paternal command and kills Clytemnestra and is almost immediately hounded by the Furies, ancient maternal goddesses who seek revenge for the matricide. In the final part of *The Oresteia, The Eumenides*, Orestes, still per-secuted by the Furies, finds sanctuary first at Apollo's temple in Delphi, then finally in Athens at Athene's temple where he is to be tried, not by Athene alone but by the Athenian citizens. The trial at Athens centres on the question of whether Orestes was justified in killing his mother in order to avenge his father's death—in other words, which murder was 'bigger': the murder of Agamemnon by Clytemnestra, or the murder of Clytemnestra by Orestes? As Apollo puts it:

> APOLLO: Zeus so ordained, and Zeus was right. For their
>   two deaths

Are in no way to be compared. He was a king
Wielding an honoured sceptre by divine command.
A woman killed him...
CHORUS (FURIES): You plead for his acquittal: have you
    asked yourself
    How one who poured out on the ground his moth-
    er's blood
    Will live henceforth in Argos, in his father's house?
    Shall he at public altars share in sacrifice?
    Shall holy water lave his hands at tribal feasts?
APOLLO: This too I answer; mark the truth of what I say.
    The mother is not the true parent of the child
    Which is called hers. She is a nurse who tends the
      growth
    Of young seed planted by its true parent, the male.
    So, if Fate spares the child, she keeps it, as one
      might
    Keep for some friend a growing plant. And of this
      truth
    That father without mother may beget, we have
    Present, as proof, the daughter of Olympian Zeus:
    One never nursed in the dark cradle of the womb;
    Yet such a being no god will beget again.
    (Aeschylus 1986: 169-170)

After this speech, which denies not only maternal rights but also the reproductive power of women, Athene exhorts the citizens, now elevated to the Athenian High Court (the Areopagus) to reach a decision. The votes are counted and are even. However, Athene herself casts the deciding vote, which 'upholds Orestes' plea' (Aeschylus 1986: 172) and thus acquits him.

In my view, Orestes' acquittal is a decisive event which, in mythical terms, marks a manic (rather than a depressive) reaction to a murder. The manic solution denies reality: the reality of the parental couple as the source of life, the reality of woman's generativity, and the reality of a slow, healing process that works through mourning—not only the mourning of the object, but also the mourning of the loss of the good self.

Instead, manic denial prevails through the insistence that 'the mother is not the true parent of the child'. However, although the denial comes from a male god, it is a *female* goddess who sanctions it and who acquits Orestes. Athene is a goddess without a mother since, according to myth, she sprang, fully armed, from the head of Zeus. This masculinised woman/goddess was the patron of Athens. The new order, the law of the father has now been established in Athens, and it has been decreed that the child belongs to father, and the daughter—Electra, Athene—has taken the father's side in this decision. Matricide is therefore sanctioned by the daughter, although carried out by the son, *in the name of the father*.

* * *

My interpretation of *The Oresteia* is in terms of the outcome of the Oedipus complex. In other words, I see *the murder of the mother* as the main outcome of what Freud regarded as 'the dissolution of the Oedipus complex'. I interpret what Freud describes as the 'ending' of the Oedipus complex as a sudden, violent psychical event which does not involve mourning, or feelings of loss, but—instead—feelings of persecution and terror. This sudden ending, due to the terror of castration, is very far from a real resolution. Although Freud talked about the genuine resolution as a 'destruction' of the Oedipus complex, so that—he suggests—it would not be present even in the unconscious (see Freud 1925a: 257), nevertheless he regarded *repression* of the complex as the norm. I would argue that this total repression or destruction of the relation to mother amounts to a psychical matricide. However, we cannot assume that the hostility towards the father follows the same fate, because it is transformed into the super-ego, and although the super-ego is partly unconscious its main task is to act as the supreme authority.

Freud saw the child as having no alternative but to repress forbidden or intolerable impulses. Although he introduced the

concept of 'sublimation' as a way of transforming these impulses, he never expanded on this. Indeed, one does not receive the
impression from Freud's description of the dissolution of the
Oedipus complex that sublimation plays any part in it. Instead
he refers to the 'destruction' (Freud 1924: 177) of the Oedipus
complex as the only alternative to repression, but he does not
explain what this means in psychical terms.

Comparing Aristophanes' myth and Freud's theory of gender development we see that Aristophanes' myth refers to a
symmetrical split which creates male and female. This is much
closer to Jung's notion of complementary opposites than to
Freud's view of sexuality (Jung 1913). Juliet Mitchell argues
that—in contrast—the strength of Freud's theory lies exactly in
stressing the *asymmetrical* development of boys and girls
(Mitchell 1975: 129-30). This asymmetrical development has
been described by Freud in the boy's and the girl's relation to
the penis and to father. From a more object-relational point of
view, it can be understood in terms of the relationship of the boy
and the girl to mother and to the maternal world.

Looking at Freud's theory we can say that Freud had two
models of development—one male, one female. The male model
was characterised by a violent dissolution of the Oedipus complex, and the creation of the super-ego and a rigid repression
barrier. The female model was characterised by a weaker super-
ego, a more fuzzy repression barrier, and by no definite dissolution of the Oedipus complex. Of course, Freud himself did not
formulate the female model in this way; instead he took the
male model as his yardstick and found the female 'lacking'. We
can see the workings of a whole culture here, a culture that has
interposed the father, or the penis, between the mother and
baby and, in so doing, has positioned traumatic loss of mother
in place of a *gradual separation* from her. This traumatic loss of
mother creates the very thing it attempts to abolish—the yearning for a merged relation with her. Freud's view of instincts as
basically conservative is, I think, related to this regressive trend,
as also is his postulation of a death instinct.

If we look at Aristophanes' myth, and the myth of
Clytemnestra, we see that they also provide two different ver-

sions of sexual development. The contrast is not simply that between an extravagant, comic tale of monster-like creatures, and a heroic chronicle of kings, queens and ancient feuds. As I see it, the former describes the separation of the sexes as a *symmetrical* affair, whereas the latter reveals development as *asymmetrical*. Like the primacy of the penis and the castration complex in Freud, the murder of the mother in the myth of Clytemnestra is an 'event' which discards any illusion of male and female symmetry. The murder of the mother by the son 'in the name of the father' cannot be an event which affects the male and female psyche in the same way. Whether we take 'penis-envy' or 'the murder of the mother' as the formative event in the structuralisation of the psyche, *asymmetry* between the sexes is unavoidable.

We can now return to *The Oresteia* in this light... Orestes kills his mother prompted and guided by Apollo. Electra, meanwhile, wants to kill her mother out of feelings of hate and suffocation, not because any god has prompted her. However, despite all her exhortations Electra does not actually murder her mother; Orestes is the one who kills her, suffers persecution, undergoes trial, and is exonerated. Electra, meanwhile, is not accused, not persecuted, not tried, and not exonerated; she is simply overlooked as irrelevant or unimportant. Neither guilty nor innocent, she has to carry the burden of her hate. Her fate is uncertain. One has the feeling that she is stranded in a blood-stained palace, yet the world has lost interest in her.

However, the fact is that Electra *cannot* leave mother behind. Being a woman, Electra identifies with her, and this identification with a damaged or murdered object is her fate. Freud expressed this situation by showing that the girl never quite leaves the mother. Her 'change of object' is not a real change, Freud seems to be saying. In 'Female Sexuality' (1931) he regards the woman's choice of a husband as based on a model of her relationship to father, whereas the actual *relationship* to the husband is a reproduction of the relationship to mother:

Long ago, for instance, we noticed that many women who have chosen a husband on the model of their father, or have put him in their father's place, nevertheless repeat towards him, in their marital life, their bad relations with their mother. The husband of such a woman was meant to be the inheritor of her relation to her father, but in reality he became the inheritor of her relation to her mother. (Freud 1931: 230-1)

The Oresteia has often been interpreted as portraying the transition from matriarchy to patriarchy. For my part, I want to stress the fact that *The Oresteia* portrays the transition only from one type of patriarchy to another, but that this represents a cultural advance. The glorious rogue, Agamemnon, is an absolute despot. He reigns in heroic times during which deception, murder, and betrayal are glorified. However, Clytemnestra—who knows the sordid truth behind the glory—destabilises a whole world of absolute male authority by murdering this arrogant tyrant, but unfortunately she creates an equally repressive regime. What follows is her own demise, the demolition of the old order and the creation of a new. The new order—as in the era of Christianity, which was to follow—is based on the *son* as the heir to the father. This symbolic patriarchy—'in the name of the father'—spells the beginning of democratic authority and the supremacy of the law. This is certainly a cultural advance on authoritarian patriarchy, but is made at a cost. It is built on the murder of the mother and of the feminine—a murder which by its very nature precludes a democratic authority based on the symbolic parental couple, a democratic authority that would *include* woman. It is no wonder therefore that Athenian democracy excluded women and remained in constant terror of female power.

The matricidal psyche takes the father as its protector. Father opens a space untainted by early anxieties—a rational space—represented in the Greek culture by Apollo and Athene. This rational space, welcomed by both boy and girl, is, however, a masculine space and exists only in a complete split from the early, murdered mother. In this sense the girl accepts a masculine space as a protection against a powerful and intrusive mother, and—later—against a murdered mother. The protection the father offers against mother's intrusiveness leads the girl to accept, or seek, the masculine solution. This protection, however, cannot act in the same way as in the boy, since the girl remains identified with mother. This classically melancholic position, in which the girl identifies with the attacked and damaged object whilst maintaining an attacking, paternal super-ego, is the girl's fate within a patriarchal psyche. However, there are endless variations and endless solutions to this basic problem, which will be explored later.

With the dissolution of the Oedipus complex a kind of parental couple is established—the only one possible under these circumstances. This parental couple does not recognise a mother and a father as equal partners, but acknowledges and recreates the socialised parental couple which sanctions the *possession* of the mother by the father and gives the father the right over the children.

All this entails that the establishment of a *genuine* parental couple in the psyche does not take place. The idealised father, as the possessor of mother and protector, keeps at bay primitive anxieties, both masculine and feminine, and creates a kind of symbolic space where *some* transformation of anxiety can take place. This paternalistic psyche, however, has to keep the murdered mother banned from the rest of the psyche, and has to replace her continuously with the reified mother. The reified mother can be loved, worshipped, mystified—or alternatively dissected, investigated, her mysteries reduced to 'facts'. In both alternatives—which are the underside of one another—the one thing that the mother or woman is not, is a subject. The terror that the murdered mother evokes can only be reduced by the protection of the paternal super-ego and by this process of reification. It also follows that where the paternal super-ego is weak, then terror will threaten to invade the psyche. The recurrent dream of a male patient expresses some of this anxiety of being invaded by terror: *He is walking along the street when he suddenly feels a strong, sinister force drawing him towards a house. He 'knows' that there is a woman behind the window and that she has the power to draw him towards the house against his will. He is filled with terror and wakes up.*

The woman in the dream has about her something ghostly and horrific, although the dreamer does not see her. One association was to the dwarf at the end of the film *Don't Look Now*. In this film a young couple lose their daughter when she drowns in the pond outside their home. The sudden nature of this tragic loss makes it difficult for them to mourn. They travel to Venice where the husband, who is an architect, is involved in the restoration a church. The unmourned loss continues to haunt them, however, and in an unforgettable scene at the end of the film the husband is lured (partly by his own death-wish, and partly by a kind of hallucinated image of his daughter, represented by a dwarf) to some of the darker, more infamous parts of Venice. He is then killed by a psychopath. Both the patient's dream and this film strikingly present a fatal attraction to a dead and unmourned object. Indeed, the patient's other associations to the dream included vampires, and the embalmed mother in Hitchcock's film *Psycho*. Death and the dead form part of all these associations.

In fact, what this patient expresses is the dread of an *undead* mother. As in any murder, the victim returns to haunt the perpetrator. The dread of the murdered and damaged mother leads increased reification of the woman, which becomes a precondition for love. One solution to this terror is promiscuity. The endless change of partner is an attempt to prevent female subjectivity from appearing and thus, in this way, to avoid persecution. This kind of love—the only kind possible under these conditions—depends on continuously maintaining the split between the undead mother and the idealised, denigrated and reified woman. Another solution—more conventional—is the absolute domination and possession of the woman. Yet another involves splitting, along the lines suggested by Freud in his papers 'A Special Type of Choice of Object Made by Men' (1910a) and 'On the Universal Tendency to Debasement in the Sphere of Love' (1912). In this split a sexual relation can only take place with a debased object—a prostitute—while a relationship with an idealised, de-sexualised woman, wife or mother is maintained.

Yet another solution may be the avoidance of any intimate or sexual relationships with women. A man's enduring relationship with a machine may, in some cases, take the place of a relationship with a woman. One male patient with a very hostile paternal image describes his love affair with the computer; another with machines of all types; yet another with the motorcar. In this case a regression from the Oedipus complex to a phallic-narcissistic, or anal phase, where no 'other' exists, has taken place.

Jim, a thirty-five-year-old man, lost his mother when he was six, soon after she gave birth to his sister. His resentment and hostility towards his mother's pregnancy, followed by his mother's death, contributed to a matricidal phantasy which is more conscious in him than in most people. Jim feels that he has somehow *caused* his mother's death. The strength with which this phantasy is upheld points to a characteristic defensive strategy, turning passive into active on the grounds that: 'Death doesn't happen just like this. I am not a passive recipient. It is under my control. I caused it'. This kind of matricidal phantasy illuminates traumatic loss and the omnipotent phantasies which the child uses to protect himself against feelings of helplessness and of being overwhelmed by them, and which are far preferable to the state of helplessness. I suggest that these kinds of phantasies mixed with rage are present, although in a more unconscious fashion, in most men, and in women (to a lesser extent), and that they constitute part of the traumatic ending of the Oedipus complex.

If matricidal phantasies are too strong, then real relationships with women are avoided and a vicious circle is established, since only through a real relationship with a woman can these phantasies be worked through.

Danny, a twenty-five-year-old man, has been trapped in an hostile and persecutory relationship, not only with his internal mother, but also with his internal father. His hatred of the parental couple, established when he shared the bedroom with his parents in his early years, had crippled both his ability to have a relationship with a woman and to succeed professionally. As therapy progressed his relationship with his internal father improved markedly, and so has his ability to succeed. His relationship with his internal mother, however, is so damaged

by his feelings of helplessness and his rage against her, that relationships with women become impossible. The vicious circle
referred to above is perfectly established in him, since only a
relationship with a woman could heal the wounds and alter the
persecutory anxiety. Yet a relationship with a woman is exactly
what is so impossible. The slow working-through of this situation, in the transference, is the only way out of this vicious
circle. [2]

I think that the structure of the psyche—as described and
illuminated for the first time by Freud—has, by and large and
with numerous variations, proved adequate since the time of
the Ancient Greeks. Now, however, for various reasons, it is
beginning to break down. The anxiety which fills the psyche as
the paternal super-ego continues to weaken is expressed in the
prevalent 'myths' of our times: invading aliens, monsters out of
control, ghosts and evil spirits of all kinds, computers or robots
taking over the world, various fears of contamination, prehistoric beasts being re-born... These appear alongside a resur-
gence of the heroic male; whether he is Superman, He-Man, one
of the Ghostbusters or James Bond, the male hero is alive and
well, as phallic defences take the place of the paternal super-
ego.

We are, in fact, experiencing at a cultural level 'the return of
the repressed'. For Freud repression was the only 'civilised'
means the psyche had at its disposal to deal with intolerable or
forbidden impulses. Sublimation, the only other possibility that
Freud introduced, received no further elaboration in his work.
Indeed, given that the father is the protector against primitive
anxieties, and a guarantor of separation from mother, is any
other model *possible*? This is an important question not only for
feminists, but for everybody interested in exploring the possibility of a different balance in the psyche.

One way of proceeding is to reformulate this question and to
investigate in what way primitive anxieties concerning love,
hate and loss *can* be worked-through, rather than repressed,
projected, or phobically avoided. For Freud this question never
arose. I think the reason for this was that Freud simply had no
model of a *slow* working-through of infantile anxieties outside

the therapeutic situation, primarily because he chose not to concentrate on the mother-child relationship. It might also be that the cultural climate within which he worked favoured rigid repression rather than slow working-through.

For Melanie Klein, on the contrary, it is the slow working-through of infantile anxieties and their juxtaposition with reality which forms the stuff of psychical development. This slow development, full of failures and setbacks, ambivalence, disappointments and intense anxiety, is an everyday reality for mothers. The reparation which the child makes to its objects, and the growth of its confidence in the goodness of its internal world, is a slow, gradual process. Anything that disturbs the capacity of the child to achieve reparation leads to intense anxiety and to regressive steps.

The outcome of the Oedipus complex as described by Freud, however, is anything but reparative. The psyche, at the peak of the Oedipus complex, is in a state of persecution. The boy's renunciation of the mother is due neither to facing reality nor to repairing his objects. Instead it is because the boy feels intensely persecuted. This intense persecution, and the impossibility of doing anything but giving up his object, is a solution which presupposes that the father is *already* between the mother and the child.

Alternative models of working-through infantile anxieties were formulated by the British School of Object Relations, which explored the mother-baby interaction in great detail. Theories like those of Klein, Bion and Winnicott have focused on the transformation of anxiety within the mother-child relationship and have, therefore, shifted their focus away from the matricidal world of the Oedipus complex. This new focus has meant that they have, on the whole, ignored the law of the father and the cultural super-ego but, in so doing, they have elucidated another way in which development can proceed—a slow working-through of anxiety within a trusting mother-child (and father-child) relationship, not unlike the psychotherapeutic experience within a trusted analytic setting. However, the way in which object-relations theory does not, on the whole, deal with Oedipal issues has had significant consequences. The two worlds of the mother and of the father have remained split apart from one another, even in theory.

Chapter 3

Masculinity and Matricide

Freud had elaborated his model of psycho-sexual development long before he realised that it was suited more to the development of the boy than to that of the girl. It was not until 1925 he realised feminine development did not follow the same path. This came as a shock to his whole model of psycho-sexual development, for Freud had not described the path 'towards masculinity'; instead he had regarded masculinity as 'normal' development, from which feminine sexuality deviated.

It was a fresh look at the castration complex which led Freud to formulate a different path for the development of femininity. The castration complex had become increasingly important to Freud, and came to occupy a central place in his conception of the Oedipus complex. It became the point of differentiation between male and female: the boy's Oedipus complex came to an end because of his fear of castration by the father, whereas the girl *entered* her Oedipus complex once she realised she was castrated. In other words, the girl entered the Oedipus complex through a 'masculinity phase'. Freud wove together the castration complex, Oedipus complex, and penis-envy, to produce what he believed to be the 'circuitous path to femininity' (Freud 1931: 229-30).

Freud chose the myth of Oedipus to describe masculinity and its pitfalls. However, it is apparent that the story of Oedipus cannot be used to describe femininity, and even for the boy the Oedipus myth does not tell the whole story. Had Freud chosen the Oresteian myth he might have uncovered some different aspects of masculinity, as revealed in the boy's dread of the omnipotent mother, the search for a male identificatory figure, and the boy's violent destruction of his attachment to mother.

The Oedipus complex, as Freud described it, was characterised by the boy's intense desire to kill his father and marry his mother. Fairbairn, on the other hand, had a much more complex view of the child's relation to his parents. He regarded the

Oedipus complex as the way in which the child copes with his ambivalence to *both* parents, so that instead of the ambivalence towards two parental objects, the child arrives at loving one and hating the other. In Fairbairn's words:

The child finds it intolerable enough to be called to deal with a single ambivalent object but when he is called upon to deal with two, he finds it still more intolerable. He therefore seeks to simplify a complex situation, in which he is confronted by two exciting objects and two rejecting objects... He thus, for all practical purposes, comes to equate one parental object with the exciting object, and the other with the rejecting object; and by doing so the child constitutes the Oedipus situation for himself. (Fairbairn 1944: 124)

However, Fairbairn also stresses the fact that below the Oedipus complex and below the situation in which two ambivalent objects co-exist, there is a third, deeper level, at which the mother is the sole ambivalent object. Stressing the immense psychic significance of the early mother, he writes:

I venture to suggest that the deep analysis of a positive Oedipus situation may be regarded as taking place at three main levels. At the first level the picture is dominated by the Oedipus situation itself. At the next level it is dominated by ambivalence towards the heterosexual parent. At the deepest level it is dominated by ambivalence towards mother. Traces of all these stages may be detected in the classic drama of *Hamlet*; but there can be no doubt that, both in the role of exciting and tempting object and in that of the rejecting object, the Queen is the real villain. (Fairbairn 1944: 124)

In this sense, then, we could say that the boy, at the deepest level of his psyche, is involved in a struggle with the ambivalent and very powerful mother. This is a very different version of events from Freud's classical Oedipus complex. Fairbairn's view takes fully into account the power of the early maternal object and the boy's dread of it.

Although Freud saw masculinity as characterised by 'repudiation of femininity', he did not go on to consider in any detail — with the exception of his study on Leonardo da Vinci (Freud 1910b)—the boy's first relation to his mother, or his struggle to dis-identify from her (see Greenson 1993: 261). Instead he viewed the 'repudiation of femininity' as the struggle against a constitutional bisexuality and a 'natural' aversion towards femininity. In Freud's words: 'The repudiation of femininity can be nothing else than a biological fact, a part of the great riddle of sex' (Freud 1937: 250-2).

For me, one way of viewing the Oedipus complex is as the boy's attempt to dis-identify from mother by eroticising his relation to her—by becoming, that is, a substitute for his father. This attempt is doomed to failure on many counts. Firstly, his identification with mother does not simply disappear with his eroticisation of the relationship. On the contrary, eroticisation binds him in a dual set of chains: identification and object-love mingle to produce a pull towards unity, that peculiar oneness experienced by people in love, when strong attraction brings about the obliteration of difference. This paradox of being in love—that is, the 'feminine' quality of this state of mind—is clearly evidenced in the way that poets, troubadours, and male lovers become 'soft', and forget masculine preoccupations. In contrast, the boy's relationship to father is adversarial, consisting of wishes to fight and replace father, as well as to be *like* him. Through desiring to replace his father, the boy projects onto father his parricidal and castrating impulses, and—as a consequence—becomes fearful of castration himself.

In 'The Dissolution of the Oedipus Complex' (1924) Freud considers various ways in which the complex might come to an end—through inevitable disappointment and the realisation of its impossibility, or simply because 'time has come for its disintegration, just as the milk teeth fall out when the permanent ones begin to grow' (Freud 1924: 173). However, Freud rejects all these possibilities in favour of the castration complex. Only the terror of castration, Freud says, is a strong enough force to put an end to the boy's attachment to his mother. Yet this fear may cause him to retreat to an identification with mother, and thus to lose his masculinity. As Freud puts it:

The Oedipus complex offered the child two possibilities of satisfaction, an active and a passive one. He could put himself in his father's place in a masculine fashion and have intercourse with his mother as his father did, in which case he would soon have felt the latter as a hindrance; or he might want to take the place of his mother and be loved by his father, in which case his mother would become superfluous... [H]is acceptance of the possibility of castration, his recognition that women were castrated, made an end of both possible ways of obtaining satisfaction from the Oedipus complex. For both of them entailed the loss of his penis—the masculine one as a resulting punishment and the feminine one as a precondition. (Freud 1924: 176)

It is the impossibility of any position—the fact that *both* positions entail castration—which prompts the child to end the Oedipus complex.

The castration complex is tied up with two things: the boy's identification with his mother, and his (defensive) perception of female castration. Freud always maintained a position of sexual monism concerning childhood; in other words, he proposed that the only sexual organ known to children is the penis. At the same time, however, he adhered to the view that *bisexuality* is the first, natural, condition of human beings. How these two positions might co-exist was never clarified by Freud.

Freud's contention that the vagina remained unknown in childhood, and was discovered only during puberty, was strongly disputed by Karen Horney. In her paper 'The Dread of Woman', Horney explores the many myths and fairy-tales in which the hero must overcome horrifying female forces, variously portrayed as witches, sirens, medusas, sphinxes, monsters, and dragons of all kinds. Horney wonders whether this male struggle does not reveal, ultimately, 'a secret longing for extinction in the act of reunion with the woman (mother). Is it perhaps this longing that underlies the "death-instinct"? And is it his will to live that reacts to it with anxiety?' (Horney 1973: 144).

However, Horney proceeds further than this. She examines the denial of the vagina as a defensive act on the part of the male child. The wish to return to the womb is only one side of this. The other side is the actual realisation by the child that his penis is too small to satisfy mother. Concerning both these anxieties, the existence of the vagina is never in question. Both anxieties are instead related to the boy's wishes, and are experienced as threats against his separate existence on the one hand, and his self-esteem on the other. This narcissistic wound, Horney suggests, leads to the denial of the female genital and a concentration on the penis. 'The female genital no longer exists for him', she writes, 'the "undiscovered vagina" is a denied vagina' (Horney 1973: 144).

Another refutation of Freud's phallic monism came from Melanie Klein. As examined briefly in the previous chapter, Klein maintained that the boy's first identification is with his mother. This phase, the 'femininity-phase', is characterised by the boy's desire to have children, and his intention to appropriate them: 'As in the castration complex of girls, so in the femininity complex of the male, there is at bottom the frustrated desire for a special organ' (Klein 1928: 190). The fear of retaliation from mother is intense during this phase. It becomes mixed up with anal anxieties, and is translated into castration anxiety:

> ...the mother who takes away the child's faeces signifies also the mother who dismembers and castrates him. Not only by means of anal frustrations which she inflicts does she pave the way for the castration complex: in terms of psychic reality she *is* also already the *castrator*. (Klein 1928: 190)

Consequently the boy, during the femininity-phase, feels a strong sense of inferiority, rivalry with mother, and a strong wish to appropriate the inside of her body, yet—at the same time—intense anxiety and fear of retaliation from the mother and also—but to a lesser extent—from the father. The boy wants to create a child using his mother's body and his father's penis. The fear and frustration arising from this lead to a displacements onto parallel achievements on the intellectual plane, but also onto an over-estimation of the penis:

> ...his sense of being at a disadvantage is then concealed and over-compensated by the superiority he deduces from his possession of a penis, which is also acknowledged by girls. This exaggeration of the masculine position results in excessive protestations of masculinity. (Klein 1928: 191-2)

Klein continues:

> In the boy's development the femininity-phase is succeeded by a prolonged struggle between the pregenital and the genital positions of the libido. When at its height, in the third to the fifth year of life, this struggle is plainly recognisable as the Oedipus conflict. The anxiety associated with the femininity-phase drives the boy back to identification with the father; but this stimulus in itself does not provide a firm foundation for the genital position, since it leads mainly to repression and over-compensation of the anal-sadistic instincts and not to overcoming them. *The dread of castration by father strengthens the fixations to the anal-sadistic levels.* (Klein 1928: 191-2, my italics)

The struggle against femininity continues throughout a man's life. Freud regarded the 'repudiation of femininity' as the 'bedrock of masculinity'. In a late paper, he wrote of the impossibility of convincing a man that being passive is acceptable, and that this does not detract from his masculinity (Freud 1937: 250-2). This continuous struggle against femininity is eased by the dissolution of the Oedipus complex and the boy's identification with the father. Whether this is attained and how it is attained are therefore of great importance for the boy.

As we have seen, although Freud regarded 'repression' as the usual way in which the ego turned away from the Oedipus complex, he described the ideal resolution as the 'destruction' or 'abolition' of the complex (Freud 1924: 177). In a subsequent paper, he even describes how the Oedipus complex is 'smashed to pieces', so that no trace at all remains—not even in the unconscious (Freud 1925a: 257). What this 'destruction' might entail in psychical terms is far from clear. My point, however, is that all these terms possess persecutory overtones, rather than conveying a sense of mourning or working-through depression. Perhaps Freud's vocabulary should not surprise us. As I have emphasised, at the moment of the dissolution of the Oedipus complex the boy's psyche is in a persecuted state. The castration complex—with all that this entails in terms of attacks on mother and father, and fear of retaliation from them—terrorises his psyche. The boy's struggle against mother and femininity mingles with his struggle against father as the possessor of mother, creating a highly intense persecutory anxiety.

I have argued that Freud's description of the dissolution of the Oedipus complex possesses a matricidal significance. Let us now look in greater detail at Freud's description of this process:

If the satisfaction of love in the field of the Oedipus complex is to cost the child his penis, a conflict is bound to arise between his narcissistic interest in that part of his body and the libidinal cathexis of his parental objects. In this conflict the first of these forces normally triumphs: the child's ego turns away from the Oedipus complex.

I have described elsewhere [in *The Ego and the Id* (1923b)] how this turning away takes place. The object-cathexes are given up and replaced by identifications. The authority of the father or the parents is introjected into the ego, and there it forms the nucleus of the super-ego, which takes over the severity of the father and perpetuates his prohibition against incest, and so secures the ego from the return of the libidinal cathexis. (Freud 1924: 176-7)

There is one important difference between what Freud states here, and what he had written earlier, in *The Ego and the Id*. In the earlier work, Freud had written on the Oedipus complex without taking the castration complex into account. In this work, the Oedipus complex was presented as an optimal situation, the best possible outcome of a process of working-through infantile anxieties and the recognition of the impossibility of realising childhood passions. Indeed, the castration complex makes an appearance in *The Ego and the Id* only towards the end of the final chapter, almost as an afterthought, where it is linked to the death instinct and the aggressive impulses involved in the creation of the super-ego:

> ...we can tell what is hidden behind the ego's dread of the super-ego, the fear of conscience. The superior being, which turned into the ego-ideal, once threatened castration, and this dread of castration is probably the nucleus round which the subsequent fear of conscience has gathered; it is this dread that persists as the fear of conscience. (1923b: 57)

Freud precedes this passage by suggesting that what the ego fears more than anything else is being overwhelmed by primitive impulses from the id. This feeling of being overwhelmed is perceived as danger, and this danger is the cause of anxiety. Thus the ego finds itself between the Scylla and the Charybdis; either it succumbs to the impulses from the id and feels overwhelmed, or else it succumbs to the castrating father/super-ego and experiences fear and dread. So, even where Freud chooses not to stress the castration complex, nevertheless he awards a central place to aggressive impulses. His analysis of the super-ego is presented with the death instinct as its backdrop. The super-ego, as Freud sees it, is a by-product of the death-instinct, filled with aggressive impulses:

> In suffering under the attacks of the super-ego or perhaps even succumbing to them, the ego is meeting with a fate like that of the protista which are destroyed by the prod-

ucts of decomposition that they themselves have created. From the economic point of view the morality that functions in the super-ego seems to be a similar product of decomposition. (Freud 1923b: 56-7)

'Decomposition products' refers here to the de-libidinisation of the parental figures, and to the substitution of a critical agency (the super-ego) in place of a relationship with the parents. This reads to me as a triumph of the death instinct. Freud himself does not quite refer to it in these terms although, a little earlier in the same paper, he describes the super-ego as a 'pure culture of the death instinct' (Freud 1923b: 53). What is clear is that for Freud the creation of the super-ego entails an identification with the aggressor (the castrating father); an accumulation of aggressive impulses and decomposition products; and the defusion of instincts. From another point of view, however, the super-ego can also be seen as the internalisation of a bad, unassimilated object which terrorises the psyche. This may not be so different from the anti-libidinal object described by Fairbairn (Fairbairn 1944: 105)—also known as the 'anti-libidinal ego', 'rejecting ego', or 'internal saboteur'—or, indeed, from the 'internal mafia' proposed by Rosenfeld (Rosenfeld 1987: 112)

* * *

If the relation to father becomes the super-ego, then what happens to the relationship with mother?

There is great uncertainty on this matter in Freud's version of events. An intriguing passage in *The Ego and the Id* points out that the super-ego consists of *both* mother- and father-identifications, forming—in other words—a kind of parental couple:

The broad general outcome of the sexual phase dominated by the Oedipus complex may, therefore, be taken to be the forming of a precipitate in the ego, consisting of *these two identifications in some way united with each other*. The modification of the ego retains its special position; it confronts the other contents of the ego as an ego ideal or super-ego. (Freud 1923b: 34)

However, in the 'The Dissolution of the Oedipus Complex' (1924), and in subsequent writings, this idea was lost and the castration complex assumed centre-stage. Freud subsequently stresses the father identification in the formation of the super-ego, and explains the cruelty of the super-ego by the fact that it represents the castrating father on the one hand, and the boy's own aggression on the other (Freud 1930: 129). Moreover, the identification with the father runs contrary to Freud's usual views on identification with the lost love object; it is, instead, an identification with the aggressor.

As I have previously suggested, traumatic loss is that which does not allow mourning or assimilation of the internalised object. On the contrary, the internalised object becomes an unassimilated, persecutory object which terrorises the psyche. This is precisely the state of the 'murdered' maternal object after the dissolution of the Oedipus complex. The repression of this object entails its total exclusion from consciousness, and a continuous state of anxiety, because the danger of its irruption into consciousness remains a continuous possibility. In my opinion, repression does not preclude projective identification; on the contrary, what is repressed can only be experienced in other people—through projective identification.[3] In this way, woman herself becomes a persecutory object. I would like to repeat here that only a real relationship with a woman can help to work through these feelings and phantasies. Less mature solutions might entail the absence of repression, and—instead—the exclusion of the mother from the psyche through more psychotic processes, such as repudiation, evacuation or disavowal, solutions which result in a state of terror and persecution.

These defences constitute an attack or, at times, the 'murder' of the mother. The banned mother exists in a state of undeadness. However, like Count Dracula, the love of the traumatised child for the mother refuses to die.[4] A state of trauma is, exactly, a state of non-assimilation. One might say that a 'natural' death of the Oedipus complex would bring about the assimilation of the maternal and the paternal objects into the psyche—in Freud's words: 'the two identifications in some way united with each other' (Freud 1923b: 34). A traumatic end, on the other hand, perpetuates a state of vampirism—a haunting of the psyche by damaged, *undead* objects. These repressed, damaged objects are in a state of 'active death', so to speak, threatening the psyche with their return. Ghosts are said to be the spirits particularly of those who died a violent death and, like any other violent incident, the dissolution of the Oedipus complex creates a 'ghost' in the psyche—a dangerous maternal object. Like Clytemnestra's ghost, the undead mother can only be kept at bay by the intervention of the gods—that is, the super-ego. The descent of the curtain of repression over the psyche does not create a state of peace, but instead a state of continuous alert. Like a country in a state of national emergency, the psyche relies on its army—the super-ego—to defend itself. This reliance on the super-ego entails that the male psyche, as described by Freud, relies on the death instinct to defend it from the bad and damaged maternal object, and also from the experience of the fatal attraction towards it.

Of course, Freud mainly referred to the mother as a love object; it is to this incestuous love that the dissolution of the Oedipus complex puts an end. In my opinion, however, the Oedipus complex concerns not only a working-through of incestuous love, but also an identification with mother. Oedipal love is infantile love, and it is part of the nature of infantile love to blur the boundaries between subject and object, and between love and identification. The battle here is not entirely about giving up mother as love object, but also about giving up mother as identificatory figure. There are different types of identification. In this instance I am referring to a type of 'merging', whereby the boundaries between self and other are blurred. In this sense the castration complex has a dual meaning; on a superficial level it concerns the threat of being castrated by the father, but it also involves a deep wish to identify with mother—to be feminine. In Freud's words: '[the castration complex] inhibits and limits masculinity and encourages femininity' (Freud 1925a: 256).

There is also the deeper fear—as described by Klein—of being castrated by the mother (Klein 1928: 190).

The Oedipus complex deserves the central position Freud awarded it, due to its role in the working-through of both object-love and narcissism, of separation from mother and the establishment of a self, of a masculine identification, of the acceptance of father and the parental couple, and of the internalisation of the parental couple. The crucial question, however, is whether the dissolution of the Oedipus complex, as described by Freud, can be said to achieve these goals, which are so important for mental health and creative living.

As I have shown, Freud's account of the dissolution of the Oedipus complex is a description of a trauma, resulting in persecutory anxiety which has to be split off, denied, repressed, or evacuated. The task of upholding the uneasy peace which results is given to the super-ego, which accords with Freud's definition of masculinity as the 'repudiation of femininity'. The super-ego, which ensures the repression of desire and of identification with mother, is regarded by Freud as the solution to the child's intolerable conflict—to lose mother, or to lose the penis. Here Freud was describing a whole culture, as well as the development of an individual—a culture based on the castration complex, and which, as a consequence, has placed the super-ego above real, libidinal relationships.

The castration complex cannot be separated from Freud's theory of phallic monism and of the ignorance of the vagina. This *denial* of the vagina, I believe, amounts to the obliteration of any representation of origins, a denial of our origins in the womb, inside mother, in the body; a denial of an origin which cannot be located in 'omnipotent creation', but only in the union of our parents. It is this denial of being 'only half', of being 'a mere broken tally of a man', which leads to delusions of masculine omnipotence.

This radical solution of the Oedipus complex—the total repression of the early mother—leads to the latency phase, a de-sexualised phase of compliance ruled by the super-ego. When puberty sets in and the 'discovery' of the vagina takes place, intense longing mixed with anxiety threatens to break down the repression barrier. The ghost of Clytemnestra looms in the air as longings and desires for the female body invade the male psyche. In a return of the repressed the terror of the undead mother is re-awakened. This is the time when adolescent boys go temporarily 'mad', out of control. Male groups become very important at this time: scouts, cadets, football teams, rugby teams, with all kinds of exhibitions of masculine prowess and heroic acts, as facilitated by practising martial arts and joining bands and gangs. The stronger the attraction towards the female body, the stronger the banding together of young males, because of the way this attraction unleashes the terror of being possessed by a woman, of being merged with a woman and becoming feminine. Thus the paradox: the ultimate expression of maleness—the sexual act—entails fears of loss of masculinity. The solution traditionally sought for this basic, masculine anxiety entails that the woman/mother becomes a possession, a part of the narcissistic self, under male control. In this type of masculine defence we encounter a reversal of the original possession by the mother.

* * *

That most gory of fairy-tales, the story of Bluebeard's Castle, starkly portrays how persecution and death are characteristic of the masculine unconscious.

Bluebeard's new bride is allowed to wander free in the castle, but there is one room she is not allowed to enter, and she is warned that if she does so she will be put to death. This is the chamber in which all of Bluebeard's previous wives were murdered, and where their bodies are kept. This room, full of dead women, is Bluebeard's deadly secret which, however, no woman can be prevented from discovering. Judith, Bluebeard's latest wife, succumbs like all the others to her morbid curiosity, and pays for this with her life.[5] Bluebeard's secret is an untenable mystery; the murdered mother simply cannot be kept separate from his present relationships. Instead Bluebeard can only rely on women to play the game of ignorance, to collude with him, or—if he is lucky—to trust him. If the woman fails to do so there is disaster in store for her, but also for him—the price is total loss. Bluebeard's tragedy is his inability to find a woman who will trust him, or—rather—collude with him and keep his secret. He is cursed to continue in this way until he finds a woman who will redeem him.

This theme of redemption through a woman recurs in many myths and fairy tales. The matricidal monster can only be redeemed by the love and trust of a woman. In *Beauty and the Beast*, for instance, it is Rose's love which turns the Beast into the prince (Perrault 1970). In Wagner's opera *The Flying Dutchman* it is Senta's love which liberates the Dutchman, who is condemned to wander the seas until he finds a woman who loves him so much she would be willing to die for him.

In Charlotte Bronte's *Jane Eyre*, a more modern version of the same tale, Mr. Rochester at first fails to attain redemption through a woman, because of the way he has concealed the mad woman in his attic. His love for Jane—and Jane's love for him— are not enough to save him. The past returns to haunt him, as the split between his ideal woman and the mad woman in the attic (to whom he is married) breaks down. It is not until he is blinded—in an attempt to save the mad woman from a fire— that his splitting-off is tragically demolished, and subsequent depressive, humbling feelings lead him to his redemption. Jane herself is not the means by which he achieves this; she returns to him only after he has achieved some kind of integration within himself. Only the blind Mr. Rochester is ready for a real relationship with a woman.

Blindness commonly signifies castration. Mr. Rochester's blindness, like that of Oedipus, indicates guilt, humiliation, but also the *insight* which is gained as a consequence of trust and dependence on a woman. It is by relying on the eyes of a woman—his daughter, Antigone—that Oedipus eventually attains his salvation. Indeed the other blind man in the myth, Tiresias, is nonetheless a *seer*, and also someone who—due to the intervention of the gods—has lived a life as both a man and a woman.

I am suggesting that some kind of voluntary, symbolic castration must take place in order to enable a real integration within the psyche and a real relationship to a woman. This symbol-ic castration represents the curbing of phallic narcissism, which is a false, defensive position that merely serves to sustain the dead and murdered mother, or the mad woman in the attic. Such voluntary castration, and the integration of femininity and the early relation to mother, cannot take place if the Oedipus complex comes to an end abruptly—under duress, so to speak. The slow working-through of the whole complex within a *real*, external relationship (as opposed to phantasies) with mother and father is very important. Very important also are the cultur-al demands to reach latency by a certain age, which encourage a split in the psyche, a repression or murder of the early mother, and a consequent exaggeration of masculine trends.

* * *

Masculinity and femininity are phantasies of one another and each relies, to a great extent, on the projections of the other. As a result, it is often extremely difficult to determine what belongs to the masculine and what belongs to the feminine unconscious. We are always dealing with endless projections and responses to these projections.

For instance, what Freud describes in 'The Taboo of Virginity' (1918) can be read as defining something characteris-tically female—which is the view Freud takes—or as male pro-jection. In this paper Freud examines certain customs found among 'primitive peoples' in which the deflowering of a bride is undertaken not by the husband but by a relative, a stranger, a priest, or the leader of the tribe. Freud suggests that the motive for these customs is 'a generalised dread of women' and that they have arisen because '[t]he man is afraid of being weakened by a woman, infected with her femininity' (Freud 1918: 198). Nevertheless, Freud proceeds to attribute the cause of these taboos to *the woman's* hostility, penis-envy, and her wish to cas-trate the man (Freud 1918: 274-5). The woman's hostility towards men is taken very seriously, because it can lead to per-manent antagonism and failure of marriage. Freud concludes it is for this reason that—in certain cultures—the first sexual encounter is assigned to another man—not the husband. It seems to me, however, that this first encounter, entailing a 'deflowering', is simply reminiscent of the violence towards the mother and—for this reason—is to be avoided. The persecutory feelings which would be aroused by this reminder would be simply too much.

Needless to say, there is an obvious difficulty here in deciding what belongs to whom—whose hostility, whose dread, whose anxiety—because of the endless projections between man and woman. One could argue either way, but there is no doubt in my mind that *both* are true, for both have a common origin in the unresolved Oedipus complex. Woman's eventual 'passivity' has as much to do with alleviating the male dread of active femininity as it has to do with curbing her own castrating wishes. After all, the female taboo on aggression is part of women's sacrifice to male fears of powerful femininity, and of the return of the revengeful mother.

Chapter 4

Masculinity, Femininity, and the Death Instinct

So far I have described the development of masculinity in terms of an opposition to mother, and the development of femininity in terms of a submission to father. Consequently there is an essential difference between the two: that whereas femininity develops as a *compromise*, masculinity develops as a *triumph*. Love is therefore different for the boy and for the girl.

For the boy, love for mother is an intensely dangerous affair which threatens his masculinity. This love is killed in an act of psychical violence which attempts to preserve his masculinity. The boy's matricidal psyche, from this point onwards, remains in dread of the early mother. For the girl, on the other hand, love for father bestows femininity upon her. This love is not dangerous, and thus is never quite given up.

Love for the parent of the same sex is also different between the boy and the girl. The girl's early love and attachment to mother is not given up easily—as Freud suggests—but sometimes continues parallel with the Oedipus complex. The boy's love for father, however, is a more risky affair which threatens, once again, the boy's masculinity. To be loved by father is to be in a feminine position.

At the peak of the Oedipus complex the boy's psyche resembles a battlefield: love has become dangerous, and persecution and threats of castration everywhere reign supreme. Freud regarded the inverted Oedipus complex as an additional evocation of castration anxiety for the boy (Freud 1924: 176); the father cannot be allowed to be loving, but becomes instead a castrating monster who forbids access to mother. To kill the father, or to kill his own love for his mother, this is the first dilemma for the boy; to lose his penis, or to give up his love for mother, is the second. The two dilemmas are finally equivalent, because to kill father (psychically) is for the boy to lose his masculinity. What seems impossible—moreover—is to allow a parental *couple* to exist, and for the boy to acknowledge his position in the family as the child of this couple. The attempt to split the parental couple is present in all the variations of the Oedipus complex—positive or inverted, male or female.

The persecution by the mother (unlike the persecution by the father, which is amenable to transformation into guilt) is much more dangerous and pervasive. It also involves more primitive part-objects, which entails that—at times—persecution by mother feels like contamination or possession. Previous ages believed these states were the result of being possessed by the Devil. Today the popular imagination has created the space-alien.

* * *

If masculinity is based on a matricidal act, at the point of the dissolution of the Oedipus complex, and if the paternal super-ego, by instituting repression, becomes the protector against persecution by the undead mother, then the father becomes a key figure for the son. However, a father *precariously* held in the psyche—because of unresolved ambivalence—will precipitate a crisis in the son. The wrath of the Furies can only be counteracted by either God or the Devil, but if the boy—due to his ambivalence towards his father—has lost God, then he might instead make a pact with the Devil. This is, of course, a common theme in legends dating from the late Middle Ages, and we have already examined the interpretations made along these lines by Freud and Fairbairn, concerning the story of Christoph Haizmann, a medieval painter.

The central theme of the myth of Faust is the pact with Mephistopheles. The story was first published in a version dated 1587. Philip Wayne, the translator of Goethe's *Faust*, describes this version as a 'good printer's thriller' (Goethe 1949). It is the purportedly true story of a practising magician, who worked sensational wonders and died in 1537. He was said to have sold his soul to the Devil and—although Humanist scholars scoffed at these rumours—they were nevertheless taken seriously by the new Protestant followers of Luther, and by Luther himself.

This *Faustbuch* of 1587 granted the legend of Faust both fame and immortality, although it was, in fact, merely a collection of tales previously told about ancient magi such as Merlin, Albertus Magnus, and Roger Bacon. Its power derives from the conviction of its anonymous author, a devoted Lutheran, who attests to the truth of the tales:

> His descriptions of the nether regions and of the fearful state of mind of his heart-hardened hero are still impressive, as can be seen from the verbatim use of such passages in the novel *Doctor Faustus* (1947) by the German writer Thomas Mann. (Encyclopaedia Britannica, Micropaedia 1982: vol. IV, 67)

The Lutheran obsession with the Devil is worth examining in greater detail. For instance, Norman O. Brown in his book *Life Against Death* (1959) examines Luther's obsession with anal imagery, and the relation of this to his struggle with the Devil. As Brown shows, for Luther everything of this world belongs to the Devil. He quotes Luther:

> The world is the Devil and the Devil is the world... Everything is full of devils, in the courts of princes, in houses, in fields, in streets, in water, in wood, in fire. (cited in Brown 1959: 212)

Luther diabolised not only human vices, but also human virtues. Traditional virtues such as 'good works' are nevertheless under the domain of the Devil. Only faith can save man:

> ...in man who does not believe in Christ not only are all sins mortal, but even his good works are sins... The Devil lets his own do many good works, pray, fast, build churches, establish Masses and holy days, and behave as if he were pious... Men of holy works (*die Werkheilen*) are Satan's captive servants, no matter how much they appear to surpass others in good works and in strictness and holiness of life. (cited in Brown 1959: 212-3)

Luther finds the Devil behind everything human, including reason. Reason is, indeed, the Devil's 'bride and whore': 'Reason is the source of all achievement in this world; but good works and achievements in this world are the domain of the Devil' (cited in Brown 1959: 213). Even conscience, which was later to become the cornerstone of Protestant morality, receives the same treatment: 'Conscience stands in cruel service of the Devil; a man must learn to find consolation even against his own conscience' (cited in Brown 1959: 213)

In the context of my argument, what emerges from passages like these is the impossibility of redemption within the parameters of this world. Luther puts all his hope on faith, but faith cannot be willed: 'No man could face the Devil with his free will' (cited in Brown 1959: 212). Faith is not determined, it is not under one's control. Instead, faith is given; it is a gift from God, an act of grace. In Kleinian terms, it is an act of generosity which leads to *gratitude.*

In this sense, then, the world of faith is fundamentally different from the world of work and action. The world of faith is mother's world, starkly differentiated from father's world. However it is precisely the world of faith which is cut off by repression—by what I have called matricide—and which leaves the world of the father under the domination of the Devil, or the death instinct.

It is noteworthy that Lutheran theology eliminates Mary. The elimination of Mary—the good mother—from the Lutheran universe means that there are only two protagonists left: on the one hand the bad mother, and on the other—father. The question is: which of these is the Devil? Perhaps it is the world of the Father which is 'diabolical'—the world of work and action—and that it becomes this way due to a lack of faith, the fact that faith has been murdered. In this case, the murdered mother becomes the Devil—the death instinct—in an attempt to create a sin-free zone, a world of idealised fathers, a world of Apollonian peace and light. Indeed Luther himself seems fully aware of the untenable, impossible nature of this 'world of light' resting on a world of Furies and devils, given that he—unlike the Greeks—chooses not to believe in the power of reason.

Luther consequently found himself in a split world, but gave expression to the demons of this world by refusing to cover them up with idealisations. A world of reason resting on repression is an untenable illusion. Freud's theory of the unconscious demonstrated this, but was unable to envisage a solid alternative to the flimsy balance that human beings often manage to achieve within this state of affairs. Instead, Freud became an apologist for that other world of irrationality and darkness, of devils and murderers, in the hope of a better balance.

Karl Figlio, in an unpublished paper, describes freedom as a moment of reparation, in opposition to attempts at *manic reparation*.[6] Freedom, he suggests, is to be in the presence of a good object. Freedom is a moment which cannot be engineered by the conscious will, but can only arise through an instance of genuine reparation (Figlio 1995). In theological terms this is a moment of Grace. The world of manic reparation can also be likened to Luther's world of 'good works' (although I am sure it is far from Figlio's intention to demonise these types of human endeavour).

My point here is that manic reparation inevitably proves ineffectual and compulsive because it does not address the main issue of the damaged mother and the damaged self. It skips over this and attempts instead to cover the hole with action, with 'good works' and 'achievement'.

* * *

In order to show how these themes impinge upon masculinity and femininity, I will examine Goethe's version of *Faust* in more detail.

At the beginning of the play Faust is a desperate man. He is gripped by meaninglessness and depression. He has studied everything: philosophy, law, medicine and theology. 'Master' and 'Doctor' are his titles—he tells us—and he has:

...outdistanced all the others
Doctors, clergy and lay-brothers;
All plague of doubts and scruples, I can quell,
And have no fear of devil or of hell,
and in return am destitute of pleasure. (Goethe 1949: 43)

Nevertheless he is in the grip of a deathly force. Death is all around him and life has retreated:

Hemmed in with stacks of books am I,
Where works the worm with dusty mange...
And shall I wonder why my heart
Is lamed and frightened in my breast,
Why all the springs of life that start
Are strangely smothered and oppressed?
Instead of all that life can hold
Of Nature's free, God-given breath,
I take to me the smoke and mould
of skeletons and dust and death. (Goethe 1949: 44-45)

Faust is not a modest man. Even in his despair he boasts to the Earth Spirit which he has summoned that he is 'in everything your equal' (Goethe 1949: 48). Significantly, the spirit replies: 'You match the spirit that you comprehend, not me' (Goethe 1949: 48). His arrogance once again lands him in despair. The Earth Spirit vanishes and he is left alone with his empty knowledge, full of dust and death. To a chorus of angels which sings of Christ's resurrection he answers:

I hear, but lack the faith, am dispossessed;
And faith has wonder for its dearest child.
This is a sphere to which, I may not venture,
This source of things sublime, this lofty strain... (Goethe 1949: 56)

Faust's 'dispossession' and his arrogance go hand-in-hand. We might be reminded at this point of the plight of the boy in the phallic phase, his substitution of the mother with the phallus in a triumphant denial of dependence (cf. Jones 1948a). Grandiosity and the death instinct combine in this narcissistic expulsion from paradise. The boy feels he has no right to enter the space of the mother. He can only obliterate it, and create the alternative, narcissistic world of the phallus, of 'knowledge'. This is an obsessional world in which milk, faeces, and babies are confused with one another. The boy negates all he was in relation to his mother, so that this becomes a world without an 'other'. The phallic phase, the anal phase, and the world of the Devil coincide. This is a dead world in which life itself is negated.

However, in reality the boy cannot live without mother any more than can the girl. If he is to reach mother, but at the same time avoid femininity, then there is only one way—to be her partner, her lover, her husband, which is—in effect—to obliterate father. This is the world of the Oedipus complex, with all its attendant fears of castration and regression, but even so, with its forbidden pleasures, it is infinitely richer and more alive than the phallic world of no other and no mother. The Oedipus complex is a world in which 'possession' of mother has returned eroticised and insistent. This is the world which Faust seeks in his despair, as a substitute for the dead place he has created for himself:

Two souls, alas, are housed within my breast,
And each will wrestle for the mastery there.
The one has passion's craving crude for love,
And hugs a world where sweet the senses rage;
The other longs for pastures fair above,
Leaving the murk for lofty heritage. (Goethe 1949: 67)

Faust's arrogance, his hubris, throws him eventually into the hands of Mephistopheles. He promises to lead Faust back to life, back to his body and the world of the senses, back to mother's body. As a perverse substitute for both mother and father, Mephistopheles promises *all* forbidden pleasures. What had formerly been denied has suddenly returned. All the negation in Faust is represented by Mephistopheles, who is himself the

Spirit of Negation. On one level, this is the return of the repressed: the unresolved Oedipus complex has returned with a vehemence, which holds out the possibility of life to someone trapped in a world of the dead.

This is also the world of Don Giovanni, as presented in the opera by Mozart, which preceded Goethe's *Faust* by fourteen years. Don Giovanni, also, turns against everything dictated by the world of the Father. Steeped in an omnipotent, phallic world, he perishes in the icy grip of the ghost he challenges to return from the underworld.[7] Don Giovanni is challenging both the Father and the Law. He is therefore in direct confrontation with what—normally—would be a protective super-ego. Instead, he is the rebellious son who denies both mother and father and, as a consequence, is left with his own deadly super-ego and delusions of omnipotence.

Faust, on the other hand—like Oedipus—finds salvation through suffering. Faust, unlike Don Giovanni, is not usually regarded as a masculine hero. And neither for that matter is Victor Frankenstein, the omnipotent creator of the first manu-factured human being. Yet it is obvious what is at stake in both: phallic omnipotence—the denial of mother's world, and of the female world which complements that of the male.

The substratum of masculinity—that which I call *primitive masculinity*—therefore oscillates between the phallic phase and the Oedipus complex, but without resolving either. It demands 'Oedipal triumph'—as in the case of Don Giovanni—or else entails becoming stuck in the phallic/anal phase, as in the case of Frankenstein.

Theoretically, mature masculinity arrives with the resolution of the Oedipus complex and the internalisation of the parental couple. However, as I have suggested, this is in fact rather rare in Western culture, in which the unresolved Oedipus complex is repressed and the mother becomes a persecutor.

* * *

Femininity, in relation to primitive masculinity, appears as both life and death, as both power and powerlessness, narcissistic wholeness and castration—the one being the underside of the other. The death-bearing mother and the life-giving mother are one and the same, as if life itself were the arch-enemy. This is clearly evident in Mephistopheles answer to Faust:

> The spirit I, that endlessly denies.
> And rightly, too; for all that comes to birth
> Is fit for overthrow, as nothing worth;
> Wherefore the world were better sterilised... (Goethe 1949: 75)

This hatred of life seems to be in the same vein as Luther's conviction that the world belongs to the Devil. Norman Brown comments:

> The doctrine of the impossibility of overcoming sin can be deduced from the doctrine of the vanity of good works, and it results in the Lutheran dualism between the inner world of grace and the outer world of works, the world of the spirit and the world of the flesh. (Brown 1959: 214)

One might argue that this dualism is the very definition of Christianity and of Western culture in general; life as 'sin', life as 'depravity' is the paradoxical statement of this position. It is as if the matricidal impulses have transformed not only mother, but also life itself into the Devil.

Just before Mephistopheles appears, Faust is struggling over his translation of St. John's Gospel:

> T's writ, 'In the beginning was the Word.'
> I pause, to wonder what is inferred.
> The Word I cannot set supremely high:
> A new translation I will try.
> I read, if by the spirit I am taught,
> This sense: 'In the beginning was the Thought.'
> This opening I need to weigh again,
> Or sense may suffer from a hasty pen.
> Does Thought create, and work, and rule the hour?

'Twere best: 'In the beginning was the Power.'
Yet, while the pen is urged with willing fingers,
A sense of doubt and hesitancy lingers.
The spirit comes to guide me in my need,
I write, 'In the beginning was the Deed.' (Goethe 1949: 71)

This takes place whilst Mephistopheles is in the room, in the guise of a black poodle. It is obvious that Faust is at this moment under his influence. What is most striking, however, is the similarity with Luther's view of action and achievement as the work of the Devil. But from my point of view both Word and Deed—as well as all the other possibilities which Faust considers—exclude life as 'life-giving'. Both God and the Devil exclude the flesh as the source of the flesh, and thus life is seen as death.

It seems to me that this is, first and foremost, a dispossession of mother and—along with her—woman, and then man himself. It is no surprise, then, that Faust's story includes the love and subsequent destruction of a woman—Margaretta. Faust's damnation also entails the damnation of Margaretta.[8]

Luther, finding himself in a dualistic world, puts all his hope in an act of Grace. Later, Romanticism—with its 'return to nature' motto—reinstated woman as the saviour of man, and love as the main force of his redemption. This love is proof of the survival of the good object and of the reparability of the internal world. Ultimately, it is as if matricide can only be overcome by love and total trust.

* * *

What I have called 'primitive masculinity' oscillates between the phallic phase and the Oedipus complex, whereas the feminine world oscillates between mother and father.

Ernest Jones makes a distinction between the 'proto-phallic phase', during which there is no awareness of sex-difference, and the 'deutero-phallic phase'—that is, the 'second phallic phase'—which follows the discovery of the sex-difference. He describes the deutero-phallic phase as follows:

There are two outstanding differences between it and the earlier stages: (1) It is less sadistic, the main relic of this being a tendency to omnipotence phantasies; and (2) it is more self-centred, the chief allo-erotic attribute still remaining being its exhibitionistic aspect. It is thus less aggressive and less related to other people, notably women. How has this change been brought about? It would seem to be a change in the direction of phantasy and away from the real world of contact with other human beings. If so, this would in itself justify a suspicion that there is a flight element present, and that we have not to do simply with a natural evolution towards greater reality and a more developed adjustment. (Jones 1948a: 454)

For Jones the deutero-phallic phase follows the Oedipus complex, and is a retreat from the terror of castration which the boy encountered during the Oedipus complex. He sees it as less sadistic, since the castration complex is no longer active.

Freud, on the other hand, regarded the phallic phase as *preceding* the Oedipus complex, or at least occurring contemporaneously. This might not indicate a disparity as such, since disappointment in the Oedipus complex might result in regression to an earlier phase. Whichever way we might choose to view it, the phallic phase entails omnipotence and a retreat from object relations. The phallic phase and the Oedipus complex might then be taken as the two poles between which immature masculinity oscillates. The challenge to the parents is evident in both phases, but whereas the Oedipus complex *engages* with the parents in a relation of love, hate and arrogance, the phallic phase *does away with* the parents altogether. There is no engagement with them at a passionate level, or with anyone else. A narcissistic phallic world fills the space, a lonely world of isolation and preoccupation with the non-human environment—whether this includes machinery, sub-atomic particles, computer science, or the cosmos.

However, we must distinguish here between phallic defences and a pre-Oedipal identification with the father. The pre-Oedipal identification with father is very important if the boy is to avoid the loneliness and deadness of a defensive phallic/anal position. Freud referred to a pre-Oedipal identification of the boy with the father, which coincides with this phase (Freud 1923b: 31-2). Jessica Benjamin writes similarly of the 'father/liberator' of the 'rapprochement period'. For the boy, the father arrives on the scene as a *deus ex machina*, which enables him to deny his helplessness and his dependency on mother:

> Recognition of himself in the father is what enables the boy to deny helplessness, to feel he is powerful, to protect himself from the loss of the grandiosity he enjoyed in the practising phase. When the boy is not playing daddy, he flies about, announcing his new name—Superman. (Benjamin 1990a: 104)

In other words, father is very important if the boy in the phallic phase is to escape the prospect of a world without objects and without life—an anal world of dead matter. If the identification with father fails, and dependence on mother is impossible, then the dead phallic world closes around the boy in all its grim and destructive reality.

* * *

Danny is a twenty-five year old man who complains of an inability to form relationships or anything approaching intimacy. He admires women from a distance, but feels that none of them would be interested in him—at least, not the ones with whom he would like to have a relationship. He falls in love with unavailable women, and develops melancholic friendships with them. He has a very low self-image and very easily feels rejected. After any such instance of rejection during the session he misses—without fail—the next session. During sessions he often withdraws into complete silence, rolls himself into a ball, and finds refuge in a world without other. During these silences he feels suicidal.

Danny loves machines. His job is to repair agricultural machinery, but any other machines are equally welcome. He has a passion for cars, power tools, diggers, bulldozers. He was very religious in the past but had already lost his faith when he entered therapy, something which left him very vulnerable because he found himself without an ideal object. It seems to me that, at this time, machines became even more important as a substitute for an ideal father. Danny is in flight from the Oedipus complex, from any kind of a parental couple, and from any kind of parents. Parents mean only one thing to him: they are persecutors. As a result, he is in the grip of the phallic defence and the death instinct.

Danny experienced his childhood as a series of reprimands, accusations and condemnations. The family lived on a farm in rural Southern Europe, where life was tough. The parents had very little time for the ten children, except when it came to reprimanding them if they did not contribute enough to the work of the farm.

Danny remembers his father as a harsh, authoritarian patriarch who had worked hard and had made some money as a farmer. He remembers very little tenderness from his father, and none at all from his mother, however she was a 'victim' in the same sense as Danny. One of his first experiences was of overhearing intercourse between his parents whilst he slept with his brother in the next room. After the birth of his younger brother, his mother resisted sex with his father, and Danny witnessed a series of marital rapes during which he thought his mother was in mortal danger. This traumatic event was a combination of a bad, rapist father, a victimised but at the same time rejecting mother, and bad sex. No identification was possible for Danny. It is as if he has remained suspended between a feminine (castrated) victimised part of himself, a male, raping, punishing part, and a rejected child. No position is safe from either attack, castration or feminisation. The primal scene—for him—is a sadistic moment, and beyond it lies a lonely life with no love and no contact. The adoption of machines as a substitute for human beings represents the death of the parents, and devoting his life to repairing machines is a kind of manic reparation which has to be repeated again and again.

When Danny emerges from the world of machinery and withdrawal he experiences me as a castrator, a devouring monster, a vampire, a fury. This coming back to life is a return to a world not only of pain and suffering, but also—more primitively—of devouring, of blood sacrifices, matricide and infanticide. He feels the dread of annihilation and retreats to a kind of womb where, curled up in the foetal position, he phantasises a world of no 'other'—only the placenta.

As I become less terrifying, moments of peace emerge. These are equivalent to being in the presence of a benign mother, to silent moments of 'being with'—without exactly meeting, or conversing, without language and without intercourse—but simply allowing mother to exist, without father. By remembering rare moments from his home-life in which mother was 'good' he becomes able to spend a whole session silently basking in my presence.

As Danny emerges from the phallic/anal position there are Oedipal moments in the transference, during which he sees himself as the seducer or the liberator. He dreams that the wife of a friend elopes with him, leaving her husband and young son behind. He catches a glimpse of a woman sitting alone inside a house and phantasises that she is lonely, despite the fact that she is married, and that he could lighten her life. He speculates that 'professional' women are especially lonely because there are very few people equal to their standards. The transferential elements here are very obvious and—I speculate—a sign of increasing hope.

However, the Oedipal constellation is flimsy. The rival father is absent, defeated, eliminated by magic means as if in a dream or fairy-tale. A single small failure on my part is enough to throw him back to a world of dead matter and despair.

Slowly, father emerges as an identificatory figure. He has a dream that he is dancing with his father at a party. They are both happy, laughing, enjoying themselves. But father and mother are never together. The parental couple is entirely absent. It is as if, for Danny, the parental couple is still the primitive 'combined parent imago' which Klein describes as a terrifying, devouring object that no child can face without terror—or, alternatively, as a mutually devouring couple (Klein 1975b: 246).

* * *

Danny is perhaps an extreme case, but he illustrates a fundamental structure present within masculinity—the oscillation between the phallic position and the Oedipus complex. This is why the Oedipus complex is such a crucial moment for the boy; below it there is only narcissistic triumph or death. The boy, during the more mature phase of the dissolution of the Oedipus complex, identifies with father and consolidates a masculine identity. This is a move towards life and away from the phallic position. However—as we have seen—if the Oedipus complex is merely repressed, or if psychic matricide has been perpetrated, then the mother will remain as a persecutor. Regression to the phallic position will occur every time the parental couple is perceived as absent, and Western culture—with its peculiar elision of the creative parental couple—is particularly prone to this. Western culture's obsession with technology can be read as a phantasy of displacing the parental couple as the source of creativity, and of re-instating the phallic position.

The post-Oedipal identification with father is very different from the triumphant, narcissistic pre-Oedipal identification—assuming, of course, that a working-through of the Oedipus complex has been achieved. In this case parental authority and parental love—the parents' love for each other and the parents' love for the child—are internalised. In the case of a mere 'dissolution' of the Oedipus complex there is instead an identification with the castrating father and a repression of the mother as the object of desire—the psychic matricide. In the additional scenario of a retreat from the Oedipus complex, there is a regression to the pre-Oedipal phallic phase which can be either a narcissistic identification with father (that is, a narcissistic state of triumph over mother), or a phallic/anal phase of no mother and no life. This sheds some light on the way in which the painter

Christoph Haizmann's symptoms began after the death of his father, and why Faust's pact with Mephistopheles also occurred after the death of Faust's father. The death of a parent is a test of identification, and may drive a man back to the phallic/anal phase.

Femininity, on the other hand, oscillates between mother and father. Trapped at a pre-Oedipal level the girl is stuck with mother and at the mercy of projected feelings of envy and hostility. The *lack of space* is the predominant characteristic of this state. Claustrophobia, agoraphobia, hysteria, psychosomatic symptoms, inability to symbolise are also often present. It is not surprising that so many fairy-tales focus on the fate of a girl at the hands of a bad (step-)mother—for instance: Snow White and Cinderella.

The phallic phase in girls can never be the same as in boys, and this makes a crucial difference. Freud posited penis-envy as the central theme of the girl's development, although subsequent authors emphasised the role of the penis in separation and individuation. Jessica Benjamin, for instance, regards the girl's identification with father during the rapprochement phase as crucial to her struggle to separate and individuate:

> Girls desire it [the penis] for one of the main reasons that boys cherish it—because they are struggling to individuate. They are seeking what toddler boys recognise in their fathers and wish, through identification, to affirm in themselves—recognition of their own desire. But they find themselves in conflict about this wish to tear themselves from the attachment to mother—often greater than the conflict of boys because of the intense narcissistic bond between mother and daughter—and seek to find another *object* with whom to identify. This other object is the father, and his otherness is guaranteed and symbolised by his genital. (Benjamin 1990b: 466)

The girl, identifying with something that does not belong to her, however, may become involved in borrowing or stealing—with all the guilt and humiliation that goes with this. The ten-

dency of women towards depression, rather than towards violence or delinquency, has its roots here. The girl is caught
between mother and father, and thus her matricidal tendencies
are interwoven with her sense of herself as female. That is why
the girl more often than not colludes with matricide but does
not attempt it herself. To kill the mother would mean to con-
demn herself to perpetual guilt and exile—estrangement from
the land of the mother in a phallic, lonely world. An alternative
way in which women avoid depression and suicidal impulses
is—often—to become pregnant. This might be interpreted as a
test of the survival of the internal mother, of the internal babies,
or of the internal couple.

* * *

Marie is a fifty year old woman who feels sadness and regret
that she never 'managed' to have children. Now that it is too late
she looks back in sadness, but still doubts whether she could
ever have 'managed'. 'Manage' refers here to the 'slavery' of
being a mother, being ruled by the baby and at the baby's power
and command. 'His Majesty the baby'(Freud 1914: 91) is viewed
by Marie as a tyrant who rules with absolute power over mother. She feels she might not have coped with such endless
demands. Another fear is that she would have damaged the
child the way she feels damaged herself.

Marie seems to be struggling with an exhausted and impoverished internal mother who has nothing to give because she is
herself struggling to survive. This mother has been exhausted
by the baby, and relegated to a half-alive state. Marie herself
escaped this state of a vampire-like symbiosis through her relationship and identification with her father. This identification
with father is felt on the one hand to be 'life-saving' yet, on the
other, to have prevented her from being a woman. 'Being a
woman' is related to having babies and to being depressed,
trapped in the vampire-like relationship with mother. 'Being a
man', on the other hand, is related to keeping the woman or
mother alive—which was her experience of her father.

In this sense, then, her father is a life-saver. Her identification with him bears all the hallmarks of manic reparation. The only beam of light in this world of shadows is Marie's love for her father *distinct from* her identification with him. This love, which is a distant echo of what must have been her first love for her mother, is her only hope of overcoming the repetitive world of manic reparation. However, this love is tainted by the bitter jealousy kindled by her sister's birth, and is therefore unable to function as a real reparative force. It is not surprising that Marie's relationships follow the pattern described by Freud in 'Female Sexuality' (1931) whereby a girl marries a man based on the model of her father, but develops a relationship with him according to that she had with her mother. In this case the relationship entails the return of a half-alive mother, the vampire or witch who once threatened to annihilate or cast a spell over Marie herself. Consequently, the wish to end the relationship becomes stronger and stronger as time passes.[9]

Perhaps it is not surprising that both Marie and her father are gardeners by profession, devoting their lives to tending mother earth and her children. When Marie speaks about her work she comes alive. She talks about her plants as if they were her children, in need of care and feeding to ensure their survival and well-being. This is not enough, however, to enrich her internal world; she feels constantly impoverished, always on the brink of losing everything. Fears of being reduced to a state of absolute poverty and disability haunt her, as well as fears of being devoured by her partner, of losing herself and having 'nothing left of myself' in a close sexual relationship. The damaged, symbiotic mother is always present. In this sense manic reparation, manifested in her identification with father, does not work as well for the girl as it does for the boy. To have a baby is—quite often—the only way in which the girl feels she might be able to repair her internal world. Having a baby is a form of manic reparation in this context, and thus Freud's equation of baby and penis is very apt (Freud 1925a: 256).

The relation of masculinity and femininity to the death instinct is asymmetrical and unequal. I hope I have shown how the consequences of the death instinct—that is, the persecution by a murdered, damaged, undead mother—plays a highly contrasting role in the construction of masculine and feminine identities. Identifications and relations with mother and father have vastly different meanings for boys and for girls. The feminine response to a damaged, murdered mother—which is mainly depressive in nature—contrasts starkly with the manic defences of masculinity, which are sometimes violent, triumphalist, 'technological', or else lonely and full of despair.

Chapter 5

Freud and Femininity

ATHENE: My duty is to give the final vote. When yours
Are counted, mine goes to uphold Orestes' plea.
No mother gave me birth. Therefore the father's claim
And male supremacy in all things, save to give
Myself in marriage, wins my whole heart's loyalty.
Therefore a woman's death, who killed her husband, is,
I judge, outweighed in grievousness by his. And so
Orestes, if the votes are equal, wins the case. (Aeschylus
1986: 172)

With these words Athene sums up her position regarding
Orestes' trial. The votes are counted and the black and white
pebbles are equal in number. Athene adds hers to the white pile,
and declares: 'Orestes is acquitted of blood-guiltiness'
(Aeschylus 1986: 173).

Here, then, we see a female goddess—unique among the
gods in that she has no mother—proclaiming male supremacy
and casting her vote in defence of Orestes, who has killed his
mother. Earlier, Electra—Orestes' sister—acts in a similar fashion, by taking the side of her father and her brother against her
mother. The father she defends is a distant father, a virtual
stranger to her, albeit a glorified stranger. This is perhaps the
point around which hinges this whole tragedy of murder,
revenge, and godly decrees: that Agamemnon's brutality is not
evident to his family, unlike that of the mother, Clytemnestra.
An absent father, it would seem, is by definition a glorified
father. And given the close, suffocating relationship which—in
contrast—Electra must endure with her mother, then the murder of the mother in the name of the father indeed appears her
only route to freedom.

ELECTRA: ...Father!
Take pity on me and on Orestes your own son.

How shall we two possess our home? We are homeless
   both,
Sold by our mother—her price Aegisthus, who murdered
   you. (Aeschylus 1986: 108)

As in so many fairy-tales, the only good parent is the absent
father, and it is the (step-) who mother dispossesses the children, especially if they are girls. The sexual couple formed by
the mother and her current partner is hated, they are viewed as
impostors, yet the glorified but absent father is idealised. In one
sense this can be regarded as the peak of the Oedipus complex
for the girl: the condemnation of the sexual couple, and of the
mother as 'whore'—on the one hand—with the idealisation of a
distant father on the other. However, it seems as if the current
sexual couple must be killed in order for the girl to reach the
father.

The idealisation of an absent father lies at the heart of femininity. The girl finds herself trapped in a bad relationship with
the mother or step-mother, who attempts to kill her or to poison
her, or who treats her with contempt and cruelty. The girl turns
to father because she wants a penis, Freud asserts (Freud 1925a:
252-3). In this sense, then, the first movement away from mother and towards father is not a change of object—not at first, any-
way—but, instead, a change in the girl's figure of identification.[10] However, the way in which Freud describes what he calls
'the change of object in women' conflates the notion of love
object and identificatory figure.

The girl's change of object from mother to father, Freud suggests, is by no means a smooth, matter-of-fact affair. It is deeply
problematic for the girl, and it was only once Freud had realised
just how problematic that he began to see the way in which feminine development follows a radically different path from that
of masculine development.

Why should the girl leave mother for father? Freud asks himself this question. After all, mother is her first object, her first
love, her first attachment. His answer to this question—'because
of penis-envy'—has not ceased to offend women ever since. The

girl turns to father, Freud suggests, because she is in search of a penis.

Freud was referring—of course—to infantile wishes and phantasies, and to the meanings which children assign to the body and to bodily organs. As we have seen, Freud's theory of penis-envy and of castration rests on the infantile notion of phallic monism—that is, the child's supposed belief that there is only one sex organ, the penis. Consequently the girl regards the absence of a penis as a 'lack': 'She has seen it and knows that she is without it and wants to have it', writes Freud (Freud 1925a: 252). For a while she clings to the hope that her clitoris will grow into a penis, but soon she has to renounce this illusion and accept her 'castration'.

This realisation by the girl that she has no penis leads to something which amounts to a narcissistic trauma. Her self-esteem appears to collapse; she blames her mother for not giving her a penis at birth, and comes to regard both herself and her mother as castrated and inferior to father. The girl turns away from her mother in anger and contempt. What she is looking for—Freud suggests—is something which her mother cannot provide.

However, the girl's wish for a penis is viewed in a different light by Melanie Klein. Klein maintains that it is the girl's *feminine* heterosexual wishes which drive her to want a penis—she desires a penis to make a child, Klein argues (Klein 1932a: 227). For Freud, on the other hand, it is the girl's *masculine* wishes which drive her towards father—that is, she wants a penis for herself, in order to replace her clitoris (Freud 1933: 119-28).

This is a fundamentally important difference. Freud is arguing that there is no *a priori* feminine, nothing 'given'. In fact, the only 'given' is sexual difference itself. This difference, however, is not understood in this way by the child, who sees only 'creatures with a penis' and 'creatures without a penis'. To the child's mind this amounts to 'intact people' versus 'castrated people'. Consequently my reading of the penis in Freud is that it functions less as a sign of difference, but more as a sign of wholeness—of omnipotence. The penis could only function as a sign of difference if the vagina were already known. I think that with his discovery of the importance of the penis Freud illuminated a crucial component of the Western patriarchal psyche—its *erosion* of difference. Within Western culture, the notion of 'difference' is substituted by the dichotomy 'castrated' versus 'intact'.

On one level, the penis must indeed function as a sign of difference, if psychosis is to be avoided. However, 'difference'—in this context—is 'difference' from the mother, and is bound up entirely with the necessity for the child to separate from her. But where 'difference' refers to the difference between 'intact' and 'castrated' people, then this carries us into what is an entirely separate domain, characterised by domination, and an entirely distinct species of delusion. This erosion of difference is also the erosion of female sexuality and of woman as subject.

The penis, then, plays a role in the separation from mother rather than in establishing sexual difference, which cannot be truly established without prior knowledge of the vagina. Consequently, separation from mother is not in fact a genuine separation at all, but instead a type of 'repudiation'. Both the boy and the girl eventually repudiate mother, but this takes place under different conditions in each case.

It was these conditions which Freud described as 'the Oedipus complex'. For Freud, the girl wishes for a penis because she feels her clitoris is inferior. For Freud, the girl has nothing if she has no penis; she is indeed 'castrated'.[11] So, for Freud the girl wants a penis because of her masculine strivings, and not because of her feminine desire (as Klein maintained). Paradoxically, then, Freud seems to be saying that the girl's Oedipus complex is not really an Oedipus complex at all, but instead an identification with father. This is a point stressed by Chasseguet-Smirgel. As she puts it: 'If we carry these statements to their logical conclusion, can we not say that in Freudian theory the father is more of an object for the boy than for the girl?' (Chasseguet-Smirgel 1986: 18). With regard to feminine sexuality, Freud reaches a curious conclusion: the girl—in effect—denies her mother and wants to be like her father. Like Athene, she upholds the 'supremacy of the male' and of the penis, and denies her own origins. Like Electra, she hates her mother, and thus places herself in a state of alienation.

Feminine development does not end here, however. For Freud, the wish for a penis must be transformed into a wish for a baby, effectively converting masculine into feminine wishes. The wish for a baby is, therefore, secondary to the girl's coveting of the penis. The other change which must come about on the 'circuitous' path to femininity is the abandonment of the clitoris for the vagina as the main erotogenic zone. Many women, Freud suggests, never attain the goal of femininity, but remain stuck in a masculinity complex or, alternatively, develop a total aversion towards sexuality and become frigid.

However Freud discovered something else, which appears to exist in a kind of parallel (or perhaps *negative*) state to the Oedipal universe he describes. In 1931, six years after his first paper on female development, he produced 'Female Sexuality', in which he describes the importance of the girl's strong, pre-Oedipal attachment to mother:

I was struck, above all, by two facts. The first was that where the woman's attachment to her father was particularly intense, analysis showed that it had been preceded by a phase of exclusive attachment to her mother which had been equally intense and passionate. Except for the change of her love-object, the second phase had scarcely added any new feature of her erotic life. Her primary relation to her mother had been built up in a very rich and many-sided manner. The second fact taught me that the *duration* of this attachment had also been greatly underestimated. In several cases it lasted until well into the fourth year—in one case into the fifth year—so that it covered by far the longer part of the period of early sexual efflorescence. Indeed, we had to reckon with the possibility that a number of women remain arrested in their original attachment to their mother and never achieve a true change-over towards men. This being so, the pre-Oedipus phase in woman gains an importance which we have not attributed to it hitherto... it would seem as though we must retract the universality of the thesis that the Oedipus complex is the nucleus of the neuroses. (Freud 1931: 225-6)

The girl's attachment to her mother is active, masculine, as well as of a feminine, passive kind. The girl's attachment to father, on the other hand, begins as an active wish to take or steal his penis, yet ends up as a passive wish to be loved by him. So, in describing the girl's transition from mother to father, Freud also describes the movement from an active to a passive sexuality.

Freud discovered that, despite this, the girl never quite gives up mother. Her attachment to mother continues sometimes even after the change of object has taken place (Freud 1931: 229-30). As a consequence, Freud regarded bisexuality as a characteristic of women more than of men. The girl—in a sense—has *two* objects: mother and father; and *two* erotogenic zones: the clitoris and the vagina. She makes a transition from mother to father, and from the clitoris to the vagina, and this constitutes the journey towards femininity. But something of the previous phase always remains in a kind of parallel state which, it seems, is not repressed.

This contrasts importantly with the way in which the boy solves the problem of separation from mother. In his case there is massive repression at the point of the dissolution of the Oedipus complex, which I describe as psychic matricide. In the case of the girl, she commits no matricide, but she does come to *accept* the matricidal world. This acceptance of matricide places her in a state of alienation. Freud writes:

We have the impression that what we have said about the Oedipus complex applies with complete strictness to the male child only and that we are right in rejecting the term 'Electra complex' which seeks to emphasise the analogy between the attitude of the two sexes. It is only in the male that we find the fateful combination of love for the one parent and simultaneous hatred for the other as a rival. (Freud 1931: 228-9)

For the boy, the Oedipus complex is also a solution to another problem—his early identification with mother. This early identification with mother might be described as an 'early castration complex', in which the castrator is the mother who threatens to deprive the boy of his masculinity. This is, of course, a projection of the boy's wish to be like mother. In this early relationship, mother love and identification are fused and confused. For the girl, on the other hand, identification with mother does not pose the same problem. Her dilemma, instead, concerns separation from mother (not in terms of gender identity, but in terms of autonomy) and the possibility of finding a heterosexual object.

Nevertheless, it is my view that the difference between the development of the boy and the development of the girl cannot be summed up by the simple statement that 'the Oedipus complex is more relevant to the boy', or even that 'the girl has two objects and two erotogenic zones'. In the case of the girl there is an entirely different dynamic at the heart of the Oedipus complex. In describing the development of female sexuality, Freud was also—I believe—describing another model of development altogether, one which is not based on repression, but on transition, integration, coexistence, and a less paranoid, more depressive and potentially reparative model. This is a model which would also apply to the boy, *if the threat of castration did not exist.*

For Freud the threat of castration is so important because it leads to the dissolution of the Oedipus complex and to the creation of the super-ego, 'and thus initiates all the processes that are designed to make the individual find a place in the cultural community' (Freud 1931: 229). But this is of course a particular type of super-ego, based not on an identification with the lost loved object, but with the aggressor. The question remains whether an identification with the lost loved object—a loss that would be neither abrupt nor forced—could lead to a different kind of a super-ego, with 'the father and mother identifications united' (cf. Freud 1923b: 34).

* * *

The repeated refrain of this book is the inability of the Western psyche to resolve the Oedipus complex by genuine resolution rather than by repression, and its perpetuation of the consequent, infantile denial of female sexuality. The revival of these conflicts in puberty entails yet more splitting and persecution, and it is within this subsequent phase that the vagina finally comes into existence, but as a passive rather than an active sexual organ. The idealisation of woman in romantic love and her debasement in pornography—two sides of the same coin—are based exactly upon this splitting and persecution, due to the castration complex, which instils the need to see woman as passive.

It is interesting that author after author has attributed this passive role to the vagina. The anus and the mouth have both been proposed as prototypes upon which the our conception of the vagina is based,[12] yet neither of these—it would seem—can be accurately conceived of as 'passive'. Nevertheless, this notion of 'passivity' has persisted in connection with the vagina, and as the general mode of female sexuality. To me, however, it seems very difficult to state what can be considered 'passive' about the vagina's capacity for incorporation.

We see here the castration complex in operation: it is *necessary* that woman remains castrated, or—if she *is* to have a sexual organ in her own right—then *it* must remain passive instead. This is not simply a male ploy to control women's sexuality. Even greater than a man's fear of female active sexuality is the woman's fear. The unresolved relationship with mother looms up here, again, and—indeed—is ready to re-emerge every time a new cycle begins for the girl: puberty, intercourse, pregnancy, or childbirth. Even more influential than this, however, is the girl's relation to her father. Her need to be loved by him overrules her concern with the maternal relationship, and forces her to adopt a passive position towards him.

One might say that Freud proposed in fact two theories of female sexuality: the first in terms of object relations (the girl's relationship to mother and father); and the second in terms of erotogenic zones (penis-envy and the renunciation of the clitoris in favour of the vagina). How the two relate is uncertain, and

Freud himself is not clear on this point. However, it is my view that the relation to mother and father (conscious and unconscious), and the parental imagos which this generates, determine the *meaning* the girl assigns to her body. The extent to which she regards the vagina as a passive organ is—therefore— a consequence of the dynamics of her object relationships.

In a poignant passage, Freud describes the devastating consequences that the turning away from mother has for the girl:

> The turning-away from her mother is an extremely important step in the course of a little girl's development. It is more than a change of object. We have already described what takes place in it and the many motives put forward for it; we may now add that hand in hand with it there is to be observed marked lowering of the active sexual impulses and a rise of the passive ones. It is true that the active sexual impulses have been affected by frustration more strongly; they have proved totally unrealisable and are therefore abandoned by the libido more readily. But the passive trends have not escaped disappointment either. With the turning-away from the mother clitoridal masturbation frequently ceases as well; and often enough when the small girl represses her previous masculinity a considerable portion of her sexual trends in general is permanently injured too. the transition to the father-object is accomplished with the help of the passive trends *in so far as they escaped the catastrophe.* The path to the development of femininity now lies open to the girl, to the extent to which it is not restricted by the remains of the pre-Oedipus attachment to her mother which she has surmounted. (Freud 1931: 239, my italics)

In this extraordinary passage Freud portrays the catastrophic consequences which the change of object entails for the girl. The renunciation of her active sexuality (one might say today: 'of her *subjectivity*') is the price she has to pay for her father's love, which is so important to her.

In 'A Child is Being Beaten' (1919b) Freud portrays the feminine wish (to be loved by the father, which is considered feminine regardless of whether it occurs in a man or a woman) as passive and masochistic. It is as if the father in the unconscious can only be a sadist, or—to put it more clearly—father's love can only be sadistic. For Freud, the father is always the castrator. In this splitting of mother-love and father-love, of mother-power and father-power, the girl reserves her anger for her (castrated) mother, and her love for her (castrator) father. This submission to father's love, which proves catastrophic for active sexuality, is, however, the only salvation for the girl, according to Freud. It is a movement forwards, towards sexual maturity, towards separation from mother and entry into culture. Anything else would mean stagnation, a mirror-relationship with mother, with endless projective identification and maybe psychosis.

Is it a case, for the girl, of 'from the frying-pan into the fire'? Freud's description is certainly very grim, and the possibilities of anything beyond submission and masochism seem very slim. He constructs the male-female relationship along the lines of a kind of non-perverse, unconscious sadomasochism. But what can this mean?

In my view, sadomasochism—even that which remains at the emotional level—denies difference. Jessica Benjamin's analyses of sadomasochistic relationships repeatedly reveal problems concerning separateness and the attempt to create boundaries between the self and the other (Benjamin 1990a: 68-78). The other, however, can *only* exist as different from the self. Thus the master-slave relationship is not a self-other relationship but instead—like all unequal relationships—it is an *appropriation* of the other. In psychoanalytic terms it is a relationship based on projective identification—in the original sense used by Melanie Klein.[13]

Luce Irigaray has concertedly stressed the lack of difference in Freud's theory of female sexuality:

In fact, this sexuality is never defined with respect to any sex but the masculine. Freud does not see *two* sexes whose differences are articulated in the act of intercourse, and more generally speaking, in the imaginary and the symbolic processes that regulate the workings of a society and a culture. The 'feminine' is always described in terms of deficiency or atrophy... (Irigaray 1985: 69)

Irigaray is highlighting a crucial element in Western psyche and culture—a superstructure built upon the base of an unconscious psychic obliteration of difference. Freud, in describing and analysing the Western psyche, but also from being part of the same culture that he is describing, and sharing the same anxieties and prejudices, became an exponent (not necessarily an apologist) of phallic defence against the early mother. It is only now, with the partial lifting of repression taking place within Western culture—a lifting that creates a state of chaos and the unleashing of primitive anxieties, as well as new possibilities—that we can observe Freud's and our culture's blind-spots and defensive manoeuvres. What Freud was aware of, however, was the monumental resistance against femininity displayed by both men and women (Freud 1937: 252). This universal repudiation of femininity exposes the absence of the father and the presence of the undead mother in the unconscious—in other words, the unresolved Oedipus complex. Phallic defences become the only weapon capable of fending off this deadly embrace with the undead mother. Woman is stuck in an identification with a damaged object—a position of melancholia—whereas man is stuck in a position which resembles psychosis, in his attempts to evacuate the damaged and murdered object. This might explain the tendency of men to physical violence and of women to mental violence, or—alternatively—to self-harm. It also reminds us of the crucial importance of the paternal, castrating super-ego to men, much more so than to women.

A woman's struggle with the mother continues throughout life in a way that is more immediate than that of a man, because it is not repressed but is bound up with the core of her femininity and her capacity to produce children. Man may overcome the dread of the undead mother within a good relationship with a woman who will not challenge his masculine defences.

Woman feels more persecuted, however, because she must remain within the ambience of her mother. Athene's solution—the total identification with father and denial of mother—leads to celibacy and childlessness. Less illustrious women, as Freud has shown, have had to tread a tightrope between a masculinity complex, a total revulsion of sexuality, and a catastrophic renunciation of their active sexuality through remaining attached to father as a love object.

Woman, however, remains a 'riddle'. In his paper 'Femininity' Freud writes:

> Throughout history people have knocked their heads against the riddle of the nature of femininity... Nor will *you* have escaped worrying over this problem—those of you who are men; to those of you who are women this will not apply—you are yourselves the problem. (Freud 1933: 113)

Woman as riddle or problem invites a 'solution' which can be codified and categorised. In this way woman becomes an object of observation, and—like nature in the scientific era—is stripped of all mysteries and terrors. Woman as a riddle is the scientific alternative to the witch; the solution of the riddle is equivalent to the hero slaying the monster. We should remind ourselves of the riddle of the Sphinx, solved by Oedipus. Freud does not draw out the significance of this aspect of the myth, but it was this deed by which Oedipus become King of Thebes and the husband of Jocasta. It is as if the 'rationalist' solution to the riddle of humankind opens at the same time the floodgates of the unconscious. The omnipotent solution of the riddle and murder of the father leads Oedipus into a regressive spiral which ends with catastrophe.

The riddle which confronts Freud—like that posed by the Sphinx—has about it overtones of early curiosities concerning mother's insides—about where life comes from, and how one might gain control over this process. Woman as the source of life leads to a particular type of female omnipotence—the obliteration of the male—and to male envy. Woman as a riddle, on the other hand, reduces both female omnipotence and male envy. She is reified as a riddle to be solved, in purely rational and scientific terms.

As a riddle, woman has no subjectivity. She is not 'other', but only an object to be known. The other—however—is in fact another subject, to whom one might relate, and with whom one might enjoy a relationship of complementarity and exchange. An object, by contrast, is devoid of subjectivity. It is totally passive. It owes its very existence to the subject, and exists *for* the subject. But relationships are risky affairs. There is always the possibility the other might *look* at the subject and thus turn him into an object; the terrifying eyes of the Gorgon are a reference to this active feminine stance—that is, woman not as object but as 'other'. The other limits the subject's omnipotence, whereas the object, or riddle, does not.

In one sense, then, Freud's theory of femininity is the story of the girl's transformation from a subject to an object. In Freud's terms, the girl is originally a little boy. But we know, of course, from the investigations of later writers, that the little boy is originally a little girl.[14] The development of masculine identity from the first relationship with mother can only be achieved through a struggle. There seems to be a paradox here, a paradox concerning gender identity and the reversal of an earlier state, as if neither the boy nor the girl—in order to be regarded as such—can remain in that original state. Where the mother is transformed from omnipotent to castrated, then the little boy is transformed from a little girl to a little boy. The girl, meanwhile, is transformed from a little boy, once father appears as a *deus ex machina* to save the day and, in the process, to help both boy and girl find their sexual identity.

According to Freud, the girl's sexual identity is to be sought in 'passivity'. To be passive, however, is to become a riddle. A riddle is meant to challenge only man's intellect; never his omnipotence. However, the notion of woman as a subject challenges precisely this. She poses the problem of an 'other' who is different, yet the same. When woman fails as an object—that is, when man comes too close to her for his own good—then what was an object suddenly becomes transformed into an alien. In her capacity as an alien, woman poses a danger of contamination. Indeed, this dread of contamination is at the root of most masculine   anxieties,   including   castration   anxiety. Contamination evokes the danger not simply of another subject separate from oneself, but of a creature who is capable of invading the self and turning it too into an alien. The gist of most stories about aliens is not merely annihilation of the population through violence, but instead concerns a subtle take-over of the body and soul of ordinary citizens, so that they are transformed into the enemy. This is also the gist of vampire stories where to be bitten by a vampire is to become a vampire. An alien or vampire is in a different category of creature altogether from a monster or dragon, which can both be slain, and which perform a role akin to the object which can be mastered, the riddle which can be solved. An alien is much more invidious and subversive. It takes over from the inside and is thus much more like the early mother, not yet separated from the self.

On one level, then, Freud's theory of femininity can be read as the attempt of a whole culture to limit this invidious invasion of early mother, by making of her an object out of a subject, and turning her omnipotence into a riddle.

Chapter 6

Mothers and Daughters

In 'Female Sexuality' (1931) Freud himself made the observation that his model of gender identity, because it is based upon the Oedipus complex, is more applicable to masculine than to feminine development. He commented that the girl's pre-Oedipal relationship to mother is at least as important as her Oedipal relationship to father.[15] Expressing his surprise and wonder, Freud compared this finding with Schliemann's archaeological breakthrough:

> Our insight into this early, pre-Oedipus, phase in girls comes to us as a surprise, like the discovery in another field, of the Minoan-Mycenean civilisation behind the civilisation of Greece. (Freud 1931: 226)

At the same time, he expressed his inability to penetrate this pre-Oedipal mother-daughter relationship:

> Everything in the sphere of this first attachment to the mother seemed to me so difficult to grasp in analysis—so grey with age and shadowy and almost impossible to revivify—that it was as if it had succumbed to an especially inexorable repression. (Freud 1931: 226)

However, he expressed the hope that women therapists would be more capable of deciphering the mother transference. This seemed likely, because female patients with a male analyst would simply tend to 'cling to the very attachment to the father in which they had taken refuge from the early phase that was in question' (Freud 1931: 226).[16] Subsequently this early phase—the mother-daughter relationship—was explored by Melanie Klein, who disagreed with Freud on a number of points.

Klein describes the girl's early relationship to mother in terms of an infantile phantasy-world which consists of both love and hate, plenitude and frustration, bliss and terror, envy and gratitude, satisfaction and cannibalism. The mother imago, at this stage, is literally 'fantastic': her body is the locus for all feelings and desires experienced by the girl, both positive and negative. In *The Psycho-Analysis of Children* (1975b), Klein describes the girl's phantasies about the mother's body at this stage, which are strongly coloured by the nature of primitive experience:

> In her phantasy her mother's body is... a kind of storehouse which contains the means of satisfying all her desires and of allaying all her fears. It is these phantasies, leading back to her mother's breast as her earliest source of satisfaction and as the one most fraught with consequences, which are responsible for her immensely strong attachment to her mother. And the frustration she suffers from her mother gives rise, under the pressure of her anxiety, to renewed complaints against her and to strengthened sadistic attacks upon her body. (Klein 1975b: 207)

The attacks on mother's body, the desire to scoop out all good things from it, result in persecutory feelings and—later—in feelings of guilt and anxiety. The girl begins to feel that she has demolished the 'reservoir from which she draws the satisfaction of all her mental and physical needs. This fear, which is of such tremendous importance in the mental life of the small girl, goes to strengthen still further the ties that bind her to her mother' (Klein 1975b: 208).

In this way, then, the girl's attachment to mother is not simply a matter of love and affection, but—perhaps even more significantly—also a matter of anxiety concerning the survival of the mother. Mother's survival is threatened both by the girl's attacks (due to frustration and hate), and to the depletion inside mother of all good things (due to the girl's greed) which—at this stage—include babies and the father's penis.

Klein suggests that the girl attempts to make reparation to mother—in other words, to give back what she has taken from her—but that this runs contrary to the girl's wish to continue to take away. Contradictory impulses to take away and to give back therefore also characterise this stage, for if the girl did give back everything, she herself would be left in danger, with nothing. Girls, at this stage, will frequently draw a house to represent mother's body, with a tree outside as father's penis, and some flowers to represent children. However, the contradictory impulses to take away and give back can lead to obsessional neurosis. In this case, a girl might become preoccupied with dolls and doll's dresses, which can be taken to represent mother's 'reconstituted' body. Restitution, governed by obsessional mechanisms, sometimes entails the return of *exactly* what has been taken. If anxiety is too strong, however, and cannot be bound by obsessional mechanisms such as these, a regression to more violent, primitive stages will occur.

Fairy-tales such as *Snow White* and *Cinderella*, as discussed in the previous chapter, also portray this persecutory phase followed by an obsessional phase. In *Snow White*, for instance, a split occurs between the projected, bad, envious and murderous mother, and the girl's attempt to reconstitute her own body, which is felt to be in danger. This anxiety about her own body is the girl's strongest anxiety, and Klein describes it as equivalent to the boy's castration anxiety:

> In addition to these many sources of anxiety a further element is added which aggravates the feminine position and the relationship of the girl to her mother—the anatomy of her body. Compared to the boy who enjoys the support of the male position and who has the possibility of reality-testing thanks to his possession of a penis, the girl child cannot get any support against anxiety from her feminine position since her possession of children which would be a complete confirmation and fulfilment of that position, is, after all, only a prospective one. Nor does the structure of her body afford her any possibility of knowing what the actual state of affairs inside her is. It is this

inability to know anything about her condition which aggravates what, in my opinion, is the girl's deepest fear—namely that the inside of her body has been injured or destroyed and that she has no children or only damaged ones. (Klein 1975b: 210)

Snow White is in flight from the envious, vicious step-mother. In the dwarves' little house—which represents her own body, and into which she has retreated—she performs obsessional rituals ('housekeeping') which amount to tending and restoring her own damaged body. However, because she has cut herself off from her projected envy and murderous feelings towards her mother—her projected matricide—she is in mortal danger from this part of herself. Within the psyche, matricide is easily reversed into infanticide. Snow White is in continuous fear for her life, but the envious mother cannot be defeated by avoidance; only the prince is able to rescue her. This rescue—which also occurs in *Cinderella* and in so many other myths and fairy-tales—expresses a fundamental psychic reality which, however, can easily become a source of female despair: the girl, it seems, can never work through her relationship to her mother without the help of the other sex. The 'other sex' should be the father, but, typically, in many fairy-tales the father is absent, away from home, or simply not mentioned at all.

The father provides a temporary refuge for the girl, a base from which she can work through her ambivalence, envy and hate towards her mother. Father's protection, as well as her own identification with him, create a new space from which she can view her relationship with her mother. The rescue by the prince, on the other hand, does not constitute a resolution, but only a manic defence which protects her from the envious mother. The Queen dies at the end of *Snow White*, and there no possibility of resurrecting her. The 'happy ending' of *Snow White*—like so many others—is in reality a defensive manoeuvre.

The other sex, the 'third term', is not the prince, then, but father—in both his pre-Oedipal and Oedipal guises. It is however significant that in both *Snow White* and *Cinderella* the father is a very shadowy figure. Because of this the girl is trapped in a world in which her anxieties and terrors are reflected back at her, and self and other become confused. In this situation goodness and bodily integrity can only be ensured by splitting and obsessional mechanisms, which can be maintained only until the onset of puberty. For instance, Cinderella's relationship to her mother is split between the good fairy godmother and the bad envious step-mother. Cinderella is, therefore, in a better position than Snow White to mobilise her good mother in order to attempt to reach her prince.

So where, then—in the psychical sense—has father gone? Has he been eliminated by the girl's possessiveness and envy? Is he too busy to care for the girl? Does mother possess him utterly and is unwilling to allow the girl access to him? Or is the father himself cruel, abusive, neglecting, absent... or even, perhaps, too over-indulgent, so that the girl's Oedipal wish to eliminate her mother seems to come true? Whatever the reason, the consequences for a female psyche which has not internalised a good relation to father—both in terms of identification with him and love for him—are always the same: entrapment with a dangerous mother, and constant fear for one's own bodily and psychic integrity.

* * *

Identification with father, in all its aspects, is—as I have stressed—very important to the girl's development. It enables her to separate from mother, and alleviates her anxiety—both persecutory anxiety and depressive anxiety. At the phallic phase, then, the girl's identification is with father's phallus. This is the father-liberator of the 'rapprochement phase', to use a term coined by Jessica Benjamin (1990a, 1990b). In this 'flight from femininity' the girl puts distance between herself and her mother by taking into herself this masculine element. However, the incorporation of masculinity through identification with father is entirely different from what Freud described as the original masculinity of the girl towards her mother (Freud 1931: 239; 1933: 126). By this he meant, simply, an *active* attitude. In contrast, masculinity through identification with father is a defence (in its triumph over mother and femininity), but also a step forward towards autonomous existence. This is because it creates a position from which the girl can move towards a different relationship with both father and with mother.

For the girl, the pre-Oedipal identification with father should not be confused with the later identification with him which occurs at the end of the Oedipus complex. The post-Oedipal identification sometimes constitutes a means of making reparation to mother, by taking on father's role of looking after her.

* * *

The mother-daughter relationship has formed the focus of many contemporary attempts to describe and explain feminine development, mainly from a feminist perspective. In my opinion, the feminist writers of the 1970s and 1980s have, by and large, ignored or underplayed the importance of the father in feminine development and have, therefore, condemned woman to a world of mirrors. Feminist literature of this time—at least in Britain and the United States—concentrates on the absence of father from child-care and, therefore, on the absence of a primary relation to him. Although I agree this is an important issue, one stresses it as the expense of underestimating the importance of the *triangular relationship* in the development of femininity, and the working-through of narcissistic defences and ambivalence. Feminine defences *against* the Oedipus complex simply lock woman into a claustrophobic world of symbiotic relation with mother.

Despite this limitation, feminist writings of the 1970s and 1980s nevertheless highlighted certain aspects of the mother-daughter relationship which are very important, including the issue of the *mother's* psychology within a patriarchal culture. This accomplished a reversal of emphasis away from the baby's mind and defence mechanisms towards those of the mother. Mother's mind and her conscious and unconscious reactions to her baby's demands are hinted at by Freud, when he describes the relationship of the mother to her male child as that which is 'most free of ambivalence' (Freud 1933: 133).[17] This implicitly acknowledges an unconscious reaction by mother towards her child. The mother's mind—and the father's mind—are important missing pieces from the puzzle of gender identity. The importance of them has been stressed, from a more pathological perspective, by Robert Stoller (1968) and Ralph Greenson (1993), but their role in more subtle disturbances of development has been largely ignored. Feminist writers have stressed mother's mind both in its social aspect (as part of a patriarchal culture), and in its more personal, psychopathological aspect. The fact that mother and daughter share the same sex is seen as the main basis for an over-identification between mother and daughter, leading to a blurring of boundaries and difficulties in separation.

I do not propose to present an exhaustive account of feminist literature on the mother-daughter relationship but, instead, I will concentrate on a few very influential books which have shaped current thinking around this issue.

Mother-daughter identification

In her book *The Reproduction of Mothering* (1978) Nancy Chodorow focuses on the mother-daughter relationship in order to explain certain characteristics of women's psychology and the development of femininity. Her analysis is a classic of its kind, and it is very difficult to overstate its importance and influence.

Chodorow's main thesis can be summarised as follows: the seemingly simple fact that, within our culture, *only women* perform the role of mother has widespread implications on the development of both men's and women's personality, gender identity, and psychic structure. The different ways in which mother relates to daughter and son, and how this is perceived by the baby boy and girl, is of paramount importance, because it sets the foundation for object relations.

There are two circumstances which are particularly significant for the baby girl. Firstly, the fact that she is the same sex as her mother, because this leads the mother to identify with the baby girl and to see herself in her child. This makes separation from mother a much more difficult task for the girl than for the boy. In a sense, then, the girl remains attached to mother, even during the Oedipal and post-Oedipal stages.

Secondly—following on from the identification between mother and the girl—little girls therefore remain in the pre-Oedipal stage for much longer than little boys.[18]

Chodorow presents many examples of symbiosis from the work of other authors, and arrives at the conclusion that a 'prolonged symbiosis and narcissistic over-identification are particularly characteristic of early relationships between mothers and daughters' (Chodorow 1978: 104).

This does not mean that the mother-son relationship is free of symbiosis, but that the mother allows the son to separate much more readily than the daughter, because mother's closer identification with the girl blurs the boundaries separating herself from her daughter. The fact that the son is an 'object' for the mother, in a sense in which the daughter cannot be, creates much clearer dividing-lines between son and mother.

The son, through his eventual identification with the father, not only separates from mother but also denies and represses his early identification with her, together with everything 'feminine' or perceived as 'belonging to women'. For the girl, on the other hand, separation seems an impossible task, because the mother is not only her first object but also the one with whom she identifies and with whom she must go on identifying, if she is to follow a feminine path. The girl will eventually turn to father as a refuge, but he is a remote figure compared to mother. He is rarely present and has little time for her. As a consequence, the girl oscillates between mother and father, and between Oedipal and pre-Oedipal attachment.

Although much of this had already been observed by Freud, Chodorow stresses that it all arises from the simple fact that only women take on the role of 'mothering' children. She re-examines the popular assumption (which is echoed within psychoanalysis) that this is all due to biological factors. Evaluating the available evidence from biology, sociology, psychology, and cross-cultural studies, she arrives at the conclusion that there is no simple one-to-one equation between genes and behaviour,

and therefore no biological necessity for women to be the exclusive or main care-givers. Women 'mother', Chodorow argues,
simply because *they* have been mothered by women. Even
Winnicott, she continues, warns us against thinking in terms of
a 'maternal instinct':

> Something would be missing, however, if a phrase such as
> 'maternal instinct' were used in description. The fact is
> that in health women change in their orientation to them-
> selves and the world, but however deeply rooted in phys-
> iology such changes may be, they can be distorted by
> mental ill-health in woman. It is necessary to think of
> these changes in psychological terms. (Winnicott, cited in
> Chodorow 1978: 23)

Most psychoanalysts, Chodorow argues, would agree that
the main factor determining the quality of mothering, in any
particular case, is the quality of mothering which the mother
herself received as a baby, because mothering is a psychological
and not a biological phenomenon.

Chodorow therefore sees in the girl's relationship to mother,
and her inability to separate from mother, the source of
women's 'relational identity'—that is, the way in which women
seek to define themselves in relation to others, whereas men
tend not to do this. Incomplete separation is also the source of
women's ambivalence towards their mothers, because of the
way the daughter feels strongly connected to her mother, yet
also strives to be independent from her.

Chodorow employs an object relations framework in her
investigation, but—within this—she understates the role of
Oedipal conflicts and the influence of the father in feminine
development. For Chodorow, identification with mother *is* the
feminine identity. This 'core feminine identity' she regards as
unalterable, and thus chooses to ignore the later re-shaping of
femininity by the Oedipus and the castration complex, and the
definition of femininity as an opposite to masculinity. Her
account is in stark contrast to Klein's vivid accounts of the girl's
early phantasies concerning the mother's body, and her drive

towards father in order to find a new object free from her sadism and greed, in the process creating a new space for relationships. For Chodorow the girl's relationship to her mother is essentially unambivalent, and reparation is not an issue.

Importance of mother's psychology

In Britain, Luise Eichenbaum and Susie Orbach have also explored the mother-daughter relationship and its internalisation, which they regard as the nucleus of the feminine psyche (Eichenbaum & Orbach 1982, 1983a, 1983b). These authors begin by defining women's social role, and then proceed to explain how a woman's personality develops in order to fulfil this role. They view woman's role within the culture as that of mother (care-giver and nurturer), but from this, they argue, follow certain requirements: that women defer to others, and make efforts to connect with others by developing 'emotional antennae'. Eichenbaum and Orbach suggest that these basic characteristics develop within the girl's relationship to mother as consequences of the incomplete separation between them.

The conclusion of this investigation, then, is similar to that of Chodorow—namely, that the girl never separates completely from the mother, and that this incomplete separation characterises the feminine psyche and forms the basis of the need (or social requirement) to live not for themselves but for others. The inevitable conclusion here is that what is usually taken as one of the strengths of women—their nurturing quality—is the result of an immature self, characterised by insecure boundaries. In other words, the nurturing qualities of women are not a mature generosity, but a compulsive wish to connect, and an expression of deep anxiety concerning separateness.

What is new in Eichenbaum and Orbach's work, however, is their understanding of the transmission from mother to daughter of a specific psychology:

The social requirements of patriarchy surround a girl from the moment of birth. This means that she has a particular psychology which she transmits to her daughter. (Eichenbaum & Orbach 1983b: 39)

The psychology she transmits is the psychology of woman *within patriarchy*.

Thus the mother's conscious and unconscious phantasies enter into the interaction between mother and daughter. These include her phantasies about femininity, about what a girl is like as opposed to a boy, and the feelings this evokes in her. The mother's personality structure therefore includes the split-off, needy little girl inside herself, whom she cannot tolerate in her daughter

The little girl discovers this very quickly, and learns to hide it (or deny it, or split it off, depending on the severity of the situation). Eichenbaum and Orbach make use here of Winnicott's theory of the 'False Self' in order to explain the little girl's precocious consideration for others, and the denial of her own needs. In order to receive love the little girl must disguise her True Self. A feeling of inauthenticity develops as her True Self, with all its needy and vulnerable parts, is split off and a False Self develops. A false sense of maturity develops alongside this, which entails that she becomes considerate towards others, towards mother, and may often begin to look after mother, as her own yearning for unconditional love is thwarted.

> Even though a daughter comes to look towards men she still yearns for mother's support and care. From girlhood to womanhood women live with the experience of having lost these aspects of maternal nurturance. This nurturance is never replaced. Women look to men to mother them but remain bereft... (Eichenbaum & Orbach 1983b: 39)

Eichenbaum and Orbach regard father as important, but his influence is bound to be limited because he arrives much later in the girl's life. Indeed, there is an additional reason why father can never be of equal importance to mother: the girl, because she is 'other' than father, cannot identify with him as a means of separating from mother (in the way the boy does). Instead, the girl turns to him for love and nurturance and for developing a sense of self *by being 'other'*.

Inadequate mothering

Adrienne Rich writes that:

> Few women growing up in patriarchal society can feel mothered enough; the power of our mothers whatever their love for us and their struggles on our behalf, is so restricted... The mother's hatred and low expectations are the binding-rags for the psyche of the daughter. (Rich 1979: 243)

She contends that although 'we acknowledge Lear (father-daughter split), Hamlet (son-mother) and Oedipus (son-mother) as great embodiments of human tragedy. there is no presently enduring recognition of mother-daughter passion' (Rich 1979: 237). However, this *was* recognised in Greece, and is expressed in the mysteries of Eleusis which are based on the Demeter-Kore myth. The story, which predates patriarchy, tells of the passionate love between mother and daughter—but this is a love now rendered impossible by a culture that devalues women and femininity. As Rich puts it: 'Until a strong line of love, confirmation and example stretches from mother to daughter, from woman to woman across generations, women will still be wandering in the wilderness' (Rich 1979: 246).

Eichenbaum and Orbach also cite evidence that mothers relate differently to their baby girls than to their baby boys: they hold them less, breast-feed them less, and spend less time with them. However, external behaviour is only a small part of what goes on between mother and baby; the quality of the relationship and the feelings involved—both conscious and unconscious—cannot easily be quantified. What seems more certain is that the devaluation of woman and femininity within patriarchal culture, which is necessarily a part of every woman's and every mother's psychology, leads to an ambivalent relationship between mother and daughter, as mother's unresolved conflict within herself (the split-off, needy little girl), is projected onto the daughter.

Inconsistency in mother-daughter relationship

As a result of the factors discussed above, the mother's relationship to her daughter is highly inconsistent. At times she will see her daughter as separate and—in that case—will be capable of being a good enough mother to her. At other times, however, she will see her daughter as part of herself, and will become either rejecting or over-involved, or both—depending on how she herself relates to the part of herself which her daughter has become. According to Eichenbaum and Orbach this inconsistency, this staccato quality, characterises the mother-daughter relationship. The extent of the mother's ambivalence will, of course, depend on her psychopathology, but I believe that Eichenbaum and Orbach have isolated a very crucial feature of the mother-daughter relationship. In this they are in agreement with Freud, who was the first to contrast the mother-son relationship with the mother-daughter, describing it as 'free of ambivalence', and thus implying that the mother-daughter relationship was not. Despite Freud's idealised view of the mother-son relationship (and this probably had a great deal to do with Freud's own relationship with his mother) nevertheless it suggests there is a *relatively* greater ambivalence between mother and daughter.

Margaret Mahler writes:

Three variables involving the mother are of particular importance in shaping, promoting, or hindering the individual child's adaptability, drive, and ego development, and the beginning of structuralisation of precursors of the super-ego:
1. The mother's personality structure.
2. The developmental process of her parental function...
3. The mother's conscious, but particularly unconscious fantasy regarding the individual child. (Mahler et al. 1975: 202)

Although Mahler did not examine the mother-daughter relationship in contrast to that of mother-son (for here she is here talking in a gender-neutral mode), I think the above quotation nevertheless supports Eichenbaum and Orbach's depiction of how the mother's specific psychology (stemming from the inferior position she inhabits in a patriarchal culture), and her unconscious phantasies about her own femininity, will affect the developing girl.

In addition, evidence from developmental psychology suggests that girls acquire language earlier than boys and are, on the whole, ahead of boys in cognitive skills and vocabulary at pre-school age. This again hints at a creation of a talented False Self in girls, in order to please others, and thus seems to support Eichenbaum and Orbach's claims. However, if taken at face value, this evidence contradicts Chodorow's (and Freud's) insistence that girls remain at the pre-Oedipal stage *longer* than boys. Indeed, Chodorow has been criticised for this. Yet the contradiction seems to me more apparent than real. As the girl attempts to separate from mother prematurely, by developing a False Self, the 'separation' can only be apparent—indeed, this is what the term 'False Self' is intended to imply. Her insecure sense of self and her ego weakness guarantee that she will never be able to separate from mother completely. In effect, the girl *does* remain longer in the pre-Oedipal stage, in order to attempt to work through her unmanageable feelings towards her mother.

What this feminist account of femininity leaves out—as I have mentioned—is the relation to father, and to mother *and* father as the parental couple. This means that the very important issue of women's collusion in their own oppression, which results from a relationship to an idealised father, is not explored. Neither is the relation of the girl to phantasies of matricide—since this too occurs within the three-party, triangular relationship. This approach also leaves on one side the whole issue of the definition of femininity in relation to masculinity, which must also take into account the girl's relationship with father, and also father's own phantasies and anxieties about to femininity. The Oedipal relation to mother, which entails an intensification of hatred and devaluation, is also omitted. However, I hope to explore these themes myself in the chapters which follow.

Contributions from French psychoanalytic feminist thinkers: Luce Irigaray

The mother-daughter relationship has also formed the focus of work by French feminists. Here I propose to examine the views of Luce Irigaray and Julia Kristeva.

Luce Irigaray regards the mother-daughter relationship as paramount in defining woman as a subject in her own right, and not as an *'homme manque'* or 'lack'. In her paper 'The Bodily Encounter with the Mother' she exhorts women to assert the genealogy of women within the family:

> Given our exile in the family of the father-husband we tend to forget this genealogy of women, and we are often persuaded to deny it. Let us try to situate ourselves within this female genealogy so as to conquer and keep our destiny... When analytic theory says that that the little girl must give up her love of and for her mother, her desire of and for her mother so as to enter into the desire of/for the father, it subordinates woman to a normative hetero-sexuality, normal in our societies, but completely pathogenic and pathological. Neither little girl nor woman must give up love for their mother. Doing so uproots them from their identity, their subjectivity. (Irigaray 1991: 44)

Irigaray accepts the view that woman finds it difficult to separate from mother. However, she points out that the girl's difficulties in separating from mother are the result of woman's position within the 'symbolic order'.[19] This symbolic order, she argues, ensures that there is only one place for woman: the place of the mother, or of the maternal function. For this reason, a great part of Irigaray's critique concentrates on the lack of symbolisation of the mother-daughter relationship within western culture. Irigaray sees this as at the very root of women's oppression; and terms this lack of symbolisation *'dereliction'*—a state of being outside culture. In Irigaray's words, dereliction is a 'state of fusion which does not succeed in emerging as a subject' (Irigaray 1991: 81). Relationships based on fusion and lack of boundaries, she insists, are in fact the result of dereliction, of being outside culture. She illustrates this state of mind by referring to the myth of Ariadne, abandoned by Theseus on the island of Naxos, whilst he continued on his journey to found the city of Athens. The story, in this context, is very interesting. Ariadne was the daughter of Minos, King of Crete, and helped Theseus to kill the Minotaur. Without Ariadne's help, Theseus had no chance of emerging from the Minotaur's labyrinth alive. Leaving Crete and her family behind, Ariadne followed Theseus on his voyage, only to have him abandon her on the island of Naxos when he returned to Athens—to the world of culture and civilisation.

Ariadne, the daughter, is therefore used by Theseus to kill the Minotaur, the maternal monster, yet is eventually abandoned on an island, representing a state half-way between fusion with mother (Crete) and culture (Athens). Neither the man nor the woman can kill the monster on their own, but when the feat is finally accomplished it is Theseus who gets the credit, whereas Ariadne is betrayed, abandoned, and left in a state of exclusion from culture. Like Electra in the Oresteian myth, she is simply forgotten.

This is the condition of woman, argues Irigaray, within patriarchal culture, which is why the genealogy of women is such an important concept to Irigaray, who is looking for a 'feminine' which is not defined by patriarchal culture. Because of these views Irigaray has been accused of searching for a pre-Oedipal feminine utopia, a state of mind which precludes conflict and the father. She has also been accused of being a biological essentialist who defines femininity as a pre-linguistic, somatic quality. Even so, what Irigaray vividly highlights is the total lack of adequate representations of the mother-daughter relationship— as Margaret Whitford writes:

By describing this relationship as unsymbolised, Irigaray means that there is an absence of linguistic, social, semiotic, structural, cultural, iconic, theoretical, mythical, religious or any other representations of that relationship. There is no maternal genealogy... Irigaray argues that we have to go back to Greek mythology to find available, culturally embodied representations of the mother-daughter relationship. (Whitford, in Irigaray 1991: 76-77)

My view that western culture is based not upon parricide, but upon matricide, is one of Irigaray's central ideas. However, what I believe is lacking from her writings is a detailed understanding of the internal world. Matricide, in Irigaray's theory, is a concept which relates not to a psychical reality and to a psychical structure, but exclusively to culture. In this way, then, her argument becomes circular. The state of fusion that is dereliction cannot (by its very nature) produce representations or symbolisations; however, it is precisely through the absence of symbolisation that a state of fusion is perpetuated. What is more, a genealogy of women—as advocated by Irigaray—can itself become just another state of fusion. For me the central question here is: how we can achieve a separation from mother which is not based on matricide?

What is missing from Irigaray, and from Lacanian theory in general, is the concept of *mourning*—that is, the gradual working-through of the loss of the mother. This basically Kleinian concept can help us more fully understand the process of separation from mother, which is—in Winnicott's words—'a separation that is not a separation but a kind of union' (Winnicott 1971: 115). This paradoxical state of mind is basically dialectical, and expresses the tension between subject and object without a resolution in either case. Indeed, this tension itself *is* life. Although Winnicott did not refer to mourning but to 'disillusionment',[20] he is nevertheless evoking the same loss of omnipotent control over the object. Mourning, with its diverse accompanying feelings—such as love, hate, rage, pining, and the gradual working-through of these feelings towards a relationship with a mother who 'goes away yet comes back'—is entirely missing from

Irigaray's theory. Yet without the concept of mourning, we simply cannot understand separation from mother—or, at least, arrive at a view of separation which is neither matricide nor dereliction. The genealogy of women, although a political weapon to attack the 'genealogy of men', does not help us understand the dynamics of an internal world based on the extremes of fusion or murder.

One of the difficulties here is that Irigaray speaks about the external world of the mother-daughter relationship, and the genealogy of women, whilst ignoring the *internal* mother-daughter relationship. From an object relations perspective, however, it is precisely this intense, ambivalent internal relationship which is the real problem. The question this raises, for me, is why contemporary western culture and the western individual are so uniquely incapable of mourning.

Julia Kristeva

Julia Kristeva awards less importance to the mother-daughter relationship, and more to the necessity of the child—male or female—to separate from mother. Although her early work celebrated the maternal world and the maternal body, her later work displays greater concern with the necessity for separation. Her early work on the first relationship to the mother was conducted at the time she was a linguistic philosopher, not a psychoanalyst. Her discovery of the maternal world of 'the semiotic' parallels Freud's discovery of the girl's early relation to mother. The semiotic, according to Kristeva, underlies and complements Lacan's symbolic. It is the pre-Oedipal, pre-symbolic, pre-linguistic world of rhythms, colours, sounds and textures which forms the *materiality* of art and of human experience. In her essays 'Woman's Time' and 'Stabat Mater' (Kristeva 1986), she explores and celebrates fundamentally female and maternal aspects of experience. However, although in 'Stabat Mater' there is some reference to separation, this thorny issue emerged fully only later when—as a psychoanalyst—she turned her attention to depression and melancholia. In her book *Black Sun* she conceptualises separation from mother as an act of matricide:

> For man and for woman the loss of the mother is a biological and psychic necessity, the first step on the way to becoming autonomous. Matricide is our vital necessity, the sine-qua-non of our individuation, provided that it takes place under optimal circumstances and can be eroticised... The lesser or greater violence of the matricidal drive, depending on individuals and the milieu's tolerance, entails, when it is hindered, its inversion on the self; the maternal object having been introjected, the depressive or melancholic putting to death of the self is what follows, instead of matricide. (Kristeva 1989: 27-28)

Although this passage does make any distinction between boy and girl, it is obvious that—if separation from mother resembles matricide—the girl will find separation more difficult than will the boy. To kill the mother, with whom the girl identifies, is therefore the prototype of melancholia—despite Kristeva's assertions. However, as I have argued throughout this book, murder can never be the basis for separation. Far from resulting in separation from the object, it leads instead, on the contrary, to the perpetual *presence* of a persecutory object and to melancholia.

For Kristeva, hatred acts as a catalyst in the process of separation, because hatred is a protection against merging and against narcissistic idealisation. Hatred, however, is not the same as matricide. Hatred can be worked-through—indeed, has to be worked-through—if depression is to be avoided. For hatred to be worked-through it has to be acknowledged, and it is here that Kristeva remarks on the difference between the boy and the girl. The boy expresses his hatred towards his father more openly, whereas for the girl the unacknowledged hatred between mother and daughter hinders separation and individuation. In this situation, having a baby can sometimes help the daughter separate from her mother. In effect, the baby acts as a

phallus—in the way that Freud described (Freud 1925a).[21]
Kristeva writes:

> ... a woman seldom (although not necessarily) experi-
> ences her passion (love and hatred) for another woman
> without having taken her own mother's place—without
> having herself become a mother, and especially without
> slowly learning to differentiate between same beings—as
> being face to face with her daughter forces her to do.
> (Kristeva 1986: 184)

Even though the daughter's giving birth to a daughter can
indeed function as the catalyst for separation from the mother,
Kristeva's account of this ignores the narcissistic use a woman
can make of her own baby—especially if it is a baby girl.

My view is that an object relations perspective is necessary to
examine in detail the working-through of aggression within the
mother-child relationship, and the eventual integration of good
and bad objects, and that Kristeva neglects this framework. As I
have argued, hatred—even if openly acknowledged—can only
perpetuate a state of non-separation from mother (although
acknowledged hatred is indeed less psychotic in nature). Hatred
can only be a first step towards separation.

Both Irigaray and Kristeva stumble when it comes to the difficult issue of separating from mother. They view the mother-
daughter relationship from its external, interpersonal point of
view, and overlook internal object relations. The way in which
the object can be split in the internal world entails that apparent
'external separation' can often be illusory. Irigaray, by making
political use of the mother-daughter relationship, leaves out its
immense ambivalence; whereas Kristeva confuses matricide
and separation. Nevertheless, both have presented us with an
immensely rich and complex account of the maternal world,
and their critique of Freud and of Lacan has doubtlessly
enhanced our understanding of the early relationship to
mother.

Chapter 7

Matricide and the Mother-Daughter Relationship

We do not know what happened to Electra, alone at Argos with a murdered mother, in a blood-stained palace.

Presumably she remained in the shadow of her formidable mother and illustrious brother, pining after her idealised father. She seems to have been forgotten by the whole world. In some versions of the myth she married Pylades, the friend of Orestes; in other versions she never married. What we do know about Electra is her hatred for Clytemnestra, the suffocating experience of being under her mother's control, her pining for her dead father, and her love for her brother. Electra is full of strong passionate feelings of love and hate, but without capacity for the actions which might accompany these feelings. The closest she comes to this is her exhortation of her brother to murder their mother.

This lack of direct action tells us something about the relationship between Electra and Clytemnestra. As Irigaray suggests, within the mother-daughter relationship there is only one position—the mother's position. Irigaray explains the eternal rivalry between mother and daughter as due to the position of woman in the symbolic order of Western culture. The only possible position assigned to her is the position of mother, hence the impossibility of separating from mother which confronts the girl (Irigaray 1991: 77). Electra's seeming inability to act, and the obscurity which consumes her after the murder of Clytemnestra, might be said to support this view. Electra simply cannot exist without Clytemnestra, even if the daughter passionately detests the mother and wishes her dead. In spite of her hatred, envy and spite, Electra is powerless to act or escape. She is reduced to waiting for her brother, just as Cinderella and Snow White wait for the prince to liberate them.

Indeed, Electra's suffocating relationship with her mother is not unlike Cinderella's subjection to the cruel step-mother, or Snow White's narrow escape from the murderous, envious

Queen. Falling into the hands of the bad mother is an intolerable experience for the girl. The only way she can deal with it is by splitting and idealisation on the one hand, and obsessional rituals on the other. The splitting can take place either between an idealised father and a bad mother, or between a good mother and a bad step-mother. The former is the classical Oedipal situation; the latter can take place at either a pre-Oedipal or Oedipal level. Indeed, the Oedipal conflicts will be manageable only if there has been adequate splitting of the good from the bad pre-Oedipal mother.

Alternatively, the girl attempts to control the relationship to a bad mother with daily obsessional rituals. Snow White, for instance, by retreating to the house where the dwarves live, is—in effect—striving to repair her fragmented inner world of phallic part-objects. The conflict with the mother is therefore succeeded by obsessional manic reparation, through a submission to phallic figures. Her state of mind is one of denial—denial of her femininity, the bad mother, conflict, persecution, envy, and love. We should not be fooled by the pseudo-feminine attitude of 'keeping house', cooking and cleaning, and playing mother to the dwarves. This parody of femininity—which is based not on identification but simply on *imitation*—betrays the state of denial which sometimes succeeds the female Oedipus complex. In the case of Snow White, the denial of the bad mother is achieved through splitting, isolation, and imitation. Snow White's world contains no other human beings; in effect, she is entirely alone with her phallic objects and obsessional rituals.

These rituals, however, fail to work in the long run. Manic reparation is evidently inadequate. The bad mother, with the help of her mirror—which she uses to ascertain that Snow White is still alive—finally catches up with her at the house of the dwarves. Here the bad mother attempts to poison Snow White. We might understand this as indicating the onset of puberty, during which all the dramas of early childhood return with a new ferocity. The obsessional rituals of latency fail, and a new phase of persecution by the bad, envious mother begins. The use of a mirror by the bad mother is very suggestive. The mirror hints at the processes of projective identification, which perhaps plays a greater role in the mother-daughter relationship than in any other. All Snow White's attempts at splitting, isolation, and obsessional control break down in the face of this renewed invasion by the bad mother.

Early incursion by the bad mother cannot be prevented, because there is no other figure present in the universe of the girl which might prevent it. The dyadic nature of the relation between mother and daughter is signalled in these fairy-tales by the entirely absent or very shadowy father-figure. These very feminine heroines depend on repetitive or obsessional works to keep the bad mother at a distance, rather than relying upon father. In Snow White's case there seems to have been no internalisation of a father-figure whatsoever. Father appears in the guise of the hunter sent to execute the mother's wishes; the hunter takes pity on Snow White, and allows her to go free. This is in stark contrast to Electra's strong investment of the paternal figure. Cinderella's father, on the other hand, complies with his daughter's wish and brings her back a twig which she plants on the grave of her dead mother.[22] We might assume, then, that Cinderella's father, as well as the good parental couple, are secure introjects for Cinderella. Maybe this is the reason why Cinderella does not submit to a phallic world of part objects, but is able to endure and survive the attacks of the bad mother. She is never in danger of her life, as Snow White is. On the other hand, her life is more miserable, since there is less denial and more slow, reparative work to be done.

For Jessica Benjamin, the girl's relationship to the pre-Oedipal father, the father of the *rapprochement* phase, is absolutely necessary for separating from mother and for a sense of autonomy and agency. In order to separate from mother, then, the girl seeks to identify with father. On penis-envy Benjamin writes:

> I interpret the desire for the penis as evidence that little girls are seeking the same thing as little boys, namely, identification with the father of separation, the representative of the outside world. (Benjamin 1990a: 108)

The girl, then, is not looking for 'a penis' as such, but instead for a father who will help her separate from mother.

The father represents the outside world as well as desire. Girls, like boys, look for a figure to represent their move away from dependency on mother towards autonomy and desire. The girl, therefore, is seeking *two* things from this identificatory relation to father: firstly, separation from mother; and secondly, recognition of her sexual desire. If this identification fails—perhaps because of father's fear of female desire—then the girl is either pushed back into a powerless relation to mother, or else subjects herself entirely to father.[23] Because the girl has no penis of her own with which to differentiate herself from mother, her identification with father is doubly crucial. As Benjamin writes:

> Thus little girls are confronted more directly by the difficulty of separating from mother and their own helplessness. Unprotected by the phallic sign of gender difference, unsupported by an alternate relationship, they relinquish their entitlement to desire. (Benjamin 1990a: 109)

It is the fairy-tale, much more than any other type of narrative, which portrays the girl's relinquishment of desire, the passive waiting for the prince to liberate her from a bad mother or from near-death.

Snow White's scrape with death raises the issue of matricide once again. The inversion should not deceive us. In the mirror-like relationship between mother and daughter, the difference between what belongs to mother and what comes from the daughter is not absolutely clear. Projective identification operates incessantly. The ferocity of the impulses involved exposes the matricidal urge which the phallic world has been unable to eliminate. This matricidal urge is never worked-through, firstly because the feelings of envy involved are simply too strong; and secondly because of the absence of the father as liberator—that is, the father in a dyadic relationship with the girl—who would have given the girl a feeling of confidence in her goodness, thus helping her work through her relationship with the bad mother.

In the fairy-tale scenario, the prince is a substitute for the father as liberator, but he represents a different form of 'liberation' which remains external, and is libidinally passive. One wonders what will happen after 'the happy ending'—whether, for instance, Freud's dictum that women reproduce their relationship to their mothers with their husbands will manifest itself, due to the way in which no real separation from mother has taken place.

In the case of Snow White, one might interpret the seven dwarves as phallic part-objects *aiding* the heroine in separating from mother. However, this side-steps the issue of the girl's identification with father. Phallic defences are a substitute for relationships with people. For Snow White the dwarves are a substitute for *both* mother and father, although it seems her subjection to these phallic part-objects is the only solution open to her.

Phallic defences also annihilate the object in the case of the boy. The boy who equates omnipotence with his own penis annihilates any dependence on an object. Ernest Jones stressed this when, in opposition to Freud, he described a phallic phase *succeeding* the Oedipus complex. He referred to a 'deutero-phallic' phase which follows the Oedipus complex (as opposed to the 'proto-phallic phase' which precedes the Oedipus complex and the recognition of sex difference). In the deutero-phallic phase, Jones maintains, there is a 'renunciation of the mother to save the penis' (Jones 1948a: 466). The deutero-phallic phase therefore erodes difference, by renouncing interest in the inside of the mother's body and clinging to the idea that everything is phallic—that is, that his mother has a penis *as well*. This phallic narcissism is a solution to intolerable anxiety and feelings of frustration.

In contrast to this phallic narcissism, the boy's early dyadic identification with father is object-relational and, as Jessica Benjamin maintains, the prototype of 'ideal love':

> I regard the identificatory, homoerotic bond between toddler son and father as the prototype of ideal love—a love in which the person seeks to find in the other an ideal

image of himself... The father-son love affair is the model
for later ideal love, just as the conflict of rapprochement
between independence and helplessness is the model conflict that such ideal love is usually called upon to solve.
(Benjamin 1990a: 107)

This father-son love is therefore based on identification, and
is precisely the kind of love which the girl may be denied. This
identificatory love should not be confused with phallic
defences. Concern for the penis is *always* defensive, whether in
the boy or in the girl. Concentration on the penis signals a failure of object-relations and of the toleration of anxiety and guilt.
Snow White's obsessional repair of phallic part-objects—for
instance—signals her anxiety due to a lack of a paternal figure,
and her fear of falling into the hands of the bad, envious
mother.

Cinderella, on the other hand, seems to have a more integrated, beneficent paternal figure. She also possesses a more
integrated parental couple (viz. the twig given by the father and
planted on the mother's grave) which she keeps apart from her
step-mother. At no point is Cinderella in fear for her life.
Nevertheless Cinderella, like Snow White, is without a paternal
identificatory figure and lacks, therefore, a desire of her own.
She thus becomes the prototypical feminine figure—the *object* of
desire.

On the other hand, Electra enjoys a strong paternal imago.
Her attachment to the idealised figure of Agamemnon is total.
This idealisation has, however, a strong passive component
which, one might assume, is the result of his previous absence.
What she lacks is a *living* relationship with a father with whom
phantasies and anxieties can be worked-through. Instead she
attaches herself to a dead father, in order to save herself from a
bad mother. Her hate for her mother is exactly correlative to the
absence of father. Her subjection to his idealised figure is the
only way she can find to retain an internalised paternal figure.

Even so, Electra's wish to kill her mother does not liberate
her. On the contrary, it consumes her with pure hatred and a
wish for revenge. Electra cannot give up her mother. She is tied

to her by bonds of hatred which are much stronger than those of love. Electra's lack of a good maternal figure makes her the prototypical melancholic. Because her love and her hate for her mother are inseparable, she can have no good object. Her matricide by proxy is an attempt to get rid of the bad mother, but— because she cannot completely relinquish her identification with this mother—we can only speculate on the disastrous psychical effect of this. Can she survive cohabitation with a murdered object? Can she make reparation or revive her dead maternal object? And if she does not, will she have to rely on liberation afforded by yet another prince? These are unanswerable questions, stemming from a profoundly damaged mother-daughter relationship.

Proud and dignified Electra is a long way from the humble, self-effacing Cinderella, or the compliant Snow White. Electra represents only one type of a mother-daughter relationship, that which is based on a denial of maternal identification. Like Athene, who proclaims 'the supremacy of the male', Electra denounces her mother's power and upholds the murder of the mother. In contrast to Snow White— and more in the vein of Cinderella—she lives with the bad mother, but has no other good mother to whom she might resort.

Another famous mother-daughter pair from antiquity is that of Demeter and Persephone.[24] There is no hint of hatred between them, although Demeter's reluctance to let her daughter go to the Underworld suggests a degree of non-differentiation. Her reluctance to allow separation also hints at a species of female narcissism which denies the male a role in reproduction, and clings to a delusion of female parthenogenesis. The wish of the mother to deny the daughter access to the male, and the illusion that women can reproduce themselves, is sometimes transmitted from mother to daughter in an insidious way. Sometimes the loss of the mother's mother (or even of the grandmother's mother) at a very early age can mark the beginning of this clinging to a female line, and a delusional exclusion of the male. A mother such as this can arouse in her daughter a panic of being trapped and suffocated. Coupled with the absence of a good father-figure, a phobic personality may begin to emerge.

Some women, who are born from an apparently stable and happy marriage in which there is affection between the parents, nevertheless find themselves shocked by the extent of their own sexual and emotional problems. They do not understand how they could have such problems, given that their parents enjoyed such a loving relationship. A closer examination, however, may reveal a mother who is attached to her husband *as if he were her mother*. A mother such as this may harbour a delusion of parthenogenesis. She may be over-protective, over-attached, or neglectful and distant towards her daughter. However, her actual behaviour may matter less than the simple fact that she clings to this unconscious phantasy.

The daughter of this mother has only one hope—a good and close relationship to her father. Such a daughter may then dream of killing her mother in the name of the father. The road to happiness and good relationships is difficult for such women. Even so, as I have stressed repeatedly, matricide is never an effective solution—for either the girl or the boy.

In the myth of Demeter and Persephone, the reality of sexual difference is seen as a trauma, a rupture of female narcissism—as indeed it is. It is also viewed as an abduction of the daughter by the male. A mother without a father finds it especially difficult to let her daughter go. In such cases the male appears not as a life-giver, but as death. It is Pluto, the king of the Underworld, who is Persephone's abductor, yet we are given no details concerning Persephone's feelings on the matter. It is as if she were just a pawn between Demeter, Pluto, and Zeus. Her fate is decided in the battle of wills between these protagonists. Demeter's possessive love for her daughter deprives Persephone of a voice of her own. Such daughters often develop somatic symptoms, eating disorders, or a promiscuous love-life.

Admittedly, this is a rather grim account of the mother-daughter relationship. Mothers are, of course, individuals, and there are dangers in defining a prototype. But there is, I think, room for both a prototype and the notion of infinite individual variations upon this prototype. The main task of individual development is the working-through of this very intense and ambivalent relationship towards the mother. Klein believed that what takes place in psychotherapy—the slow working-through of defences and anxiety—takes place also in childhood (Klein 1959). In this case, constitutional factors such as the capacity to contain anxiety, as well as mothers and father's personalities, and the cultural container, are all very important. The ability to work through murderous impulses towards mother is, however, of paramount importance, and the lack of an ability to achieve this can leave the daughter with severe problems.

* * *

What follows is the clinical example of a woman for whom the myths of Clytemnestra and Electra were a vivid reality.

Mary, an attractive professional woman of thirty-three, came to therapy because of an unhappy relationship and her inability to put an end to it. Mary had been in this relationship for five years prior to the commencement of therapy.

Mary's relationship with Nick might be described, loosely, as 'sadomasochistic'—not in a sexual but certainly in an emotional sense. Mary felt crushed, humiliated, and constantly attacked, but was unable to break away because this would mean being left with nothing inside—with only 'a big, gaping gap', in her words. It was as if she was stating that Nick was not only her only possible object, but also part of herself.

For his part, Nick had declared himself at the very beginning of the relationship as 'polygamous'. He had told her that if she wanted a nice, boring, monogamous man who would settle down into a nice, boring relationship, then she had better look elsewhere. If she ever complained or made a scene about his behaviour, he would threaten to leave, or else he would completely demoralise her by saying that she was childish, selfish, stupid and inadequate. Every time she made a serious attempt to break away from the relationship, however, he would then tell her that he loved her, and that she was the only one who mattered in his life. The blame for the ups and downs of the relationship was placed on her for being jealous, possessive, and unable to accept Nick as polygamous.

Mary was close to despair when she came to see me. She could neither remain in the relationship, nor break away from it. She felt trapped in an impossible situation. What I have not yet mentioned, however, is the fact that Mary was deeply attracted to Nick. She found him physically attractive, intelligent, interesting and immensely superior to any other men she knew. She announced again and again that she found other men boring, and her many attempts to become interested in them had all been in vain.

As therapy progressed she came to realise that she only found attractive men who rejected or tantalised her. Nick, with his provocative behaviour—giving and withdrawing almost in the same instant, or else giving just enough to ensure Mary knew what she was missing when he withdrew—was the perfect 'alluring bad object', in Fairbairn's sense (Fairbairn 1943).

Mary's attachment to a rejecting object was both a repetition of her relationship to her mother, and an attempt to repair it. Mary had one thing in mind as she persisted in her desperate attempt to make this relationship viable, which was to make Nick love *only* herself. It seemed to Mary that the way to achieve this was to change herself—that is, to make herself be what Nick wanted her to be. However, this was impossible, because what Nick wanted from her was for her to accept him 'as he was'— namely, to accept his 'polygamous' nature and his affairs with other women. The stalemate was absolute, but the raging battle had continued for years.

Mary's sessions often took the form of long, cruel attacks on herself and on her inability to rid herself of jealousy, insecurity, and the wish to appear mature and non-possessive in Nick's eyes. The attacks on herself were, however, disguised assaults upon the internal libidinal object—in the way that Fairbairn (and Freud) have described (Fairbairn 1943; Freud 1917)— which would predictably change their focus and direction towards Nick, who would then become the main target. This took the form of, on the one hand, accusing him of being cruel, insensitive and immature, whilst—on the other hand—trying to change him. The deep wish that he remain the same (as a rejecting object) was deeply unconscious, and was manifested only in

Mary's inability to form a relationship with a man who was not rejecting. Mary's immense ambivalence towards this tantalising figure was correlative to her deep feelings of worthlessness and guilt, and the wish for self-punishment which she harboured.

Mary was the eldest of three sisters. She described her relationship to the others as full of jealousy, envy, and competitiveness because, as the eldest, she was excluded from the alliance between the other two. She felt rejected by this, but she also wanted very badly to be the best in everything, which provoked further rejection and exclusion. The deep feelings of envy, jealousy and hate towards them—especially towards the one chronologically closer to her—felt unmanageable. Her sense of herself as 'bad' was intense. At one time she slept with the door of her bedroom locked, because she feared she might get up in her sleep and kill her sister.

Her relationship to her mother she described as one of continuous rejection on her mother's part. Mother seemed to have been unable to tolerate Mary's feelings of jealousy and envy towards her sisters. Mary received from her mother the message that these feelings were unacceptable and dangerous. It is possible that her mother saw Mary as an unacceptable part of herself, so that there was nothing Mary could do to win her love. However, if mother could not stand Mary's competitiveness, she was equally unable to bear her neediness. The more Mary begged for love, the more she was rejected. The more Mary tried to be the best at everything, in order to attract mother's attention, the more she was told to stop showing off. Mary spent her childhood trying to figure out what she had to do or what she had to be in order to win mother's love—which sounded also like a very good description of her relationship to Nick. Her anger and hatred of mother was deeply unconscious, and had been turned instead towards herself.

This grim state of affairs was alleviated only by Mary's relationship to her father, whom she described as loving and supportive. Here was the father as 'refuge' or 'haven' (Freud 1933: 129)—or as the 'second chance', which Kohut describes in cases where mother fails in her mirroring function (Kohut 1971). I wish to draw a distinction here between the father as object in a triangular relationship, and the father as a mirror in a dyadic relationship. The triangular relationship to father as an object is full of guilt, since it entails competition with mother. The dyadic relationship to father as a mirror, on the other hand, is non-ambivalent, and can help repair some of the damage to the self.[25]

As Mary became a teenager, she began to grow more aware of her anger against her mother, and embarked upon a rebellion against her which, had it succeeded, might have helped Mary work-through a great deal of her ambivalence. Unfortunately, mother fell ill and died when Mary was sixteen. During mother's illness, which lasted for some time, Mary felt unable to be supportive towards her, or to express any feelings whatsoever. At the time of her mother's death—Mary reported—she felt numb and unable to mourn. She blamed herself for having refused to visit mother the night before she died, and knew that she would have to live with this guilt of this for the rest of her life. The conviction that she had literally killed her mother was, of course, deeply unconscious, but the consequences of this were to haunt Mary from that point onwards.

Significantly, one of the few feelings she was able to describe was her immense pity for her father, coupled with the feeling that she—as the eldest—would now take mother's place. This was mixed with fears that her father, now without a sexual partner, would claim her as his partner instead. She began locking her door at night yet at the same time felt ashamed of these thoughts.

The Oedipal feelings, fears, and wishes are hardly disguised here, but to have attributed all her struggles with her mother to Oedipal strivings and rivalry would have been a great mistake. To begin with, Mary's continuous aim was to win the love of her mother rather than her father's love. (According to Fairbairn, mother remains in the unconscious as the first rejecting object for both sexes [Fairbairn 1944].) Secondly, her attempts to change herself or to change Nick were *direct* attacks on the self and the object, entirely without regard to the intervention of a third party—the father. In this sense, then, her relationship to Nick can be described as a form of projective identification without the possibility of a third space. What is also clear is the super-imposition of an Oedipal situation on top of a pre-Oedipal set-up which, of course, proved highly unsatisfactory. In this sense the Oedipal situation is highly defensive, serving merely as a way of escaping the trap of an extremely ambivalent, two-person, mother-and-daughter relationship.

One might object at this point that my clinical example offers an exceptionally rejecting mother, and also exceptional circumstances—such as the death of the mother at the height of the daughter's rebellion—which artificially elevates Mary to the unconscious status of an Electra. My contention is that however exceptional this particular situation might be, nevertheless it highlights a fundamentally female situation: the identification with an ambivalent, attacked and damaged object, where attacks on mother are followed by abysmal horror and guilt. We also see here the difficulties of escape through identification with father. The idealised father cannot serve as an identificatory figure—at least, not in the same way as for the boy. At best he serves as a benevolent, protective, external or internal figure. Because the girl is unable to identify with the idealised father, he cannot be viewed as the figure upon which relationships such as that between Mary and Nick are based. Indeed, these are modelled instead on the relationship to mother. In relationships such as this the woman is attempting to make reparation to the object by serving it, yet her simultaneous attacks upon it are poorly disguised as 'attempts to change him'. This is also a situation in which the woman is projectively identified with her attacked object. As we have seen, in Mary's case it is the relationship with her mother which is relentlessly repeated in her relationships with men (before Nick she had a similar relationship with another man), whilst the relationship to her father remains an ideal.

The conflict between mother and daughter need not always take the same form as in Mary's case. For instance, it might not be externalised and projected onto a relationship. It might remain instead a purely intrapsychic conflict, between an internal mother and an internal daughter. In cases in which, for one reason or another, open conflict between mother and daughter is avoided or forbidden, the woman carries the whole burden of guilt and depression, and an extremely poor self-image is often the result. External conflict with mother is necessary for many reasons. Among these is the way in which, for the girl—and maybe to a lesser extent for the boy—it is an attempt to create boundaries in the 'no-man's land' that is the mother-child relationship. In the absence of the father as a care-giving figure, this no-man's land consists of a confusion of identity between mother and daughter, and of the daughter's entanglement in mother's projective identification. However, external conflict has a further beneficial effect, in the sense that it enables phantasies and internal conflicts to be tested against reality. If the mother survives the external attacks without either retaliating or being damaged, then the daughter can eventually come to trust her own reparative powers. But if external conflict is either discouraged or retaliation follows, or—even worse—if the mother seems too fragile to withstand the child's aggression, then the girl will be locked into her own vicious circle of never-ending attacks on self and internal objects. The feeling of 'being bad' is then unavoidable, which fosters further compliance, and thus the vicious circle is completed.

To return to Mary, I will now comment on certain aspects of the transference which, at first, I found quite puzzling, as I often find is the case with many women patients. At the beginning of the treatment, Mary kept me at a safe distance. For a while she used therapy as a place where she could come and complain about Nick and express her despair and her conviction that nothing could be done. It might be said that, in this way, I represented father for her, a benevolent but powerless figure. But maybe I represented father in a further sense: I was a 'third person' to whom she could talk about her relationship with Nick, for Mary went nowhere without him. Indeed, Nick was so much part of herself and her internal conflicts, and the oppressiveness of the relationship was so much a part of the oppressiveness in her internal world, that therapy felt the only place in which a 'third space' was possible. However, this was only tolerable if she brought Nick with her (figuratively), so that she was not alone with me.

Slowly I realised that, underneath the trusting therapeutic alliance, she did not expect anything from me because I was perceived as useless in helping her to solve her problems. More than that, I *had to be* useless, because she did not really want to free herself from Nick or from her submission to an internal sadistic object. Indeed, she felt she thoroughly deserved the treatment she received. There was, of course, the other fear that if I was acknowledged to have any power I would cease to be father, and would then become very dangerous and invasive—like her mother—and, also like her mother, I would be in mortal danger.

It would have been easy to overlook mother's invasiveness by concentrating instead on her rejection of Mary, and it would also have been easy to have failed to recognise that mother's rejection was actually based on seeing Mary as an unwanted part of herself. Indeed, I think that this type of projective identification is often overlooked and interpreted instead as 'withdrawal', whereas the real dynamic is confusion of identity due to fusion and lack of boundaries. The difficulty is deciding *whose* invasiveness we are talking about—Mary's, the mother's, or both.

Mary's fear of her mother's invasiveness took the form of keeping me at a safe distance, whilst Mary's own invasiveness was acted out in her relationship to Nick. This had the advantage of keeping me safe from her anger and aggression. In this way, then, the mother transference proved difficult to unravel. The primitive fears which accompanied it were expressed only as symptoms in her relationship with Nick, and were thus kept safely out of therapy, or expressed in therapy only as a deep resistance against dependence.

The first months of treatment consisted of Mary telling me the same story again and again. The story had endless variations as Mary recounted, session by session, all the events and twists in her relationship with Nick. There was nothing else either in the world or in the consulting room. I was just a pair of ears to listen to Mary's monologue of self-revilement. I found myself first growing bored and then wanting to stop her, to interrupt. Needless to say, any interpretations on my part were met with: 'yes, but...'

I slowly realised that by concentrating my interpretations on Mary's aggression I had done what Fairbairn had warned against—namely, I had joined forces with Mary's internal saboteur, in this way increasing her self-hatred (Fairbairn 1943: 74 n2). As I slowly started concentrating instead on her low self-esteem, her immense sense of guilt, and her fear of her own love and needs as dangerous and depleting, I began to sense a change in the transference. I was no longer bored by Mary. Instead I began to feel very close to her, very motherly. On her part Mary seemed to be more trusting, but there was no obvious relationship to me. I was important to her, yet I was not. Breaks were difficult and she felt, at times, that she could not cope by herself. Yet the relation of this to me was vague, blurred. I was puzzled, although this was a phenomenon I had come across with so many women patients. The concept of projective identification was helpful but did not quite fit because it had connotations of envy and destructiveness, and this situation did not feel like that.

My supervisor, the late Helle Munro, helped me by providing the image of a pregnant woman and her relationship to her unborn baby: so close and yet so distant, so tangible and yet so vague. Mary had lodged herself inside me in a non-aggressive way, waiting to be born again. This is a phenomenon akin to what Bela Grunberger has termed the 'monad'

The monad is a nonmaterial womb which functions as though it were material; on the one hand, it encloses the child in its narcissistic universe; on the other, it prepares it for the partial dissolution of that universe—or, in other words, for the dissolution of its own essence. (Grunberger 1989: 3)

This is a situation which produces the illusion of narcissistic perfection, the experience—according to Grunberger—of the baby in the womb. Grunberger regards the analytic setting as promoting the monadic situation, with the aim of eventually dissolving it. It is a kind of 'regression in the service of the ego'. In my experience, this is a predominantly feminine situation, as masculine defences usually prevent men from such a regression. For women, on the other hand, this seems to be a state of bliss before the rivalry between mother and daughter had begun.

In my experience, the blurred boundaries between mother and daughter are often reproduced in settings where both patient and therapist are women. These blurred boundaries might entail destructive projective identification, during which unwanted parts of the self are projected into the other who is then experienced as a persecutor—or it might mean something much more benign, such as re-living an experience of fusion, a harking back to a point before the conflict between self and object (either internal or external) had begun. This harking back in search of a safer relationship has to be distinguished clearly from projective identification. It is a return to what Winnicott called the stage of absolute dependence (Winnicott 1965: 46) or, even further, to a kind of pre-natal bliss. Only then can the therapist be trusted as a container. I think that Mary had moved from her profound distrust of me, produced by projective identification, to a deep trust produced by a species of fusion experience. Needless to say, the two often appeared to co-exist, and she was capable of moving from one to the other very rapidly.

Mary provides us with an insight into just one possible constellation of relationships in the girl's life: the rejecting mother and the helpful, highly idealised father. This type of woman often becomes seemingly active and independent, because she has formed a strong—but nevertheless secondary—identification with her father. Below this identification, however, lies the more fundamental identification with a fearful and damaged mother, and the unending battle between mother and daughter. Women with this psychic constellation, then, although active in their professional life, are emotionally very fragile and insecure, and frequently end up in relationships like Mary's.

Identification with a damaged or dead mother, which precludes the possibility of making reparation, would be fatal not only to ego-structure, but also for the development of femininity and the capacity to bear children. One often hears from women doubts over whether they could or should have children, and the fear of damaging them in the same way they have been damaged. But here—precisely—lies the woman's dilemma and her discontent, which led Freud to cry so exasperatedly: *was will das Weib?* For her to identify with father poses major problems to her femininity, yet fails to solve her problem of the damaged internal mother. To identify, on the other hand, with the damaged mother leads to severe self-doubt and, perhaps, to depression. In my view, the structure of the traditional patriarchal family offers few opportunities for the resolution of this conflict, because a flight to the idealised father—a figure idealised by culture and untarnished by early ambivalence—is possible, and is even prescribed, as Freud's description of the girl's path to femininity has shown. The girl's flight to father, and the father's collusion with it, does nothing to help her resolve her ambivalence towards mother, whilst the boy's identification with father helps to locate the 'bad object' outside himself and to project it onto woman.

One way in which the girl works through her ambivalence and repairs her damaged objects, is by working-through the damaged relationship with mother in her relationship with her father. If this relationship is close, it can provide opportunities for reparation. It is, maybe, no coincidence that another famous daughter of antiquity—Antigone—rises to the status of a heroine and independent agent only after she has made reparation to her blind and unhappy father, the exiled Oedipus, for something for which she was not even responsible. It is Oedipus who accepts Antigone's love and care as from his own mother. Antigone becomes his guide, his eyes, his non-dangerous, nonseductive 'mother'. We are told nothing of Antigone's hatred for her mother, yet one cannot help wondering how she could possibly escape blaming her mother for what has happened. The journey of Oedipus and Antigone through the wilderness of exile and disgrace develops into a voyage of reparation and redemption. Oedipus reaches a peaceful end, and Antigone goes on to become the most noble of all heroines, representing Love, Freedom, and—as Nina Lykke reminds us—the 'mother right' (Lykke 1993).

Luce Irigaray, commenting on Clytemnestra's murder, writes:

...what is now becoming apparent in the most everyday things and in the whole of our society and our culture is that, at a primal level, they function on the basis of matricide. (Irigaray 1991: 36)

The symbolic reproduction of this murder in the psyche is a 'necessary' pre-requisite for entering the culture, in stark contrast to the taboo which arose from the murder of the father. From the heroic times of Clytemnestra, down to our nuclear age, the demise of the mother is the single fact which haunts our culture and creates the asymmetry that is characteristic of male-female relations as well as the relation between our culture and nature. It is true that there has been a partial restitution of the mother through Christianity, but in a position that is both powerless and objectified, poised between an all-powerful Father and an all-powerful Son, and excluded from the Holy Trinity.

It is because of this asymmetry that I find it impossible to talk about the mother-daughter relationship without talking about mother-son, father-daughter, and mother-father relationships. If this chapter has spread itself too thinly over all three of these it is because I believe that we cannot understand the mother-daughter relationship without approaching the context within which it takes place. However, at the present time, and for the first time since Clytemnestra, the mother is rising from the ashes and demanding rights equal to those of the Father. How difficult it is for us to conceive this actually happening is reflected in Freud's theory of infantile development, in which the level of the father and the level of the mother are strictly separated and their functions split. Freud's blind-spot—his relationship to his mother—is also our culture's blind-spot. We have overlooked the fact that it is Electra, the daughter, who carries the burden of guilt for the whole of humankind.

Chapter 8

The Father-Daughter Romance

CORDELIA: Unhappy that I am, I cannot heave
My heart into my mouth. I love your majesty
According to my bond; no more nor less.
LEAR: How, how, Cordelia! Mend your speech a little,
Lest it may mar your fortunes.
CORDELIA: Good my lord,
You have begot me, bred me, lov'd me; I
Return those duties back as are right fit,
Obey you, love you, and most honour you.
Why have my sisters husbands, if they say
They love you all? Haply, when I shall wed,
That lord whose hand must take my plight shall carry
Half my love, with him, half my care and duty. (*King Lear*,
I. i, ll.90-101)

With these words Cordelia disburdens Lear of the illusion that
she belongs to him. But it is a truth he cannot bear.

LEAR: So young, and so untender?
CORDELIA: So young, my lord, and so true. (I. i, ll.105-6)

Consequently, Lear disowns her. Soon after, Cordelia marries
the King of France, whilst Lear himself proceeds towards madness and destruction.

The father's 'ownership' of the daughter, enshrined in law
within many societies, exposes the underlying dynamic of the
relationship. The illusion of ownership enters into the relationship between father and daughter very early. It is part of the
illusion of ownership of children in general, but it has a special
quality—namely, *erotisation*. In other words, the father's illusion
is that he owns the girl's love. The girl, for her part, wants more
than anything else to be loved by the father. For Cordelia to be
so forthright about her divided allegiances is an act of unusual

independence and spirit, especially given the fact that she has not yet had a relationship with another man. The scenario we are used to—and the scenario which Lear expects at this moment in the play—is undivided love and devotion. Lear desperately wants to *hear* it, as well as to have it; he would much rather hear empty words of devotion from Cordelia than be confronted by this declaration of divided love.

Although I do not intend to address the theme of Lear's individual psychopathology, I will treat him as a prototypical father, in the sense that he represents an authority figure which demands not just obedience, but also absolute domination of the girl's mind and love. Freud's prototypical father—the castrator—exists only in relation to the son. In relation to the daughter, however, the father becomes the charismatic leader, a seductive authority-figure. His domination is not achieved through threats of castration, but instead through demands for ownership of the girl's soul. Her love is the redeeming feature of this exceedingly unequal relationship.

Love is indeed what the girl is looking for, as she moves from the unsatisfactory relationship with her mother to an idealised relationship with father. To be acknowledged and loved by this ideal figure is all that she desires. To this end she will renounce a great deal of her autonomy and aggression. As Chasseguet-Smirgel has pointed out, the girl represses her anal-sadistic instincts as she enters into this idealised relationship with father, because they are incompatible with idealisation (Chasseguet-Smirgel 1985). I argued in the previous chapter that the girl gives up her aggressivity for the additional reason that she perceives her father's woundedness and dread of independent femininity, and of the undead powerful mother. The girl sees to it that anything which might bring this persecutory anxiety to life in the father is avoided.

The question arises whether there is anything new in the girl's relation to father, or whether this is just a repetition of her relationship to mother, but with a male object. Freud—on this point—seems contradictory. He writes:

...where the woman's attachment to her father was particularly intense, analysis showed that it had been preceded by a phase of exclusive attachment to her mother
which had been equally intense and passionate. *Except for
the change of her love-object, the second phase had scarcely
added any new feature to her erotic life* . (Freud 1931: 225, my
italics)

On the other hand, in the same paper he states:

The turning-away from her mother is an extremely
important step in the course of a little girl's development.
It is more than a change of object... we may now add that
hand in hand with it there is to be observed a marked
lowering of the active sexual impulses and a rise of the
passive ones. It is true that the active trends have been
affected by frustration more strongly... But the passive
trends have not escaped disappointment either. With the
turning-away from the mother clitoridal masturbation
frequently ceases as well; and often enough when the
small girl represses her previous masculinity a considerable portion of her sexual trends in general is permanently injured too. The transition to the father object is accomplished with the help of the passive trends and in so far as
they have escaped the catastrophe. (Freud 1931: 239)

Here Freud describes the unequivocal change in the girl's
sexuality which takes place upon the introduction of this new
relationship. Freud suggests that the girl's anger towards mother is provoked by the fact that the she did not give her daughter
a penis—in other words, the daughter blames the mother for
making her a woman (Freud 1931: 234). Anger at womanhood
in general, therefore, is a consequence of the girl's experience of
being stuck within a relationship of the same, a relationship in
which projections and mirroring prevent a clear emergence of
separateness.
    On the other hand, to be in a 'refuge', as Freud put it (Freud
1933: 129), entails exactly a retreat by the daughter from all the

things she cannot deal with. The splitting between a bad mother and an idealised father is a solution to the girl's ambivalence. If it becomes overly polarised, she may never work through her ambivalence, in which case she may develop 'a secret chamber', an internal feminine equivalent to Bluebeard's forbidden room, in which the girl stores her feelings for her mother, and for herself in identification with the mother. If the father colludes in this—that is, if he has his own blood-stained secret room, which (as I have argued) is often the case—and uses his daughter as a refuge from this gory reality, a kind of *folie à deux* may develop, whereby idealisations prevent the formation of a relationship with real people.

The father has been generally regarded as the agent which ushers the child from the symbiotic relationship with mother into reality. He is the one who stands between mother and child, puncturing the child's narcissistic illusions. Yet although this might be so in the case of the boy, where the girl is concerned something quite different may happen, something which actually itself resembles an illusion—the *folie à deux* previously mentioned—yet which, at the same time, ushers the girl into the social reality of female passivity. We should not forget at this point how, for Freud, the female Oedipus complex often remains unresolved. This does not constitute a pathology, however, as Freud himself asserts. It is simply because the lack of a fear of castration in women implies that the main impetus for the dissolution of the Oedipus complex is also absent (Freud 1925a: 257).

This, to me, is a curious statement, which appears to regard the relationship between father and daughter as *dyadic*. The mother as a rival, and the persecutory relationship to her which a 'romance' with father can create, is entirely absent from this statement by Freud. It is as if mother has been eliminated 'as mother'—that is, as the father's partner. This might be conceived of as a female 'Oedipal victory', but often the triumph is more apparent than real; the relationship with father is instead more of a 'haven' or 'refuge'.

'No matter whose theory you read', Jessica Benjamin writes, 'the father is always the entry into the world' (1990b: 464).

Benjamin stresses the dyadic relation to father as that crucial relationship which can either lead to a sense of agency in the girl, or else to submission to an idealised other. Benjamin refers to a pre-Oedipal, homoerotic love for the father—that is, the 'exciting father' of the rapprochement phase. In my opinion, however, the Oedipal father also functions as a dyadic figure for the girl when the split between the mother-world and the father-world is excessive.

In the light of the above, we must ask ourselves whether the father actually is synonymous with 'the entry into reality'. After all, the confusion which surrounds this issue is due, I think, to the presumption that the father must always represents the third term. As an alternative object on to whom the girl transfers *her relationship with mother*, the father decidedly does *not* fulfil the criteria of a third term; he merely represents another dyadic relationship. This dyadic relationship can be as full of illusion and avoidance of reality as that enjoyed with mother. The collusion between father and daughter in order to maintain this illusory reality can lead to sexual disturbances in the girl.

The romance between father and daughter, then, is itself a *dyadic* relationship. The only triangular relationship open to the girl—and to the father—would be to acknowledge the parental couple. This acknowledgement would, indeed, be a recognition of reality. The father as the idealised lover, however, is an illusion which—if promoted by the father—creates a very severe split in the psyche between bad mother and idealised father, and which proves extremely resistant to analysis. Women with a bad relationship to mother and a solid idealised relationship to father live securely in this split. In therapy the idealised father transference can fool the therapist for a long time, whilst the patient's relationships in the outside world exhibit the characteristics of the relationship with the bad mother or, alternatively, a lack of depth and commitment. The resistance to a mother transference in these cases is very strong and persistent, and when it does become manifest it possesses a markedly delusional quality.

We must not underestimate the importance of the father as a helpful figure—that is, as a good object with a key role in ego-development. However, this aspect of the father is much less clear and much less explored or acknowledged than his role in structuring gender identity. Maybe the only major theorist to have acknowledged his role in ego-development is Kohut, who regarded him as offering a 'second chance' where the mother has failed. This second chance cannot entirely make up for mother's failure, but can prevent serious psychopathology from emerging. The blind Oedipus at Colonus, in spite of his total dependence on Antigone, or maybe even because of it, represents this 'second chance' for her.

Clinical examples

It was a series of female patients, each of whom relied heavily on father's affirmation for their basic self-esteem, which first caused me to realise the full significance of the father in ego-development. Yet, for all of these patients, the mixture of 'good object' and 'lover', and the split in the psyche between bad mother and idealised father imago which resulted, had caused confusion and had led to difficulties in their relationships and in their capacity to have children.

These women were all seemingly independent and active, although the degree of their professional success varied. Their secondary identification with father acted as a defence against their experience of mother. Underneath the secondary identification lay the identification with a mother who was both oppressive and damaged, and who regarded the daughter as an internal bad-object. For these patients, reaching the father—both as a good object *and* as an identificatory figure—had been crucial to their development into relatively healthy women. Even so, the 'romance' with father had given each a grandiose, dazzling image of herself as 'father's girl' to which she clung in opposition to the impoverished, down-trodden image of herself as 'mother's girl'. The double persona of Cinderella is an obvious parallel here. In fact, one of these patients referred to herself in exactly these terms.

The defences which developed within the father-daughter relationship were so very firmly entrenched because it was these which had proved so successful in providing them with basic self-esteem. It is the introjection of the good qualities of the object which leads to secure ego development. This introjection of the good object is, however—in these cases—intimately related to identification and to the perception of gender difference. In other words, qualities which are perceived to belong to the opposite sex, and which the father dreads in the girl, are not internalised by her. The father's dread of powerful, independent femininity, and of female aggression, acts as a motive for repression—as a kind of 'external super-ego'—for the girl.

Equally, then, the difficulties arising from identification with the father must not be underestimated. They include the frightening possibility of entering into competition with him, and confusion over gender identity, often leading a woman to choose a man who either acts out the repressed mother-identification, or with whom the woman can act out her original relationship to mother, and thus with whom the woman soon finds it impossible to live. The problems which relate to being 'father's little girl'—that is, entering into competition with mother—are indeed terrifying. The consequences of the guilt and persecution which this entails are immense. In these women a healthy Oedipal relation of love, hate, conflict, jealousy and reconciliation has not been possible; thus they have always lived in fear of their own destructiveness.

Monica

Monica, a vivacious, intelligent, professional woman of thirty-four came to therapy with the presenting problem of whether she should go back to her country of origin (a Northern European country), or stay in England. Behind this dilemma, however, lay the problem of her relationship with a man whom she described as 'kind, but aloof and depressed', and who could not communicate his affection for her. As she saw it, behind this wall of non-communication lay the man's own damaged relation to his mother.

Monica's therapy centred on what she experienced as a hunger for love. She experienced herself as a kind of female

Tantalus, always thirsty, always stretching out for water—of which, apparently, there was plenty—but which, however, receded as soon as she reached out. Underneath Monica's confident veneer of an adult, professional woman was a little child, father's favourite girl; and underneath this an even younger little girl, perhaps a hungry baby, longing for mother's love and affirmation.

Monica's idealisation of her father had been exaggerated because her parents had separated when she was seven. The week-ends—when he came to visit—had been festive occasions, with father as the Prince Charming, rescuing Monica and casting some glamour over her mundane existence.

Monica claimed that there was a kind of split within the family; mother always sided with her sister, and father always sided with herself. She maintained that she had always been aware of mother's preference for her sister, and she attributed this to the fact that mother was—like herself—a second child, but who, at the age of four, had been given up for adoption. Monica maintained that all through her childhood she had witnessed the growth of a mother-sister alliance from which she was excluded. When she later confronted her mother with this, and the fact of her resentment, her mother expressed complete surprise and exclaimed that, in her opinion, she had loved Monica more than her sister.

It was difficult to ascertain what exactly had happened, and the reasons why. However, in the transference Monica was definitely a hungry and greedy little girl who could never get enough. At times I experienced the sessions as exhausting and depleting, and was very aware of Monica's dissatisfaction with what she received. I experienced myself as the frustrating mother who had everything but gave nothing, or very little. At other times there was a kind of playful competition between Monica and myself, which put me definitely in the place of the father. Her competitive impulses were a defence against the hungry, dependent and envious child, but also a source of enjoyment and satisfaction in their own right. It was evident that they belonged to another level and another relationship. A competition with mother over father would have given rise to immense guilt, but this never arose, because Monica scored an easy victory over her mother, since father had bestowed his favour upon his daughter so ostentatiously. Monica loved her mother with a kind of hungry, frustrated love, but—at the same time—denigrated her. Although this denigration of mother is in many people unconscious and denied expression in personal relationships, it was a living reality for Monica. 'Poor mum' had married beneath herself, had endured faithlessness and hardship, and had brought up her two daughters in near-poverty more or less alone, with father visiting at week-ends, demanding his laundry to be done and his dinner to be ready. 'Poor mum' worked in a factory, had no money to spend on herself, and the little she earned she spent on Monica and her sister. Father, on the other hand, was a more glorious figure. His faithlessness and selfishness were ignored by Monica. When, during therapy, she finally accessed her very powerful feelings of anger towards him, she commented: 'As a child I could not possibly have allowed myself to know these feelings. If I had, then the whole world would have looked bad. Father was my only hope'. This is a statement I have heard in one form or another from many women, each of whom experienced a similar pattern of a 'bad' relationship to mother and 'good' relationship to father.

The point I wish to stress here, however, is not the way in which father was the 'good' object, or even the way in which Monica was father's 'little princess', but instead the extent to which this relationship helped Monica repair some of the damage which her unsatisfactory relationship to mother had caused, creating 'compensatory structures', in Kohut's use of the term.[26] It is easy to dismiss Monica's idealisation of her father, and the positive feelings about herself which the relationship to him engendered, as a 'manic defence'. Although this is true to an extent, there is another dimension to this relationship which might be overlooked if we regard it as dominated simply by manic defences—because it was father, not mother, who indicated to Monica that she *was* good enough. Unfortunately, however, there was also a seductive dimension to this relationship— an indication that she was 'special' and 'better than mother'. The two levels co-existed: the good-enough and the idealised;

the relation to Monica as a daughter, and as a compensation for a bad marriage; the relation to Monica as a separate person, and father's projection onto her of a part of himself. Added to this were also the de-sexualised relation of adult to child, and the sexualised relation of male to female.

Monica's choice of a partner, then, was a depressed man who had experienced problems of his own with a depressed mother. Onto this constellation Monica projected her own relationship to her mother, and found it unbearable. At the same time as attempting to 'cure' him she also wanted to make him 'acknowledge her'. In cases such as this, where heterosexual object-choice has been maintained, the identification with father can only be secondary and rather superficial. Underneath lurks the identification with a damaged and denigrated mother.

Kohut suggested that the early idealisation of the parents was slowly withdrawn, as a consequence of 'optimal frustration'. In other words, when the parent 'fails' or disappoints the child, the child *internalises* that attribute of the parent which has failed, rather than continuing to idealise that attribute *in* the parent. However, this occurs only if the failure is 'phase-appropriate'. The internalisation of bits of the parents, or of their functions, creates an internal structure which is capable of dealing with frustration and regulating impulses and drives. Providing he is not over-idealised, the father can help compensate for maternal failure, as part of this process (Kohut 1984). In Monica's case, her father enjoyed a lot of early interaction with his daughter, before his separation from mother. Until Monica was seven the family lived and worked on a farm, and her father was present much more than is usual in most households. 'Seductive' behaviour on his part gave Monica the impression that she was his partner, and kept her in a state of delusion, hindering her development towards a mature identity. In later years, her father's removal from the family meant that he was not close enough to be seen to fail or disappoint these expectations. Nevertheless, Monica was a reasonably well-functioning woman with a great deal of enthusiasm for her job and her life. Her split-off relation to her mother was apparent only in her relationships with men.

Marie

This was also the case in the development of another woman, Marie, who presented the same pattern of a 'bad' relationship to mother compensated for by a 'good' relationship to father. Marie came to therapy complaining of very low self-esteem. She felt that people did not like her, could not like her, and that she was essentially unlovable.

Marie suffered from an intense sense of shame and inadequacy. She felt that, basically, she was not good enough. When faced with a group of people she felt exposed, defenceless and shamed. This feeling involved intense humiliation and the wish to hide, and prevented her from joining any groups—even from studying, since taking up a course entailed being with a group of people.

Marie had, however, many friends with whom she enjoyed close relationships, but a small disappointment with them or a little comment on their part, which Marie would interpret as a slight, was enough to throw her into self-doubt. Did they really like her after all? Did they find her too needy, too demanding?

Marie had an intense hunger for close relationships but at the same time an intense dread of exclusive relationships, which she linked on the one hand to her parents' relationship or, on the other, to her relationship with her mother. Marital relationships felt to Marie like a trap. A previous relationship with an older man, which had lasted for a few years, made her feel completely ensnared. Marie described the man as charming and cultured, yet possessive and demanding. It was difficult from Marie's account to ascertain whether this man did indeed make excessive demands on her, or whether he had just wanted a 'normal' marriage, something which Marie experienced as a threat to her very identity. As therapy progressed Marie began to wonder for herself about the truth of this relationship. Marie loathed 'married couples'. Marriage seemed to her a cannibalistic feast in which mutual devouring took place. A 'couple' was a unit which consisted of two non-persons who always did the same thing—slept in the same bed, ate together, went everywhere together—and which implied the surrender of individuality and identity.

However, it would be a distortion if I described Marie only in these terms, for she was also capable of great joy and richness of feeling. She experienced moments of deep happiness when she was alone in nature, or when she was with a close friend—in other words, when she did not feel the threat of being either invaded or rejected. When Marie did not feel threatened she was full of life and joy which, I believe, were genuinely non-defensive; there was nothing about these moments of rich emotion which seemed to me 'manic'.

I will attempt a reconstruction of her family constellation, based partly on her account and partly on the transference, although I am fully aware of the dangers involved in such an endeavour, and the warnings of many analysts that it is impossible to know what the original relationships were like. I think that these warnings successfully draw our attention to the distortions which the original objects may have undergone in the internal world, and the danger of colluding with our patients in forming distorted views. Human beings might never be certain of having discovered the absolute Truth about anything but, even so, a series of relative truths, which can act as guiding principles, might be possible. The family constellation might be one of these relative truths, and clues to the nature of this seem to present themselves by analysing the patient's internal object relationships and the transference.

In Marie's early years her mother seemed to have had very low self-esteem and a particular inability to communicate with her children. 'She made door-mats out of my sister and myself for anyone to tread on', said Marie in one of our first meetings, 'because she herself was another door-mat'. She described her mother as a 'non-person': extremely conformist, insecure, extremely unsure of herself and, above all, without any flesh on her body, no curves, no warmth. She likened her to an ironing board—as if she were a piece of flat wood with no breasts, no womb, sexuality, or life—and went on to state that everything which came into contact with her mother had to be ironed out, straightened and smoothed. Austere, unsmiling and non-sensuous, obsessively clean and tidy, yet at the same time totally 'unreal', Marie's mother sounded like a fatal combination of being too present and too absent, intrusive and rejecting at the same time. She sounded to me like a dead mother who only played at being alive.

During therapy Marie allowed herself to lift the lid of what she called 'the cauldron' of her feelings for her mother. Marie, the witch, in an intense identification with her mother, found that uncovering the 'cauldron' for anything more than a short time was intolerable. Feelings of intense anger, hate, disgust, sadness, abandonment, began slowly to emerge. Gradually, the undifferentiated mess which was Marie began to differentiate itself from mother.

Because my theme is the father-daughter relationship, I shall not proceed any deeper into the details of Marie's therapy. Given her extremely damaged relationship to mother, Marie had survived relatively well. She had sustained deep narcissistic wounds, but retained the capacity to make relationships— even if restricted—and to enjoy life. In my view the idea of the father as 'second chance' sheds a great deal of light upon this situation.

'Thank God that my father was there', Marie exclaimed in an early session. 'He gave me the little self-esteem that I have, and gave me a love for life and nature.' Father was described as warm, sensitive and loving, but at the same time shy, weak and non-assertive. He gave Marie love and affirmation but was unable to protect her from either mother's invasive presence or from the aggressive cousins who lived next door. Father was a benign figure, a 'good object', although not an 'idealised' object, in Kohut's sense, because Marie had witnessed all too often his humiliation at the hands of his aggressive brother. Father's submission to mother, in order to avoid conflict and hysterical tears, was also witnessed by Marie often enough. So although Marie introjected and identified with a good and benign father who loved nature and life, this father was, at the same time, a denigrated object—like mother and like herself.

These are not the optimal conditions under which Kohut's 'transmuting internalisation' might take place—that is, the development of a stable ego.[27] Yet Marie had considerable ego-strength, and an ability to survive disturbances in self-esteem which occurred all too frequently. We are obliged to hypothesise, therefore, a time when Marie was unaware of father's humiliation and denigration, a time when father was the Prince Charming, the glorious liberator. It was during this early period that Marie's ego developed considerably, but the development came to a halt, possibly for the following reasons. Firstly, the removal of Marie from the pedestal when, at the age of four and a half, her sister was born. And secondly, father's removal from the pedestal when Marie began to realise his true position within the family, and his position in relation to his brother. Nevertheless, in my opinion whatever ego-strength Marie possessed had originated from her relationship with her father, who made up for her mother's deficiencies. However, the fact that this 'compensatory' ego-structure can never prove as deep and secure as that based upon the mother-infant relationship becomes all too clear, once we consider how father exists 'at a higher level' in the internal world. He cannot 'undo' but can only *compensate for*, an unsatisfactory mother-infant relationship—at least under the present conditions of child-rearing, in which mother is the main care-giver.

Father provided something very important to Monica and Marie: a spark of life, a feeling of being, a joy in existence. Winnicott has termed this sense of life and energy within the individual 'the True Self'.[28] Winnicott, however, never considered the True Self has having a direct connection with the father. Indeed, for Winnicott this would have been incomprehensible, since he asserted that the True Self is dissociated in cases where good enough mothering is not available (Winnicott 1960a). The cases of Monica and Marie, however, point to the possibility of paternal compensation for inadequate mothering, especially if the father is present during the early life of the baby, as was the case in the lives of these patients.

Neither Monica nor Marie had children, and all of them doubted their capacity to bring up children.

Also part of this pattern is the partial identification with father, which lent these women a sense of independence and a fear of dependency, on a rather masculine model. The lack of potential space between themselves and their object (mother), is resolved by recourse to the 'outside' rather than 'inside'; the consequent fear and longing for an experience of merging with the object is very similar to that encountered in masculine psychology.

Marina

For these two women, whose father played an important and compensatory role in their development, I will contrast a final female patient whose father was 'no more than a shadow'. Marina came to therapy for what she termed 'depression', but which seemed to me more like a schizoid withdrawal from the world of external relationships. She complained of feelings of futility, of lack of interest in life, people, work, reading—just about everything. This condition had already been with her for about two years by the time she came to see me. Therapy, seeking 'help', was the last thing Marina wanted, but she was desperate, and the hope that 'it would just go away' had evaporated with the passage of endless grey days and months.

Marina was forty-eight when she came to therapy—an independent, 'no-nonsense' woman in the helping professions, with a dry sense of humour which she often used to describe herself. She was a lesbian and lived alone, in spite of continuous pleas from her partner, who wanted to move in with her. Marina would not risk this because she had bitter memories of previously 'living together' with another woman; she had found the dependence this aroused in her very threatening. The present relationship was described as 'good', but I had the impression of a rather lukewarm connection; the other woman seemed dependent on Marina for support.

From what Marina told me of herself, she had never been a spontaneous person and had never enjoyed life. Life was to be 'managed', not enjoyed. She was reliable, efficient and helpful, in a matter-of-fact way, but something was missing from her personality—a spark of life, a *joie de vivre*. Moments of ecstasy seemed totally unknown to her. Marina's relationship with her mother seemed to be (and to have been) a reversal of the mother-child roles. Mother was an immensely unstable and persecuted woman, apparently kept sane by the tacit pledge made by Marina and—to a lesser degree—by her sister to remain completely loyal to her. This is not how Marina would have put it, for she was totally unaware of the absolute reign of her internal mother. She had, after all, moved away from home as soon as she could—at eighteen. However, she had not moved very far. She was always within fifty miles or so from home and visited her mother quite often. Since father's death she and her sister took turns to visit mother every weekend, staying from Friday to Sunday evening, although both of them dreaded it. According to Marina this was understandable behaviour, because mother was all alone; and besides, was it not evident that she, Marina, was an independent woman who could see mother objectively, criticise her, and laugh about her peculiarities?

Around the same time that Marina began to think about starting therapy her mother started to deteriorate. Firstly, her mother developed tinnitus; she swore that her neighbour was drilling all through the night so that she could not sleep. Gradually she began to accuse all the neighbours of plotting against her. Marina was quite desperate, yet felt increasingly guilty as she responded more and more to the need to free herself from the aggressive internal mother. Unconsciously she sensed that her move towards freeing herself had triggered her mother's deterioration.

The symbiotic relationship between a (probably) psychotic mother and her daughters, who kept their mother sane by agreeing not to separate from her, was unbroken by the intervention of a father. Marina's father was a shadowy figure, despised and denigrated as socially inferior and uncouth by the whole family, and completely dominated by his wife. There seemed to be collusion between the whole family not to rock the boat and trigger, in this way, the mother's breakdown. But this maternal brittleness, obsessionality and lack of warmth, so similar to Marie's family romance, was not balanced—as in Marie's case—by the warmth and love of father. The father, kept at a distance, was simply one more pawn in the hands of an omnipotent, jealous mother. In the course of her therapy Marina uncovered her feelings of sadness and anger at the way her father had been treated by the whole family, and the way mother had kept him away from her. However, she could not progress beyond the image of him as denigrated and debased. The internalisation of two damaged and denigrated parental figures left Marina completely bereft of any helpful objects or any compensatory internal structures.

This absence of the father as both an idealised and a desired object can spell psychical disaster to the girl who is struggling to free herself from the stranglehold of a symbiotic relationship with a latently psychotic mother. Marina lacked an idealised figure altogether and seemed to have grown up prematurely in order to become the only 'adult' in the family, making sure everybody was okay. The internal mother-image, however, continued to rule her internal world unchallenged, because to challenge it would mean to risk the deterioration of the external mother. The cruelty of the internal mother, and Marina's devotion to her, were therefore linked with the fragility and brittleness of the external mother.

Identification with the denigrated father might have acted in Marina's case as a barrier against psychosis, but it did not lead to any kind of ego-development or growth. On the contrary it led to a rigid, frozen structure which precluded, by its very nature, any change. It entailed a denigrated self-image, an attitude of extreme control over the self and the internal objects as well as the external world, and an absence of anything that resembled spontaneity, love of life, or creativity. Marina's dry sense of humour was the closest she could get to a moment of spontaneous enjoyment of the self and its creativity—but typically this creative moment was self-denigrating.

Chapter 9

Beauty and the Beast: the Father-Daughter Relationship

The father, as the third party in the family drama, is inevitably regarded by the girl as the complementary opposite of both herself and her mother. The girl's sexual identity, then, will develop according to this perception—in other words, according to the way in which the girl positions herself as 'opposite' in relation to the man. The father's psychology—his unconscious and conscious feelings and phantasies—are therefore essential to the girl's sexual identity and sexual development, because these will determine the position she will adopt in relation to her father.

As we have seen, Freud's view was that the girl moves from mother to father in search of a penis in order to heal her 'castration' (Freud 1933). Even in classical Freudian terms, then, the father is the healer of a wound—the narcissistic wound caused by the recognition of sexual difference. However, this 'wound' has an even greater significance than that awarded to it by Freud: it also entails the experiences of birth, weaning, and infantile helplessness, as well as experiences of frustration and envy, once the mother is recognised as the possessor of all the riches in the world. The concentration upon the penis—in the case of both the boy and the girl—is therefore an entirely defensive manoeuvre, undertaken in order to escape the experience of powerlessness and helplessness which the relationship to mother inevitably involves.

Previously I have shown how the girl's relationship to an idealised but absent father leaves her stranded with an envious mother, from whom she can only escape by being rescued by the prince. However, even a relationship with an idealised and present father has its difficulties, as a consequence of the girl's idealisation and its corollary, persecution.

The idealisation of the father by the girl is one of the main characteristics of the father-daughter relationship. Freud explains this by describing how the girl's first relationship—

with mother—is full of frustration and conflict. Janine Chasseguet-Smirgel (1985) agrees with Freud that the girl's first object is frustrating, and that by turning away from it she is bound to idealise her second object. According to this model, a split occurs between these first and second objects—that is, between the mother and father, who represent (respectively) the bad object and the idealised object.

The wish for a penis—on the other hand—is a wish for a part-object that annihilates the relationship with *both* mother and father. For instance, Maria Torok (1964) regards the girl's wish for a penis as a way of revenging herself on her mother in the anal struggle between them; the penis stands for faeces, which are retained by the girl as an indication of her defiance. This penis does not help the girl separate from mother; instead, it locks her into a position of opposition and defiance.

The girl's phallic phase, in this case, must be clearly differentiated from her relationship to father. If the girl desires a penis either in order to use it as a weapon with which to fight her mother, or else in order to use it as a signifier of separateness from her mother, in both cases it functions as a *part-object* and, as such, is a repudiation of relationships to both the mother and the father. If, however, the girl desires her father (and his penis) then this is a full object relationship—which may be of either the 'narcissistic' or 'anaclitic' type.[29]

The narcissistic type of identificatory relationship with the father has been explored in detail by Jessica Benjamin (1990a). She regards the girl's identificatory love for her father as the road to autonomy.

> By shifting our focus from the Oedipal to the pre-Oedipal stage, we were able to explain the 'masculine' aspirations of girl toddlers—their tendency to identify with their fathers as well as with their mothers—as a legitimate avenue of psychic development. While masculinity no longer appears to be the original orientation of both children, it does remain associated with strivings toward difference—toward the outside world, toward separateness—which are just as important to the girl's sense of

agency as to the boy's. For girls as well as for boys, the homoerotic identification with the father informs the image of autonomy. (Benjamin 1990a: 122)

The identificatory love between father and daughter is, however, doomed. It is not simply that the girl realises that she is not like daddy but more like mummy—although this can be considered a factor. The main difficulty is that *the male matricidal psyche views with terror any sign of female power or autonomy*. This is indeed true both for men and women, but it is men who are more persecuted by the repressed and murdered early mother.

Father, given his dread of female power, will consequently find it difficult to allow his daughter the same autonomy, aggressiveness, and competitiveness as he allows his son. He will, instead, relate to her as to 'a sweet little girl', and thus does not—on the whole—strive to maintain an identificatory relationship with his daughter. In this sense, then, it is father's masculine defences which usher the girl into the Oedipus complex. Within the Oedipus complex itself the idealisation of the father is sustained, but the persecutory undercurrent of the idealisation is more obvious.

For Klein idealisation is both a corollary of persecution and a defence against it; where there is excessive idealisation there is also persecutory anxiety. In the Freudian model, persecutory anxiety is assumed to belong to the first object, the mother, whereas the relationship with father is described as a 'haven' or 'refuge'. I am arguing, however, that the father himself is also perceived—at some level—as a persecutor, and that the idealisation of the father by the daughter is simultaneously a defence against the father *as persecutor*. I would also like to suggest that the girl's fear of persecution by the father, which she carries within herself, is not purely a phantasy resulting from her Oedipal desire (as Freud would say), but also a more or less accurate perception of the father's unconscious. The father's unconscious masculine identity is, of course, related to his own struggle with the early mother, his Oedipal entanglement, and his 'matricidal' dissolution of his Oedipus complex.

Lemoine-Luccione remarked that 'men and women are the fantasy of each other' (Lemoine-Luccione 1976). My question here is what governs the interaction of fantasies between the daughter and the father? Because Freud—and psychoanalysis in general since Freud—concentrated mainly on the child's own phantasies about his or her parents, this question has not been asked. What is more, Freud assumed that repressed phantasies cannot be directly communicated at all. A single notable exception to this stance can be found in his paper 'The Unconscious', in which he writes: 'It is a very remarkable thing that the *Ucs.* of one human being can react upon that of another, without passing through the *Cs.*' (Freud 1915a: 194). Several decades passed after Freud's death before Robert Langs decided to concentrate on precisely this phenomenon—that is, how the unconscious of one person (the patient, in this case), can accurately perceive the unconscious of another, the therapist.

I would like to expand on the idea that the daughter accurately perceives the father's unconscious experiences, and also—therefore—his persecutory anxiety. In order to do so, we must first take a closer look at the Freudian version of the father.

Freud comes very close to postulating something which amounts to an 'archetypal father' when, in *Group Psychology and the Analysis of the Ego* (1921), he refers to a frequently reactivated father-imago which consists of the image of a 'paramount and dangerous personality, towards whom only a passive-masochistic attitude is possible, to whom one's will has to be surrendered' (Freud 1921: 127). Freud is elaborating here upon what he has termed the 'archaic heritage' of humanity, the self-confessed 'scientific myth' which he first described in his book *Totem and Taboo* (1913). He is, however, referring predominantly to the phantasies of the boy. Nevertheless, the assumption here is of a phantasy of a persecutory figure which is based—somehow—on real events, albeit far removed in prehistoric times. As I see it, this persecutory father-imago can be interpreted as a metaphor for Freudian unconscious, the id, or—more specifically—for the *masculine* unconscious. As must be apparent by now, I believe that Freud's description of the id is in fact a description of the masculine unconscious, which—I have argued—is characterised by the murder of the mother and subsequent persecution by her as a murdered undead object.

As Freud's description of the primal horde itself suggests, images of the masculine unconscious often form part of pornographic, sadomasochistic literature. In contrast, there are very few images of the masculine unconscious which focus upon the boy's early relationship to his mother, because of the sense of the persecution and sadism this is likely to evoke for the masculine psyche.

Fairy-tales, however, are linked more directly to the unconscious, and among them we encounter the most horrific of all accounts of unconscious masculinity—the story of Bluebeard, to which I have already referred in some detail. It is easy to concentrate solely on the horror of this story—the sealed-off part of Bluebeard's psyche in which he is condemned to repeat the early matricidal story, again and again, with his subsequent wives. However, alongside this there is also the despair and loneliness of Bluebeard, whose hopes of finding a woman who might lend him her absolute trust are dashed again and again. All his wives have failed him, but what if Bluebeard had a daughter: would she, as a less threatening woman, have repaired her father's monstrous psyche? Or would we have witnessed just another replay of the scene between Lear and Cordelia, once the daughter had begun to assert her autonomy?

Oedipus—of course—killed his father. But we tend to forget the Sphinx. Only after Oedipus had negotiated the obstacle of the Sphinx, by answering her riddle, was he able to enter Thebes as a hero and take Jocasta (his mother) as his bride. In other words, then, the murder of his father, Laius, did not by itself lead Oedipus to his mother; it was the solution of the riddle posed by the Sphinx which most directly led him to her.

By killing his father, then, Oedipus was exposed to persecution by the bad mother, in the shape of the Sphinx. Unlike the Furies, whose eyes drip blood and whose hair is made of snakes, this bad mother—in a truly rationalist manner—simply asks questions, and sets logical traps. Men who cannot answer her question must die. Her riddle concerns the naming of Man. She therefore possesses the secret of naming, and her power rests on this. She asks Oedipus to name the creature 'that walks on four legs and two legs and three legs' (Oxford Classical Dictionary 1970: 924). By providing the correct answer Oedipus defeats the Sphinx, who dies. It is Oedipus who has now become 'the one who can name things'.

The solution of the riddle of the Sphinx amounts to an appropriation of the mother's power, and thus establishes the matricidal psyche. Mother, as the power which holds sway over the riddle of existence, is deposed by the new, rationalist Oedipus. In a sense, Oedipus kills *both* his parents, since Jocasta—when she learns the unspeakable truth that she is both Oedipus' wife and his mother—hangs herself. Oedipus, meanwhile, in a moment of abysmal horror, blinds himself and allows himself to be led by his daughter, Antigone, who becomes his eyes and his guide. The blind Oedipus wanders through the wilderness with Antigone, until he arrives at the holy ground of the Eumenides at Colonus near Athens. 'What is this ground? What god is worshipped here', Oedipus asks. 'It's untouchable, forbidden—no one lives here', answers an Athenian citizen. 'The Terrible Goddesses hold it for themselves, the Daughters of Earth, Daughters of the Darkness... The Ones who watch the world, the Kindly Ones' (Sophocles 1982: 285-6). These are the Furies— the same Earth goddesses who persecuted Orestes after the murder of his mother. 'Let them receive their suppliant with kindness!' responds Oedipus. 'I shall never leave my place in this new land, this is my refuge!' (Sophocles 1982: 286).

The 'untouchable, forbidden' ground brings to mind the mother's body. Oedipus who killed his father, overcame the Sphinx, and then succumbed to incest takes refuge on this 'untouchable' ground, guided by his daughter, in a kind of symbolic return to the place of origins—to the 'Daughters of the Earth'.

The crime against the mother in the myth of Oedipus is not explored by Freud, who concentrated instead on the desire for the mother. Even so, this crime underlies the whole tragedy. We should not forget that Oedipus' power stems from the fact he solved the riddle of the Sphinx, which led to her destruction. The murder of the father is therefore compounded by the murder of this early, omnipotent, bad mother. The crime of Oedipus is thus a double crime, the destruction of *both* parents. A child abused and abandoned by his own parents in infancy, he in turn destroys them and then destroys himself. The last words of *Oedipus Rex* are spoken by the Chorus:

People of Thebes, my countrymen, look on Oedipus.
He solved the famous riddle with his brilliance,
he rose to power, a man beyond all power.
Who could behold his greatness without envy?
Now what a black sea of terror has overwhelmed him.
Now as we keep our watch and wait the final day,
count no man happy till he dies, free of a pain at last.
(Sophocles 1982: 251)

The father-daughter relationship, in the case of Oedipus and Antigone, involves a form of mediation: the daughter mediates and facilitates a symbolic return of the father to the place of the mother (the 'untouchable, forbidden' ground). Oedipus seeks refuge and, in the end, finds redemption.

In contrast to the masculine world of war, political intrigue, and revenge—as represented by Oedipus' sons—and to the female world of entrapment and deathly desire (the Sphinx, Jocasta), the place occupied by the daughter represents, for Oedipus, a refuge. Blind, disgraced and impoverished, cast out by the whole world, Oedipus has only his daughter to care for him. Her love and unlimited devotion humanises him.

The transformation of the monster into a human being, through a woman's love and devotion, is yet another recurrent theme in fairy-tales. This transformation refers to the split in masculine identity between the idealised father and the beastly, monstrous part of the father. Underlying both is the wounded human being, which the daughter recognises. Although the daughter might collude with the father by idealising him, nevertheless she 'knows' that beneath his glory there is the phantasy of a monster and the reality of a wound.

The split in man, and the ways in which it is perceived, maintained, and healed by the daughter, are beautifully portrayed in the fairy-tale *Beauty and the Beast* (Perrault 1970). In this story, a rich merchant has three daughters. The youngest is Beauty, whom he loves the most. When the merchant sets off on a trip he asks his daughters what they would like him to bring home for them. The elder daughters ask for beautiful clothes, but Beauty asks for a red rose. On his way back the merchant loses his way in a dark wood but finally, exhausted and hungry, he arrives at a mysterious castle. He finds a table laid for him and dines alone, and then he finds a bed ready for him, lies down, and goes to sleep. The next day, his strength restored, he sets out for home. About to leave the grounds of this mysterious place, he suddenly remembers Beauty's request and cuts a red rose from a tree. At that very moment the Beast appears, and announces to the merchant that he has cut the Beast's favourite rose, abused his hospitality, and must therefore die. The merchant pleads with him and is finally allowed to go home, but under condition that he sends his daughter to stay with the Beast, otherwise the death sentence must be carried out. The merchant accepts and goes home, having decided not to keep his promise. But when Beauty hears about the incident she insists on going to stay with the Beast, in order to save her father's life.

Beauty stays at the castle for a long time as the Beast's guest. He dines with her every evening, is courteous and kind to her, but every evening he repeats his request to marry her. Beauty always refuses, feeling disgusted by the Beast, and the situation remains unchanged for many years until one day Beauty's father falls ill and Beauty receives permission from the Beast to visit him.

Beauty stays with her father for longer than she had promised, and the Beast sends her a message that unless she goes back to him he will soon die of a broken heart. Driven by pity, and apparently by some kind of love for him, Beauty returns to the Beast and accepts his proposal of marriage—at which point, of course, the Beast turns into a handsome prince.

The story portrays vividly the splitting of the father into an idealised figure and a Beast. Beauty, in order to keep her idealised father in existence, is compelled to split him off, otherwise he may become confused with the Beast. I must stress here that I do not consider the Beast simply a phantasy in Beauty's mind—as Bettelheim (1978) suggests—but instead *a real split within the father*. This is revealed by the fact that it is the father who first brings the Beast into being. It is the father who loses himself in the dark wood, and who descends into the dark side of himself to find the mysterious castle where the Beast resides. To the father, the Beast can be helpful, nurturing, energising, and restorative. However, once the father is confronted with his daughter's desire, and his wish to comply with it, then the Beast becomes threatening and devouring. In this same moment primitive masculinity takes hold of the father, and the split in his psyche is now revealed to Beauty. Now she can either be with the Beast, or with father, but not with both of them at the same time. While she lives with the Beast she can only go on worshipping the father's idealised image from a distance.

It is also important to realise that the healing of the split comes about by a lessening of both idealisation and persecution—that is, in the story, by the father falling ill, and the Beast in danger of dying of a broken heart. The moment Beauty realises the vulnerability of both of them, she perceives their humanity. Consequently, the extremes of idealisation and persecution collapse. By recognising the vulnerability of the Beast, Beauty is now ready to love a man. And the Beast can become a man only through renouncing his own beast-like powers and receiving Beauty's love.

The split is healed by a similar process in the case of Oedipus and Antigone. Her love is centred solely upon the wounded father. More mature and less narcissistic than Beauty, Antigone humanises Oedipus during his long journey in the darkness towards the place of the Goddesses of the Earth. Finally Oedipus is accepted back into human society by Theseus, The Athenian king, and given a place of honour. The beast is humanised through the mediation of a woman who is devoted to the father, yet who lacks all the power of the early mother. This is perhaps the most crucial component of the father-daughter relationship.

As I have remarked, the humanisation of the beast by a woman's love is a common theme in fairy-tales and myths. Bettelheim interprets this as the overcoming of infantile feelings of revulsion towards sex. Following Freud, he explains these feelings of revulsion as part of the incest taboo. These feelings dissolve with the movement away from the parents and towards a lover (Bettelheim 1978: 308). Although I do not disagree with this view, nevertheless I believe there is much more to these stories. They also refer to the phantasy—common to males and females—of the beast which resides within man. The phantasies of matricide and incest, which underlie the phantasy of parricide, are projected by woman onto man and worked-through in her relationship with him. This is nowhere more apparent than in the father-daughter relationship. Here, more than in any other relationship, aggression is kept at bay as father and daughter use one another to achieve acceptance of the contra-sexual, and a reconciliation with the matricidal beast (as well as the parricidal).

However, there are also pitfalls to the relationship. For instance, a girl's relationship to a wounded father can turn her into an eternal nurse and carer. If the relationship to father is nothing else but 'taking care' of him, then nothing is worked-through, and this repeated manic reparation can continue for life.

Similarly, excessive projection of the beast onto man renders woman a helpless victim. This victimhood is portrayed in Milan Kundera's *The Unbearable Lightness of Being* (1985), through the character of Tereza. In the novel Tomas—a brain surgeon and eternal womaniser—meets Tereza, an infinitely faithful, docile and submissive woman, and falls in love with her. This union of opposites, in which each acts as a mirror for the repressed self of the other, leads only to fraught unhappiness and unsatisfied love. Although the novel is much more complicated than this short account suggests, I shall concentrate here only upon the way in which Tereza projects the image of a sadist onto Tomas. In a dream Tereza sees herself naked in a swimming pool, together with other naked women. They are expected to walk around the swimming pool and sing and perform for Tomas, who is sitting comfortably, enjoying the spectacle. If one of the women should stop singing she is immediately shot dead, and her body falls into the swimming pool which is full of blood and corpses. Tereza feels exhausted and humiliated, and wants to stop performing, but she is terrified and must go on, despite realising that at some point she will collapse from sheer exhaustion.

So, the terrifying image of a male tyrant, as portrayed in Bluebeard, in Tereza's dream, and in Freud's *Totem and Taboo*, is part of the phantasies about masculinity harboured by both men and women. It is, in other words, part of the masculine unconscious for both sexes. This masculine unconscious is acted out in the stories of Oedipus and Orestes, but is (ideally) worked-through in the father-daughter relationship. Oedipus does find redemption in the end, although this is only in relation to a single woman, not to men in general. Oedipus does not forgive his sons.[30] Oedipus the son, having become Oedipus the father, now hates his son:

OEDIPUS: My son, king—that son I hate! His words alone
would cause me the greatest pain of any words,
any man alive.

THESEUS: But why ? Can't you listen?
He cannot make you act against your will.
Why should it hurt you just to hear him out?

OEDIPUS: Just that voice, my king,
the sound is loathsome to his father.
Don't drive me, don't force me to yield in this! (Sophocles
1982: 355)

And to his son , Polynices:

You—die.
Die and be damned!
I spit on you! Out!—

your father cuts you off ! Corruption—scum of the
   earth!—
out!—and pack these curses I call down upon your head:
never to win your mother-country with your spear, never
   return to Argos ringed with hills—
Die! (Sophocles 1982: 365)

If Oedipus cannot forgive his son, then we might feel sure he
cannot forgive his own father either. The father-son relationship
becomes the locus for the acting-out of hatred and aggression.
John Steiner (1993) interprets Oedipus' lack of forgiveness and
spite towards his son as a consequence of his growing delusion
that he himself is innocent, and that he has been only a pawn in
the hands of the gods. For Steiner this retreat from truth—the
truth that Oedipus himself is responsible for his actions—is a
retreat into omnipotence. Personally, however, I am unable to
see Oedipus' condemnation of his sons in this same light.

This father-son constellation within the psyche represents, I
think, an 'all masculine exclusion of mother', which is the prototypical denial of truth. In this respect I disagree with Steiner
that Oedipus cursing his son represents a retreat from the truth.
Oedipus could have returned to Thebes, with Creon, to be reinstated; or he could have allied himself with Polynices, against
his brother. Ultimately he vehemently refuses to do either, and
curses them both. In effect, then, Oedipus condemns the whole
masculine, phallic world of feuds, wars and corruption. To me,
Oedipus blinding himself is a symbolic castration—that is, a
refusal to be part of a phallic world any longer. There is indeed
an element of denial in this, but it is the denial of the specific fact
that Oedipus is part of this phallic world, whether he likes it or
not. Indeed, the murder of his father demonstrates exactly this,
as Freud was the first to show.

Oedipus' relationship with Antigone, however, is something
entirely different. It helps him reach a part of himself which is
untouched by father-son feuding, and which relates to attempts
to repair the internal mother. The feud between father and son,
in contrast, merely denies the damage which has been done to
mother. In his relationship with the daughter, the father reaches

another dimension of himself which has been banned from consciousness. However, he can attain this only if he is blinded—only if, in other words, he can renounce the phallic world of illusory 'clear-sightedness', and seek 'in-sight' instead. Not many fathers are willing to do this, because they are plagued by masculine fears of castration and femininity. Instead they accept the projection onto themselves of the beast, and regard themselves as guardians of masculinity. The projection of the beast onto man is, however, merely a convenient refutation of masculine dependence on mother.

The phantasy of the beast is accepted by both men and women. It can prove a highly persecutory delusion, and—unless it is worked-through in the father-daughter relationship—can force the girl into the role of victim (as in the case of Kundera's character, Tereza). It is in situations where the father is absent, or remote—or, of course, cruel or abusive—that working-through cannot take place. The experience of men as persecutory monsters is then the projection onto them of the girl's own matricidal psyche. Only a real relation to a real father, which is solid and affectionate, will help both daughter and father attain some kind of reparation.

But we have seen, instead of a working-through of matricide, sometimes something else occurs within the father-daughter relationship. The father's dread of femininity may lead him to relate to his daughter in a way which might encourage her submission, or collusion, in order to keep mother—and woman in general—under control. This is what we encounter in the case of Antigone, as she leads her powerless and blind father through foreign, unknown lands. For all his blindness and disgrace, Oedipus still behaves like a king, and Antigone does not challenge his determination to cling to authority. However, during the long years of wandering with blind Oedipus, evidently she has learnt much about the vulnerability and fallibility of kings and tyrants, for it is she—alone amongst the citizens of Thebes—who challenges Creon, by flaunting the tyrant's phallic decrees, and pays with her life for her adherence to the moral law.[31]

In *The Odyssey*, Homer paints in vivid colours and unforget-table images more scenes from the endless struggle of man against woman and her engulfing presence. From the moment Odysseus escapes from the Cyclops—that formidable part-object—he encounters woman in all her fantasised power. In Antiphates' wife he encounters a literally cannabalistic woman (Homer 1946: 158). In Circe, meanwhile, he encounters the anal mother who enjoys trapping and humiliating men. In the Sirens, and in the Scylla and Charybdis too, he faces yet more formida-ble and engulfing feminine forces, while Calypso, a more benev-olent and gentle goddess, is nevertheless still dangerous because she seeks to keep Odysseus on her island forever, and to prevent him from reaching Ithaca and regaining his kingdom. It is remarkable how *all* the forces of regression encountered by Odysseus during his travels are represented by women or female forces, which he must overcome or outwit in order to reach Ithaca and fulfil his masculine destiny.

As I see it, *The Odyssey* portrays the struggle of man to estab-lish his masculinity in a continuous battle against femininity, yet at the same time it illustrates the humanisation of masculinity through woman. One should not forget that *The Odyssey* follows the events depicted in *The Iliad*, a poetic portrayal of one of the most savage wars of antiquity in which primitive masculinity runs rampant. It is also significant that Odysseus begins his story with the capture of the city of the Cicones—a recapitula-tion, in miniature, of the more savage capture and destruction of Troy:

> 'I sacked the place' Odysseus tells with pride, 'and
> destroyed the men who held it. The wives and the rich
> plunder that we took from the town we divided so that
> no one, as far as I could help it, should go short of his
> share.' (Homer 1946: 140)

Odysseus' self-evident pride in destroying a city, and treat-ing the women in it as material goods, are the basic characteris-tics of primitive masculinity. In Homer's heroic era these were still part of a conscious masculine identity, and exhibited with pride. This primitive masculinity inevitably makes an impact on the father-daughter relationship. However, the extent of the father's wish to dominate and objectify his daughter will depend on how far he has succeeded in working-through his fear of femininity, the nature of his identifications with his father and mother, and the extent to which he feels secure in his masculine identity. For her part, the girl experiences her father as 'opposite' to herself, and therefore the way she perceives her father will also shape her perception of herself as a woman. We must not forget how much the daughter wants to be loved by her father. This is, perhaps, her strongest desire.

Women with fathers who are insecure in their masculinity, and whose struggle with mother continues unabated into their adulthood, are deprived of the chance to work-through their relationship to mother, the idealised father, and their phantasies of masculinity as 'the beast'. Any of these phantasies can become harmfully entrenched if the father is either abusing or over-remote.

The girl may even identify with the father. This identification, however, will not release the girl from her unconscious equation of femininity with submission, based on her perception of primitive unconscious masculinity and her fear of her mother's power. On the contrary, the daughter's identification with father is often a defence against this unconscious equation—it is as if the girl is saying: 'If that's what femininity is, then I don't want to be feminine'. However, things can become much more complex if the identification is with a father who is not experienced as masculine. The case of Marie (which I have previously referred to in chapters 7 and 8) illustrates this state of affairs.

Marie's father was a passive, quiet man, manipulated by his controlling and very insecure wife, and by his brother who lived next door. The brother was brutal and aggressive, and terrorised Marie as a child whilst humiliating her father repeatedly. Marie's father invariably gave in to him, which she perceived as a terrible defeat. For Marie, the uncle represented masculinity; that was 'how men were'. Her father, meanwhile, belonged to some kind of intermediate category, a kind of confusing 'no man's land'.

I began to sense that Marie's confusion actually went much deeper than this, and that—in fact—it was her father's confusion which Marie was expressing. The father, like Marie, seemed to be saying: 'Masculinity is violent and inexpressible'. It was as if he was afraid of his own repressed, phallic masculinity, and had taken flight into a passive, conciliatory attitude. Marie thus identified with a non-masculine father, which led to a curious mixture of independence and extreme vulnerability. For instance, Marie had lived alone in extremely remote places, but felt uncertain, unwanted, and doubtful of her own femininity when faced with any kind of relationship. When confronted by men, she wanted to hide, believing that they would find her unattractive and unfeminine.

The bind in which she found herself could be summarised as follows: to be attractive she must be feminine, but to be feminine meant to be vulnerable, weak, and prone to assault and rape. Marie had split men into two categories: the few men with whom she was friendly were gentle and understanding; the rest of them she perceived as aggressive, macho, and seeking to devalue women. The split between the father and the uncle (who represented phallic masculinity and also manifested her father's unconscious) is more obvious, but there is also the split in herself between a compliant femininity, based on her perception of the masculine unconscious, and her identification with her father.

As I see it, the intermediate place inhabited by both Marie and her father is expressive of a fear of both femininity and masculinity. Marie regarded both as depriving her of her individuality. All intimate relationships were therefore perceived as devouring and, instead, identification replaced relationship.[32]

Fathers with an intense fear of their mother's power to devour will encourage a tendency towards identification—rather than towards the formation of relationships—in their daughters. Marie's fear of violent men had as much to do with her father's unconscious phantasy of a beast within himself as it did with her uncle's manifest aggression. Her confusion found expression in the phantasy of a monstrous formation inside herself, which was invisible to the outside but which any intimate relationship would reveal. We see here the superimposition of the relationship with father onto the earlier relationship with mother.

Her fear and her longing for an intimate relationship with a man found expression when she fell in love with a homosexual man. Through this compromise Marie was able to love a man who, like her father, inhabited an 'intermediate' area, through the way he had apparently renounced his interest in women. She believed that homosexual men were disgusted by women's bodies. This built a very powerful defence in her mind against her fears of assault and rape.

What emerges here, then, is that if there is no genuine working-through of anxieties in primary relations, and thus if no sense of self has been securely established, there will be an attempt to fill in the gap with a kind of masquerade of masculinity and femininity. This is what phallic defences amount to, in the cases of both boys and girls. The attempt to attribute gender identity solely to an organ, an attitude, a type of dress, profession, or possession, reveals the way in which the phallic defence is a denial of reality. The relationship with father is extremely important when it comes to working-through this repudiation of sexual difference.

Chapter 10

Aggression and Femininity

There is a great deal of writing on the mother-daughter relationship, and the profound influence it has upon the internal world of women and upon women's gender identity.[33] Many authors attribute feminine character traits—such as relatedness, interest in people rather than things, loose boundaries, the tendency to defer to others, and lack of self-assertion—to this first relationship. Over-identification, unduly prolonged symbiosis, and lack of separation from mother have all been cited—within a patriarchal culture—as causes of these feminine traits.

More than one commentator has also remarked on the way 'little girls do not play'. Instead, they seem simply to *prepare* for their role as future mothers; their play with dolls is 'object related', as opposed to 'making use of the object', in the manner described by Winnicott (1971: 101-11). Winnicott has suggested that the external world can only be established through the *use* of the object—that is, through the attempt of the subject to destroy the object, and the object's survival of this attack. In effect, this places the object outside the subject's omnipotence, and thus plays an important part in the movement towards the reality-principle. The girl playing at being mother to her dolls may present a somewhat stereotypical image, but—like all stereotypes—it nevertheless contains a lot of truth, whose full significance only becomes apparent later when the division between the 'relational female' and the 'scientific' or 'entrepreneurial' male emerges as a clear division between the sexes.

Here, then, I propose to concentrate instead on the way women seem to find it difficult to 'use objects' and to play. I will concentrate in particular on the dynamics which govern the early mother-daughter relationship, and the way that these affect mother's ability 'to carry the baby over from relating to usage' (Winnicott: 1971: 104).[34]

The early interaction between mother and baby is inevitably dominated by unconscious processes. As I see it, the baby's reading of mother's unconscious follows those lines indicated by Robert Langs in his detailed exploration of the unconscious communications between patient and therapist. Langs maintains that the patient can accurately read and is deeply influenced by the therapist's unconscious (Langs 1988). The concept of 'projective identification', especially as it is used by Bion in his theory of the container and maternal reverie (Bion 1962), serves a similar function in explaining unconscious communication between patient and therapist. In this context, however, projective identification usually refers to the therapist's reading of the patient's unconscious in a direct, non-verbal sense. Similarly, it is usually taken for granted that it is the *baby's* unconscious communication which is received by the mother; her own projective identification is not usually taken into consideration. It is precisely this, however, which I propose to examine here: the mother's mind and the mother's unconscious will form the focus of this chapter.

* * *

In a consulting room within which both the therapist and patient are women, the difficulty patients experience with using objects often manifests itself as a symbiotic, or early narcissistic relationship with the therapist. The early mothering situation is readily re-established, and a variety of different terms have been used to describe what amounts to the same consequent phenomenon: 'the monad', 'the cocoon', 'the environment mother', 'the symbiotic bond', and so on. This situation is sometimes maintained with dogged resistance to any kind of change.

'To use an object', Winnicott writes, 'the subject must have developed a *capacity* to use objects. This is part of the change to the reality principle' (Winnicott 1971: 105). The opposition here, then, is not between 'primary narcissism' and 'object relations', but rather between primary object-*relatedness* and the ability to *use* the object. This is an interesting juxtaposition, which completely bypasses the debate on whether object relations exist from the beginning. Instead, Winnicott suggests:

In object-relating the subject allows certain alterations in
the self to take place, of a kind that has caused us to invent
the term cathexis. The object has become meaningful.
Projection mechanisms and identifications have been
operating and the subject is depleted to the extent that
something of the subject is found in the object, though
enriched by feeling... When I speak of the use of an object,
however, I take object-relating for granted, and add new
features that involve the nature and behaviour of the
object. For instance, the object, if it is to be used, must necessarily be real in the sense of being part of shared reality,
not a bundle of projections. It is this, I think, that makes
for the world of difference that there is between relating
and usage. (Winnicott 1971: 103)

The contrast here is between object-relating which is always
governed by projection and introjection, and object-usage which
relates to an object *outside* the subject's omnipotence. Therefore
the baby emerges from narcissism not through object-relating
(which is always governed by various degrees of omnipotence)
but instead through object-usage.[35]

The use of the object therefore implies the employment of
aggression, in the service of development. This in turn entails not
only the capacity of the object to survive the subject's aggression, but also an adequate phase of omnipotence and a non-
traumatic disillusionment. Winnicott described the early relation of the baby to mother as characterised by illusion: the illusion that the baby has created the breast, and that the breast
belongs to baby. The good-enough mother *allows* this illusion,
by adapting almost perfectly to her baby's needs. This stage is
important, because it allows development of what Winnicott
terms the baby's 'spontaneous gesture' and its 'True Self'.
However, unless psychosis and denial of reality should pre-
dominate, the stage of illusion comes to an end. For optimal
development it is important that the mother *disillusions* the baby
gradually and in a non-traumatic fashion. If this is not accomplished gradually then guilt, persecution, and the creation of a
False Self will ensue, as reality floods into a baby not yet

equipped to deal with it. Providing disillusionment proceeds smoothly, the baby proceeds to create or discover (crucially, he is not sure which) the *transitional object*. This is an object which is a possession, a creation, but also a discovery—and which therefore lies outside the baby's omnipotence. Object-usage in itself is 'ruthless', prior to the infant's development of the capacity to feel concern for the object. However, in order for concern to develop (as opposed to guilt) the subject must first proceed through this experience of a thoroughly ruthless use of the object, and the consequent making of reparation to the it. For this to happen, then, it can be appreciated how the continued survival of the object is absolutely essential (Winnicott 1965: 77). It can also be seen how the response of the mother to the child's aggression and his or her use of the object is also crucial. If mother is fearful, forbidding, or somehow appears to the child to have been destroyed, then a sense of guilt and persecution will take the place of the capacity for concern, and an overly compliant child—with a 'False Self'—will develop instead.

* * *

I have argued that, in her relationship with her father, the girl responds to the father's dread of feminine power by repressing her own aggression and by constructing a non-threatening femininity. In this case, a woman's unconscious is created as a response to father's unconscious dread of the mother and of powerful femininity. This primary dread of femininity arises from the boy's first identification with and envy of the mother and her capacity to give birth, and his subsequent over-valuation of the penis as a means of denying both identification and envy in order to construct a masculine persona. The dread of powerful femininity remains in the male unconscious and is synonymous with the threat of castration—which is usually disguised, in a face-saving exercise, as a threat from the father. I have also argued that the dissolution of the Oedipus complex for the boy results in matricide, in the sense that the first relation to mother—both object-relational and identificatory—is repressed, denied or evacuated, depending on the quality of the object-relations involved.

If the feminine unconscious is indeed formed from the relationship with father's unconscious, then it too will contain an image of an all-powerful, devouring and revengeful mother, as well as a 'castrated' mother who is pliable, non-aggressive and passive. An illustration of this is the image of the virgin mother and virgin birth, encountered in Christianity. This is, in effect, the transformation of powerful female narcissism, which denies the need for a male in order to produce children (the 'virgin birth') into a devout, obedient woman at the behest a powerful male God (the 'virgin mother'). This transformation occurs afresh in the mind of both girls and boys, on the dissolution of the Oedipus complex. It is not a genuine transformation, however, for it bears all the hallmarks of disavowal and delusion. It is as if the child were saying: 'This is *not* the powerful, bad, murdered mother. This is a weak mother who is totally under the control of an omnipotent, just and benevolent father.' In this way the whole drama of the Oedipus complex is denied, and the notion of the parental *couple* erased from the map. The terror of the murdered mother is also denied or split off.

The father's fear therefore joins forces with the girl's own hatred of the frustrating mother, and her wish to curb her mother's power and to create distance between them. The girl's love for her father, and her wish to be loved by him, are therefore the main motives behind her willingness to collude with his wish for a non-threatening, non-aggressive femininity. Her wish to love him and serve him unconditionally echoes his own wish to be loved and served unconditionally by an infinitely pliable mother. In this sense, then, the daughter becomes the castrated, non-threatening mother of the father.

Although the repression of aggression in the girl comes about as a consequence of her relationship with her father, its roots nevertheless lie in her relationship to her mother. However, the version of the mother I have in mind here is one *whose own unconscious has been formed through her relationship with her own father*. Winnicott ignored this dimension of the mother, whilst feminist writers—at least in Britain and USA—have concentrated instead on the mother-daughter relationship, tracing back an entirely female genealogy to mother's mother and mother's grandmother, and so on. By introducing the dimension of the mother's unconscious, however, we are forced to acknowledge the influence also of the father, the parental couple, the super-ego, and the culture.

In other words, the mother's mind is *gendered*, and has already recognised father's vulnerability to female power as well as his idealised image and power within the culture. The mother's mind contains irreconcilable imagos of her own power and narcissistic omnipotence—as symbolised by pregnancy, and identification with the pre-Oedipal mother—as well as her own powerlessness, and her narcissistic wound, as expressed in the notion that she 'lacks' the phallus.

The mother's unconscious contains, therefore, both male and female omnipotence, and male and female narcissistic wounds. What I wish to stress, however, is that due to its inevitably gendered structure, the mother's unconscious also embodies an intense dread of powerful femininity. This *must* be stressed, because, in my view, it is precisely this dread of femininity which constitutes the entrance into our culture.

Ideally, the mother's unconscious also contains a parental couple, joined together in loving intercourse. However, this cannot be taken for granted, because this does not constitute most people's experience of the relationship between their parents, and neither is this image an established part of Western culture. Instead, the image of the father as 'possessor' of the mother has prevailed. Western culture conspicuously lacks a symbolic parental couple in its founding myths. For instance, both the creation of Adam and Eve, and the notion of the virgin birth, exalt the Divine Father as omnipotent, and deny a divine parental *couple*. The omnipotent creation depicted in the monotheistic religions not only establishes a principle above nature—that is, 'spirit' or 'Logos'—but clearly defines this principle as all-powerful and male—God the Father. The mother is excluded from the Trinity, the most powerful Christian symbol, and the 'couple'—according to Christian mythology—is instead the Father and the Son.

What is clear, however, is that the idea of the father as 'possessor' of the mother serves to deny man's narcissistic wound. Possessions—as Freud pointed out—are a form of narcissistic confirmation: 'Everything that a person possesses or achieves, every remnant of the primitive feeling of omnipotence which his experience has confirmed, helps to increase his self-regard... [which] has a specially intimate dependence on narcissistic libido' (Freud 1914: 98). In this sense the 'possession' of woman restores man's omnipotence by denying both the loss and the lack—the loss of the breast, and his lack of a womb and the ability to give birth.[36] The narcissistic wound is, therefore, situated at a more fundamental level for the boy than for the girl, and is denied in two ways: firstly through the elevation of the penis into a phallus; and secondly by the 'possession' of woman. The dual meaning of the phallus itself reflects this: on the one hand it is a narcissistic symbol of omnipotence, but on the other an instrument with which to reach out to woman or the mother. In its second aspect, the phallus is not merely a symbol of the boy's narcissism, but also of his acceptance of his lack, a more mature acceptance of the incompleteness of *all* human beings. This second meaning of the phallus remains unrealisable, however, as long as woman is a 'possession', whether in reality or in the unconscious. For the penis to be fully realised as a vehicle for reaching the other, then the otherness of woman from man— that is, *sexual difference*—must first be established and accepted.[37]

Woman, then, has responded to man's fears of castration (or of powerful femininity) and has accepted a castrated version of femininity in order to alleviate his dread. However, a 'castrated woman' is not a woman, as such. This becomes evident after considering Freud's model of female sexual development, which suggests—in essence—that the little girl is, in fact, a little boy (Freud 1933: 118). The girl is 'castrated' only if she is considered in this light—that is, as a 'boy'. The absence of the notion of the vagina in childhood (if one agrees with Freud that this notion is indeed not available), guarantees the subsequent 'non-existence' of a female subject. This pseudo-complementarity of 'intact male' and 'castrated female' is not therefore a complementarity at all, but a collusion and a defence which seeks to establish a certain power relation between the parental couple, rather than a recognition of the sexual difference between them. Within this state of affairs the only possible parental couple is one in which the woman is regarded as a commodity. Because anxiety about the existence of the vagina remains unworked-through, the woman with a vagina can only be dealt with by making her an item.

The view of woman as a possession denies any aggression on her part. All aggression is projected instead onto man. She is masochistic and persecuted. She is a victim: someone who denies her own power and aggression. In a complementary fashion, man—as the possessor—denies his vulnerability and his relatedness to others, and assumes instead the position of the aggressor. If this description of men and women looks more like a caricature than a portrait, this is because it is based on traditional rather than contemporary notions of femininity and masculinity. My argument, however, is that these cultural and traditional images persist in the unconscious, where they form powerful internal objects which clash with the values consciously held by both men and women. One need only remind oneself of the furious and often undignified arguments which surround the issue of the ordination of women—for instance—in order to realise the power which these imagos still possess both within the culture and within the unconscious. Similarly, one need only glance at children's cartoons and films to realise that the male aggressive hero is alive and well, and that masculinity is equated in the unconscious with aggressive heroism—the slaying of the monster.

Woman, as the mother, is invested with colossal power by the baby but not by the father. This contradiction is the basis of patriarchal culture. The baby situates omnipotence firstly in itself, then the mother, then father, before passing it onto the Law as represented by the Father. This might indeed constitute a cultural advance from primitive anarchic masculinity, but it does nothing to establish a parental couple in the unconscious. The establishment of a parental couple in the unconscious would mean the acceptance of difference between mother and father, and the working-through of both womb-envy and penis-envy.

* * *

As we have seen, Winnicott regarded aggression as essential to the creation of the sense of an external world:

> The assumption is always there, in orthodox theory that aggression is reactive to the encounter of the reality principle whereas here it is the destructive drive that creates the quality of externality. This is central to the structure of my argument. (Winnicott 1971: 110)

For Freud, part of the girl's development is the renunciation of a great deal of activity, and the acquisition of passive aims (Freud 1933: 115-6).[38] It would thus seem unlikely, then, that a mother who has denied or repressed her own aggression, in the process of assuaging her father's castration anxiety and becoming a woman, could allow her baby girl to express anything similar.

Those feminist writers who have noted that mother can relate to the boy as 'other' from the beginning, but that she relates to the girl exclusively as a part of herself, have therefore implied that only the father can break up the symbiotic relationship between mother and daughter. Winnicott, on the other hand, is suggesting something quite different. He stresses the role of aggression in the separation of baby from mother, which occurs without guilt, provided the object—that is, the mother—manifests the ability to survive the baby's aggression. This position is also markedly different from that of Klein, who regarded development as a procession from persecutory anxiety to depressive guilt and anxiety. The baby's capacity for guilt acts as the crucial point of change, and appears alongside increasing ego integration (Klein 1948: 35, 1952: 72).

Winnicott, unlike Klein, did not admit the existence of a death instinct, but regarded an active and aggressive baby as the healthy precursor of a secure, non-compliant self. Guiltless aggression—as Winnicott saw it—necessarily preceded the baby's sense of responsibility. However, for guiltless aggression towards the object to be possible, the object itself must survive the baby's attacks. As Winnicott saw it, the destruction of the object is in fact best understood as the consequence of the object's non-survival:

> ... although destruction is the word I am using, this actual destruction belongs to the object's failure to survive. Without this failure, destruction remains potential. The word 'destruction' is needed, not because of the baby's impulse to destroy, but because of the object's liability not to survive, which also means to suffer change in quality, in attitude. (Winnicott 1971: 109)

In other words, a mother who reacts to the baby's attack with angry, distressed, forbidding or depressed feelings, has not survived the baby's aggression. She is a different mother. The good-enough mother is gone, and this new mother—who is unable to tolerate the baby's aggression—appears instead as persecutory, or else inflicts a premature sense of guilt upon the baby. This type of pathological guilt is, in fact, quite common among women, and acts as a break on aggressive feelings and on object-usage, and often leads to depression. Depending on the mother's response to the baby, then, the baby's use of non-destructive aggression in the creation of both self and object can be blocked.

One female patient, for instance, suffered from depression and was convinced that she could not drive a car because 'she was not meant to'. Another was convinced that if she did learn to drive she would be a public menace, and would kill someone by accident. I have found fears about driving quite common in women patients, hand in hand with their fear of their own aggression and an exaggerated view of male aggression. In other words, the fear of their own aggression in these women was closely connected with their fear of becoming a victim or an object of attack. As Winnicott puts it:

...the babies that have been through this phase well are likely to be more aggressive *clinically* than the ones who have not been seen through this phase well, and for whom aggression is something that cannot be encompassed, or something that can be retained only in the form of liability to be an object of aggression. (Winnicott 1971: 109)

The repressed, denied, and then projected female aggression of these patients, which—in spite of developments in the social world—is coupled with the perception that the external world belongs to men, points to an early disturbance in object-usage. As we have seen, for Winnicott it is the mother who performs a crucial role in the baby's capacity for object-usage: 'Mothers, like analysts, can be good or not good enough; some can and some cannot carry the baby over from relating to usage' (Winnicott 1971: 104).[39]

For the initiation of object-usage two circumstances need to be in place: the capacity of the subject to destroy the object; and the capacity of the object to survive. If either of these two conditions is missing the use of the object cannot develop to any great degree. Winnicott avers that the first is dependent on the second.

What is clear from experiences in the consulting-room is the difficulty women experience in *using* their therapist. As I have mentioned, a kind of symbiotic relationship is readily established when both therapist and patient are women. In this relationship neither ruthless love nor object-usage are present, but instead an 'environment mother' is established, wherein no aggression is experienced. This situation might be described as akin to a benign drug addiction, in which painlessness, obliviousness, and endless feeding are the main features. Unless we become aware of this, and of the patient's inability to use us, we can create a situation of collusion which might last for years.

It is not that these patients never experience aggression or conflict, but that they experience it outside the analytic situation, and any attempt to interpret it as part of the transference leads nowhere. This is a peculiarly female transference situation. Not all women establish this type of transference, but I have encountered it frequently enough to warrant its description in these terms, and have experienced it only once with a male patient. This patient, who was homosexual, ended therapy suddenly, as a consequence of his increasing awareness of his anger and guilt towards his father, who had died three months previously. The passivity of this homosexual man bore all the signs of a feminine identification, and of a rejection of an aggressive masculine identity which, however, persisted in the unconscious.

* * *

In this chapter, I have attempted to expose the roots of the difficulties women experience in the area of object-usage. As I see it, these originate in the mother-daughter relationship which, more than any other, is governed by the baby's response to the mother's unconscious. I have, therefore, also attempted to provide an account of the feminine unconscious, and its origins in the father-daughter relationship. By concentrating primarily on gender issues I have deliberately left to one side other factors, such as the mother's psychopathology, ego-strength, and her ability to act as a container for the baby. To me it seems that difficulties with object-usage cause such fundamental problems in the lives of women that an investigation of gender issues in relation to the mother-baby couple cannot be postponed.

I seek to distance myself from those writers who have separated the mother-daughter and father-daughter relationships, by attributing to the former a privileged position as the attainment of a feminine identity which is not yet influenced by patriarchal culture. The mother-daughter relationship served as a metaphor for women's redefinition of themselves in the 1970s and 1980s. Unfortunately, however, this argument falls into the trap of presuming a 'female reserve', a corner into which patriarchal culture has not yet entered. My response is that this 'genealogy of women', as Irigaray describes it (Irigaray 1991: 44), is *not* 'culture-free'. Even the mother's body—supposedly the least culture-bound element in the mother-daughter relationship—is in fact socially defined. So too is the way the mother experiences her body—her ease with it, or her lack of ease; her love or her hate for it—and her phantasies about it will influence the way the baby experiences it too. None of this is ever free from patriarchal culture, because the mother's mind itself contains repressed aspects of patriarchy—the murder of the mother foremost amongst them. In this way, then, unconscious images of femininity (and of masculinity) are just as powerful as ever, despite changes in the external world and in consciously held values and beliefs.

Chapter 11

Two Women in the Consulting-Room

In the preceding chapters I have shown how many women, in their struggle to separate from mother, resort to father and his matricidal internal world. By doing so they become entrapped in a position whereby attacks on themselves and on the object, alongside repression of their aggression, become an established part of their feminine identity.

In the previous chapter I examined the difficulty girls experience in using their mother as an object, and the way in which this prevents them from experiencing their own aggression, and from working it through. In my opinion it is this difficulty in particular which locks the girl into a position of unresolved ambivalence towards the maternal object. As I see it, this is the key reason why the girl never attains a clean split between one hated and one loved parent, to the same extent that one observes in the boy.

For Julia Kristeva the pervasive ambivalence of the mother-daughter relationship is only resolved through matricide:

> For man and for woman the loss of the mother is a biological and psychic necessity, the first step on the way to becoming autonomous. Matricide is our vital necessity, the sine-qua-non condition of our individuation... The lesser or greater violence of matricidal drive, depending on individuals and the milieu's tolerance, entails, when hindered, its inversion on the self; the maternal object having been introjected, the depressive or melancholic putting to death of the self is what follows, instead of matricide. In order to protect mother I kill myself. (Kristeva 1989: 27-28)

I think that here we witness a confusion which equates matricide, on the one hand, with separation from mother and, on the other, with the avoidance of the melancholic position. There is no notion here of a working-through of aggression towards mother (Klein 1959), nor of transitional phenomena, use of the object, the development of concern, or of potential space (Winnicott 1971). Instead there is only a simple dichotomy of 'murder of the mother' versus 'murder of the self'.

In actuality, matricide is the single psychic event guaranteed to bind us forever to the mother, in a way which is at once insidious, invasive, and without hope of resolution. In pathological cases the murder of the mother acquires a ghostly, persecutory quality which terrorises the psyche, and creates an air of unreality. For Kristeva to advocate matricide as an effective means of separating from mother is to give up entirely on any genuine working-through of ambivalence. This can only ever be a slow and laborious process, and can only take place within a relationship which is secure. Working-through also presupposes the ability to use objects and this ability—as we have seen—is often damaged in women. Nevertheless, awareness of this damage enables the mother-daughter relationship to become a locus for the development of the self.

An object towards which one is ambivalent can neither be assimilated nor renounced. The relationship one has with it is not of a type which might enhance the ego's capacity to grow, or the ego's independence. An ambivalent object remains lodged in the psyche like a foreign body, always provoking attempts to expel it, yet always resisting these attempts through evoking the bonds of love and hate by which it remains attached.

Fairbairn's model of endopsychic structure reflects this situation very clearly (Fairbairn 1944). He maintains that infantile dependence is—basically—repressed ambivalence, which remains in the psyche in the form of an attachment to a 'tantalising object' (which is split into 'libidinal' and 'rejecting' components). Although Fairbairn did not envisage this situation in terms of gender, nevertheless it is perhaps important that he arrived at this model after analysing in great detail the dream of a woman patient (Fairbairn 1944: 95-101). Although this endopsychic structure applies fundamentally to both sexes, it is women who are more at the mercy of the 'tantalising object' since the manic defences which can be utilised during the phallic phase prove less successful for women than for men.[40]

In this chapter I shall examine a specifically female type of transference, in which merging with the object is utilised as a means of avoiding aggression. The tendency of many women to merge with their objects appears alongside their intense guilt concerning their aggressive feelings. In many instances this takes the form of a taboo on overt aggression. Retreat to a state of merger and passivity is—for many women—a method of avoiding aggression, but also a means of searching for a pre-ambivalent experience. The search for a pre-ambivalent experience may be one way of avoiding the guilt and persecution which an ambivalent relationship to mother has evoked. Equally, however, it may assume the significance of a search for an important experience which, because of mother's own ambivalence towards her female child, was missed at the appropriate stage. Here, then, I propose to concentrate on the difficulties associated with living with this ambivalence, and the various ways in which women attempt to resolve it or avoid it within the transference.

There are a number of ways of understanding what is meant by the term 'merged relationship'. I have found that it is possible to distinguish several types within the transference:

1. *A passive submission to the object, which is phantasised as all good and powerful.* This is, then—in effect—fusion with an omnipotent object. The type of submission involved here is, however, very different from submission to the superego. Here, the poor degree of differentiation between subject and object creates an experience of security and elation rather than of persecution. Kohut has put this into words as: 'You are perfect and I am part of you' (Kohut 1971: 27), whereas Grunberger has named it 'the monad' (Grunberger 1989: 1-13).

2. *A tyrannical control over the object, which is regarded as existing simply in order to mirror the self, and therefore is not allowed any independent existence.* This is Kohut's 'merger

transference'—a variation of the 'mirror transference' (Kohut 1971). This kind of transference appears to be a resistance to the first type, in which the subject becomes part of the omnipotent object. Here, on the contrary, an omnipotent self demands that the object mirrors the self. In this way an abolition of difference is achieved, but always according to the demand of the omnipotent self.

3. *A resistance against powerful impulses towards merger, which are often manifested through a split: one aspect of the self becomes merged, whilst a more conscious part puts up a fierce resistance.* Resistance to merger can take the form of overt aggression. This third type can be seen as a reaction to an underlying situation of either the first or the second type.

Types 2 and 3 are often encountered in male patients, but the first type seems to constitute as much of a taboo in men as aggression is for many women.

For some authors, experiences of merger are understood as 'pre-ambivalent'. By this I mean that they are not viewed as a 'defence' against intolerable conflict, but as an *original state* of being merged with the object. Writers who take this position include Winnicott (1960b), Mahler (1975), Kohut (1971: 1-34), and Grunberger (1989). Of course, in a clinical context—properly speaking—regression to experiences of merger can only ever be defensive, but even so the therapist's theoretical stance towards merging will influence the way we view and treat the clinical manifestations of merger in the transference. Other theorists who emphasise object relations from the beginning of life regard the phenomena of merger, as manifested in the transference, as a parasitic activity which is motivated by envy or destructiveness, and which is aimed at annihilating the object.

From the first perspective, merging harks back to original pre- and post-natal experiences of being one with mother or the placenta. Bela Grunberger, referring to pre-natal experiences, describes this state as the very source of narcissism (Grunberger 1990). This state of being is—according to him—one of omnipotence, elation, harmony and security, of being one with mother, God, or the universe.

Modern observational techniques have questioned the supposedly 'ideal' nature of pre-natal experience (Piontelli 1992). Even though these studies suggest the existence of foetal distress and discomfort, this need not be taken as demolishing the argument for primary narcissism. For Grunberger, for instance, it is the way in which the baby does not yet have to fend for itself—because everything is provided—and the fact that its instincts are not yet operative which produces the feeling of perfection and elation. After birth, and the commencement of the operation of the digestive tract, both libidinal and aggressive instincts come into play. Grunberger suggests that it is this confrontation between the instincts and primary narcissism which constitutes the vicissitudes of development (Grunberger 1990).

It is important to me to state that I see merger not as a 'stage' of development, but as a *state* of being. In other words, it can coexist (indeed, it always does) with a paranoid-schizoid mode of being, since this implies a splitting of the object into an idealised as well as a persecutory object. Any failures of maternal care which are experienced as persecutory are simply split from the ideal state of merging with the object.

Fusion with an idealised object—which, later, might become pathological submission to a charismatic leader, or a manic defence against mourning—is, at this early stage, not pathological but instead an absolute necessity. I do not believe that the concept of primary narcissism precludes an object. In fact, we could argue that the placenta is the first 'object' for the child, the first 'environment mother', as Michael Balint has shown (Balint 1979: 64-72). What defines primary narcissism is the type of relation involved—which entails omnipotence and elation. As I see it, the balance between ideal and persecutory experiences in early childhood will determine the strength of the ego, and thus its ability to separate from its objects. It will also determine the capacity for guiltless aggression which is so essential for object-usage. The greater the extent to which the subject has been able to live these kinds of experience to the full, then the more smooth and complete the separation from mother will be.

Winnicott expresses this as the necessity for a stage of omnipotence followed by gradual disillusionment (Winnicott 1951: 240).

Indeed, Winnicott views aggression in a very different light from Klein. As we have seen, he considers it absolutely necessary for the separation of Me and Not-Me. Aggression, in this sense, disturbs the experience of oneness and harmony and promotes separation. A relatively guilt-free expression of early aggression will depend then, I think, on two things: a firm belief in one's reparative abilities; and the mother's ability to survive her child's attacks. The two are, of course, closely related.

At this point we must ask whether there is a difference—as regards aggression—between boys and girls. Freud maintains that the little girl's sadism at the anal stage is as strong as the boy's, and that it 'leaves nothing to be desired' (Freud 1933: 118). Other authors disagree. Chasseguet-Smirgel (1962), for example, regards the repression of aggression during the anal phase as one of the essential features of female development. Melanie Klein (1975b: 210) and Ernest Jones (1948b), meanwhile, refer to anxieties about damage to the inside of the subject's body, as a retaliation for the attacks of the subject on the mother's interior. These phantasies are common to both sexes; both fear retaliation from mother. However, Klein and Jones stress that whereas the boy is able to check he is intact, the girl is in no position to do so, and that this is the reason she represses knowledge of her vagina. The fear of attack from mother is thus the girl's deepest fear. In comparison, the boy's castration anxiety follows much later and has father as its object. Consequently the boy's curbing of his aggression also occurs much later—during the latency phase—and is therefore not so immediately related to issues of separation, but more to rivalry with father.

To gain another perspective, let us consider again the feminist position. The highly ambivalent nature of the mother-daughter relationship, as described by these writers (which implies—first of all—the ambivalence of the mother towards her daughter), would serve to rupture the girl's fusion with the maternal object, and to usher in prematurely the phase of separation or individuation. This is the deceptive 'maturity' manifested by little girls in comparison with boys. As I see it, this is a pseudo-maturity, because it is based on a pseudo-separation from mother. This underlying lack of separation from mother will exert its effects on the girl for the rest of her life. The mother-daughter relationship, then, is characterised not by a prolonged symbiosis—as Nancy Chodorow (1978) suggests—but on *the lack of a conflict-free symbiosis*. This difference is important to how we choose to regard the clinical manifestations of merging. If we adopt Chodorow's idea of a prolonged symbiosis between mother and daughter, then for the therapist to tolerate fusion within the transference would simply entangle the female patient in an increasingly symbiotic position. If, on the other hand, we view the clinical manifestations of fusion as a regression to the point of the original trauma, in order for the self to heal, then fusion should be regarded as a natural and expectable position in the case of many female patients.

Searles (1986) suggests that a period of 'therapeutic symbiosis' is both necessary and unavoidable for both male and female patients. Searles, however, conducted most of his work with schizophrenic patients, and I do not know to what extent he intended his findings to be applied to neurotic patients. In my experience, an overt merger within the transference is by no means a general phenomenon amongst patients as a whole, but is quite common among women. (I think that in the case of non-psychotic male patients masculine defences prevent such a regression.) Of course, if we sought to unravel all the layers of a conflictual transference in a male patient we might indeed discover an underlying symbiotic transference. In this case, however, conflict is being used as a defence against fusion and loss of self, or of gender identity.

* * *

It was due to a series of female patients, who—at least in the therapeutic situation—seemed to have no symbolic means by which to make their wishes and fears known to me, that I began to think about the way these women had fought so fiercely against merging with mother. It was as if the internal mother had been parasitically 'stuck' to their ego, such that they continued to spend their lives and their therapy fighting against her. This 'parasitical internal mother' is the negative—so to speak—of a healthy state of merger. She is experienced instead as an envious, internal mother who engulfs and prevents growth. This situation might be called 'symbiotic', but by no stretch of the imagination is it 'conflict-free'. Far from having experienced a normal phase of merging and absolute dependence on the mother, these women experienced mother as absolutely dependent on *them*.[41] A narcissistic mother such as this sees herself in the baby, and the baby—if it is to survive—must go on supporting mother's ego. This is more a case of the mother merging with the baby, than of the baby merging with mother. What these patients are seeking in therapy is a conflict-free merger *on their own terms* even though, at the same time, they view this wish as dangerous and entrapping. Such women often adopt an identification with father, and from this position of security seek to look after mother and themselves, or else to ward off mother continuously.

Marie—the same patient I discussed in Chapter 7—illustrates this type of mother-daughter relationship particularly vividly. Marie described her mother as a very controlled, brittle woman, with extremely low self-esteem, whom the rest of the family had to support and preserve from disintegration. Marie's anger and guilt over carrying this inadequate mother are immense. In the transference these feelings became manifest as a fear of damaging me, or as a lack of trust in my ability to contain them. In the first session Marie brought the following dream: *She was on the toilet having diarrhoea. I handed some toilet paper to her but she continued to have diarrhoea and needed more and more toilet paper. She was afraid that I would run out of toilet paper and felt frightened.* Her phantasy of herself as both dirty and uncontainable, and her fear of exhausting my resources, are both evident, alongside her inability to trust me to help her.

When Marie spoke about her mother she shivered, as if her mother was inside her and the mother's coolness and deadness were affecting the daughter's body. As mentioned previously, she described her mother as an 'ironing board', unable to conceive of her as possessing any interior space or being capable of any containing function. The 'ironing board mother' is wooden and lacks all warmth; she is flat, and lacks breasts and flesh. 'I would like a big, fat mother who would embrace me and make me feel warm and safe' said Marie. She described her feelings of being bulldozed and flattened every time she went to visit her mother. During these moments, then, mother ceased to be an 'ironing board' but became instead a huge impersonal machine, dangerous and out of control, which flattened her daughter and extinguished her. In this image it is Marie herself who becomes the 'ironing board', flattened by a gigantic 'steam-roller mother'. However, if Marie were to express her discontent, anger, anxiety or despair, then the unthinkable fear of causing mother's disintegration might come true. This fear arises from Marie's wish to invade her mother and retreat to a protected space inside. Yet this could only be achieved if mother were a 'fat', 'containing' mother—not an ironing board. Marie yearned to be allowed inside, but instead felt herself invaded by mother's uncontainable feelings. It was this yearning, alongside the fear of being engulfed and trapped inside a hostile environment, which was expressed in her relationship with me.

Perhaps we should also distinguish here between two distinct types of engulfment. The first is engulfment by an *invading object*; and the second by *an object which oneself has invaded*. The former, then, is akin to letting into oneself a kind of Trojan Horse; the latter is like visiting a friendly country, only to find out that the border has suddenly closed and one is trapped inside an enemy state. Marie experienced both of these types of engulfment and, consequently, was unable to find a form of intimacy with which she was comfortable.

In the transference, however, Marie was conscious only of the first type; the second type she was aware of only in her other relationships. However, for Marie—and here lies the essence of her dilemma—not to invade is to be left outside, in the cold and at the mercy of her desolate feelings of being unwanted and alone. A relationship which is not an invasion of some kind was difficult to imagine, and she could only picture it as a form of feeding. This was often the case in her friendships with women, and also in her relationship with me, which indeed felt like feed-ing—but 'spoon-feeding' rather than breast-feeding. The latter would imply the possibility of a devouring mother, or of letting in a Trojan Horse. 'Spoon-feeding', removed from mother's breast and body, was the only possible form of feeding for her.

The fear of being trapped inside me was not the only fear for Marie. There were also fears of damaging me inside with her badness and her anger, of poisoning me, of causing some kind of disintegration within me, or simply soiling me. In other words, she feared that she would herself become the Trojan Horse she so dreaded—or else, alternatively, that I would do this to her. This latter fear was deeply repressed, and only allowed expression in dreams.

Marie left home when she was seventeen and spent her life trying very hard to avoid every situation that might 'entrap' her. This included permanent jobs, studying, and therapy, as well as permanent relationships. When she began therapy her main fear was that she would be trapped in a situation from which she could not escape, reflecting precisely the situation of her child-hood and her internal relationship with mother. She needed to know that she could leave at any moment, yet at the same time was terrified I might send her away.

Therapy, like mother, was potentially a prison. She could not allow herself to relax too much otherwise she would be taken over unawares, and there would be nothing left of her. If she were to entrust herself into my hands, then I must be made *all* good. Nothing negative could be allowed into the consulting room.

Marie's idealisation of me was both a defence and a repeat of a necessary but missed developmental step. By idealising me Marie was saying, firstly, that I was all good and strong and could therefore be trusted to contain her; and secondly, that if I was indeed all good, then she would have absolutely no reason to hate me, despise me, or attack me. Thirdly she was implying if she were to grow into a self-respecting woman with good objects inside herself, then she would have to experience me as all good and direct badness outside onto other people; in other words she would have to maintain a good, clean split inside herself—something which she had never experienced satisfactorily.

Marie's fear of her destructive impulses was very strong and largely unconscious. It was manifested mainly in her inability to allow herself to succeed in any kind of way, and also in the persecutory anxiety which accompanied most of her social interactions. Her yearning for merger was very well defended against, since—in her experience—the object is parasitically attached to the self, from where it seeks to distort and stifle the self. This internal symbiosis of self and object had prevented Marie from forming any good and lasting relationships. Her strong defence against her own wishes to intrude and invade I experienced as a demand to abandon the boundaries of psychotherapy and to treat her as a personal friend.

This suffocation of the self by the object made itself felt in all her intimate relationships, and the confusion between the good and bad aspects of the object rendered her unable to form a good self-image. I think that it was because father was not an idealised object for Marie that a secure split between the bad and the idealised object could not take place. The idealising transference, therefore, was a necessary and inevitable means of creating this split between good and bad objects. In this situation, she was enabled to find a secure place in me from which to view (with me) her envious, attacking part, as projected onto other people who 'cannot let her be'. From this situation—which entails clear splitting—the work of integration could begin.

I discovered that this state of inadequate splitting is not uncommon in women patients, and I would speculate that this is due to the repression of aggression in little girls. The lack of clear splitting is experienced by the individual as feelings of being 'messy', 'dirty', and confused. Subsequent attempts to separate the good and bad objects, and to attain some kind of internal cohesion, often result in paranoia.[42]

I think that Marie attained some degree of splitting between the good and bad object, but only partly. By this I mean that the good object was projected onto father and the bad onto mother. However, this process was disturbed by the fact that father was experienced as good but weak, and thus unable to protect Marie from either her mother or from the very aggressive cousins who lived next door. Also, splitting which occurs later in life does not affect the maternal object; everything belonging to Marie's early relationship with her mother remained diffused and undifferentiated. Once, when she was talking about her mother, she had an image of a huge cauldron full of greenish stuff pouring down from the ceiling of the consulting room, making her feel very sick and endangering us both. This sickening stuff, which was really inside herself—and perceived at times to be right in the depths of her stomach—totally permeated her, destroying any possibility of a well-differentiated, good part of herself.

For a long time Marie was unable to tolerate interpretations of the transference, which she viewed with suspicion. It was as if she were saying that she would not allow me to jeopardise her newly-found security with any clever interpretations. Only gradually did Marie seem more ready to look at the transference. Tentatively she began to listen and—often—to agree that I must be right: 'It looked like that, didn't it?'. However, at these moments she would hasten to remark that she 'could *see* it but could not *feel* it'. It was as if she were becoming an observer—together with me—of herself and of her relationship to me, but that she stood outside it, so to speak. I think that this was the first step towards the development of a 'third space'.[43] Even so, *genuine* third space entails an experience of both inside and outside; in other words, a genuine third space observation is not split off from the feeling and experiencing self.[44] A genuine third space is essential to being able to tolerate transference interpretations and use them in a meaningful way. This is because an exploration of the transference relationship entails an appeal to the separateness of therapist and patient, and thus to the creative space in between them.

To return to my classification of types of transference, as presented near the beginning of this chapter, Marie represents the third type, in which the powerful need to merge with the object is resisted. This resistance is due to the way in which the distinction between good and bad objects has become blurred, and fears of being trapped inside a bad object have arisen. In Marie's case, idealisation was the intermediate solution between the twin dilemmas of fusion and separation.

* * *

In contrast to Marie's idealised transference, which formed an intermediate state, the relationship to me of another patient—Anette—was of a fused, but denigrated type. There was no resistance to merging here, no fears of being taken over, but simply a passive surrender to being looked after, a surrender to the 'environment mother' in the absence of the 'object mother'.

Anette, a thirty-eight-year-old French woman, described her mother as very unhappy and totally dominated by an authoritarian husband who had terrorised her and the whole of the family. Anette talked often of her 'poor' mother, meaning that she had no money because her husband gave her none. However there was another connotation here, of somebody terribly impoverished and with extremely low self-esteem. She could not remember any good experiences with her father. She remembered him as mean, tyrannical, rigid, and somehow strange. She suspected some kind of sexual perversion, but was not able to substantiate her suspicion. When he was absent the family felt able to 'breathe', but when he was there everybody felt suffocated.

Anette, the second daughter of four children, took to looking after her unhappy mother. She became extremely sensitive to mother's moods and state of mind, and protected her from any demands on her own part.

Living inside a good but impoverished mother can take many different manifestations. These might—for instance—include an identification with father, in which case 'living inside mother' serves the purpose of replenishing her, servicing her, restoring her. Indeed, this is often the case when a good, positive identification with father has been attained, and thus it acquires a more positive, reparative function. However, in Anette—for whom father was a sadistic object, and towards whom submission rather than identification was the predominant attitude—this 'living inside mother' possessed an altogether different meaning. It was not connected with restoring mother, but instead with preventing her (and Anette herself) from dying. This cohabitation with a moribund mother manifested itself in the transference as a kind of passive surrender to a minimal form of existence—a bare survival.

Anette—unlike Marie—considered her relation with her mother 'good'. Although she seemed completely unsatisfactory, mother nevertheless served Anette as a good object. Even though Marie regarded her relation to her mother as a disaster, in actuality *both* women had a mother with very low self-esteem, and who was totally unable to act as a container of early anxieties. Marie's relation to her father, as well as her parent's relationship with each other, was—however—totally different from that of Anette. Marie had a very good relationship to her father and identified with him, thus putting some distance between herself and her mother. In this sense her attempts to repair mother by acting as father were more risky, since the danger of becoming stuck inside a bad mother filled her with terror. Marie's relationships with others remind me of Freud's reference to Schopenhauer's porcupine fable (Freud 1921: 101, n1).[45] She expended a vast amount of mental and emotional energy trying to work out the 'optimal distance' between herself and her partner: Too close, or too distant? Did she really want to have a relationship, or didn't she? Was he the right man, or was he not? In other words, Marie was constantly trying to ascertain whether her partner was father or mother. Anette, on the other hand, had given up on all relationships (after a few catastrophic liaisons) and had concentrated herself fully upon her own daughter, who was supposed to make up for all the failures in her own life. Unwittingly, then, Anette was repeating the cycle of mother-daughter symbiosis.

Marie saw her father as a very good influence on her life.[46] The parental relationship also seemed less sadistic and more benign than in the case of Anette. Marie, then, represents a case in which father presents a 'second chance' where mother has failed.[47] For Anette this second chance never arose. Father—in her case a hated and feared figure—became a sadistic super-ego to whom she submitted in a totally masochistic way. For Anette the only choice available was between herself (in total identification with a denigrated mother), and a sadistic, aggressive father who dominated the unified mother-daughter. Any sadism on the part of mother or herself was totally denied. The situation, in Anette's mind (and, no doubt, in her mother's mind also), was a clear-cut vision of master and slave, of aggressor and victim. In this situation any possible third term was negated. Indeed, there was no 'conflict' as such, only terror and persecution.

Throughout her life Anette had fought constantly against her tendency towards utter passivity, which sometimes took her over completely. During these periods she had a strong urge just to stay at home and go to bed. In any other place she felt unsafe and persecuted.

Anette experienced therapy as being looked after by a mother about whom she did not have to worry. In this new mother-daughter relationship she submitted herself completely to me. As with Marie, I felt as if I were spoon-feeding a hungry baby who had difficulties with breast-feeding. Suckling at the breast is an active, libidinal situation which goes beyond the mere satisfaction of needs. The baby as hedonist is the model presented by both Freud and Winnicott. The spoon-fed baby, in contrast, passively accepts food; his active, libidinal self has turned either to thumb-sucking or some other autoerotic activity, or perhaps to a narcissistic love of self and mother. The *healthy* spoon-fed baby—on the other hand—accepts being an object, but only after having been (within the illusion of omnipotence) the active subject. Anette gave the impression of never having been the libidinal subject. Mother's inability to tolerate the baby's ruthless love or aggression created guilt, withdrawal, and premature ego-development. Anette's submission to me in the transference had about it the feeling of an 'endless feed'. She seemed a permanently hungry baby, spoon-fed, and constantly avoiding the aggression entailed by breast-feeding and the use of the object. There was a masochistic element in the way she submitted to me, with hunger and with gratitude, but without any real conviction that things would change. As she sees it, I, like her mother, was incapable of making any difference to her predicament, surrounded as she was by a hostile male world onto which she projected all her aggression. We—two women united by our powerlessness and lack of aggression—were unable to change anything. She looked up to me as a presence that might bring her some relief, but which offered no real solution to her suffering.

Passive submission to a pre-Oedipal object is, of course, not an exclusively female phenomenon. However, men tend to defend against this through the use they make of the phallus and of the Oedipus complex. Thus they may, for instance, eroticise the transference, introduce a third person (thus establishing a defensive triangular situation), use aggressive phantasies, or mechanise or rationalise the transference.

It could also be argued that because of the dynamic established between mother and daughter, the girl is less likely than the boy to have enjoyed a non-conflictual symbiosis, or—in Winnicott's terminology—to have been allowed a state of omnipotence. This *state* (not stage) of non-conflictual symbiosis is absolutely necessary for the structuration of the psyche. Whatever the reason for it, this is a type of transference which I have often experienced with women but not with men—except in the single, notable instance of a young homosexual male who, however, broke off therapy abruptly following the death of his father (p. 183, above). We might speculate here that the death of his father in the external world triggered fears of becoming stuck in a fused state with me, or that it had aroused the notion that his phantasied attacks on father (through regressing to a pre-Oedipal situation), had actually killed him. As the patient was very much at the beginning of therapy I have no way of answering these questions.

Anette, in the transference, used me as a buffer against a hostile, male world of violence. By performing this function I protected her from all her own aggressive feelings towards mother and me, which were to be directed at men instead. Anette had frequent dreams of being attacked or persecuted by men, who spied and followed her—ready to entrap her—or forced their way into her home. This was an instance of splitting in which the good and submissive object was mother, and the bad and sadistic object the father. Through this, Anette avoided her own ambivalence towards her mother and myself, and her fear of retaliation if her aggressive feelings were externalised.

The formation of an ego-ideal around a weak but good mother, and the projection of aggression and sadism onto father and the sadistic, paternal super-ego, has many consequences in the lives of women like Anette. In these cases, the Oedipus conflict disappears and—instead—we encounter a cohabitation of the daughter with a good but impoverished mother, alongside a masochistic relation to a bad and potent father. The relation between the parents is regarded by the daughter as wholly sadistic. The self, unable to own any sadism, due to the fear of disintegration, becomes totally persecuted. Passivity in the transference is, therefore, inevitable. However, this passivity can be a submission to an idealised object, as well as a cohabitation with an impoverished mother. It is very important to distinguish between the two. Idealisation constitutes an attempt to combine a good and a containing, surviving object. Symbiosis with an impoverished mother, on the other hand, is a hopeless avoidance of persecution, resulting in a near-death state—and maybe leading to problems akin to drug addiction.

A merger transference is 'inevitable' in the sense that it repeats—and attempts to heal—a crucial deficit: the absence of a good-enough mother. It is dangerous, because the idealisation of the therapist, and the splitting off of all sadism from the transference, can prove very difficult to influence. However, within this framework a secure base may be created from which to begin the difficult work of integration.

Submission to a *pre-Oedipal* object—including idealisation of that object—has about it a passive and masochistic quality which is quite different from submission to an Oedipal object. In the first instance, submission borders on merging; it leads to phobic reactions and to fears of being trapped inside the object. In cases of submission to the Oedipal father, however, there is an active quality alongside the passive one, which may lead to fanatical activity which has as its goal the continuation of father's work or world.

* * *

I shall now examine another type of merger transference: the domination of the object by the self, which demands that the object be the same as the self. This type of transference was explored by Heinz Kohut (1971). Kohut describes it as follows:

> The analyst is experienced as an extension of the grandiose self and he is referred to only insofar as he has become the carrier of the grandiosity and the exhibitionism of the analysand's grandiose self and of the conflicts, tensions and defences which are elicited by these manifestations of the activated narcissistic structure. (Kohut 1971: 114)

He continues:

> Since in this revival of the early stage of primary identity with the object the analyst is experienced as part of the self, the analysand... expects unquestioned dominance over him... the analyst experiences this relationship in general as oppressive. (Kohut 1971: 115)

I wonder here whether—contrary to what Kohut is saying—the unquestioned domination of the analyst is not in fact a defence against *being dominated by* a frightening, non-empathic, omnipotent object. In fact, this is indeed what emerges when the domination of the therapist by the patient breaks down.[48]

In the cases of both Anette and Marie I encountered the absence of a secure idealised object, and of symbolic communication in the transference, including a creative response to interpretations. However, the wish to merge with an idealised object can manifest itself in various forms within the transference, one of which (a very archaic form) entails merger not with mother but with the pre-natal environment. This involves a state of 'constant supply', without the need to make any demand. This form of merger can be terrifying, because it threatens to pull the subject back to a state of no identity and no separateness.

Aggression can then be used as a defence against merging, and also a means of repeating a relationship to a 'bad' mother, as in the case of another patient—Sylvia.

The first two years of Sylvia's therapy were a continuous battle between her as an innocent victim, and myself as the sadistic mother. Interpretations were experienced as attacks on the self designed to deprive her of autonomy. Interpretations, therefore, bound us together in a master-slave relationship. Through interpretation I seemed to acquire horrendous power over her—power to define, reify, and turn her into a part of myself. Her reactions to interpretations were aggressive and often hysterical protestations, or else contemptuous dismissals. Her attacks on me had such a venomous edge that I often felt as if stung by a poisonous snake. I often felt frightened and put in the position of a terrified little girl—a girl faced by a sadistic mother. Alternatively—in fact, just as often—she would become the deprived and greedy little girl, hungry for love and understanding, who could never get enough and who could not find anyone who would endure her hunger.

In her ordinary life Sylvia seemed to have acquired quite a reputation as an aggressive 'bitch' whom people were afraid of. When she first realised this she was shocked and baffled, because her experience of being with others was one of fear and uncertainty. What appeared to her as reality was that she could never be accepted by anybody, that people ignored her or put her down, and—consequently—that she had to defend herself in order to survive. This seemed a repetition of her relationship to her mother. It was another shock to her, however, when she realised that in this repetition she herself became her mother—the venomous, envious, attacking mother who had terrorised her childhood. In the transference I experienced the terror of the little girl. What Sylvia experienced as an invading, envious mother was spat out at me, and reduced me to the attacked child.

The excessive use of projective identification and aggression served, I think, as a defence against being merged with the mother. Return to this level was both a wish and a nightmare. It was the place unconsciously craved for as the state of no need, a pre-natal bliss with no mother, just the placenta as an infinite source of nourishment. The wish for this kind of merger was manifested in the way she demanded to be loved, nourished, and understood, yet rejected me as the source of nourishment and understanding. We might speculate here that Sylvia had missed the state of early omnipotence, postulated by Winnicott as a normal phase of development. Her attempt to attain it in the transference was, however, a very convoluted affair, since the reality of my existence as a separate, frustrating, and potentially terrifying object kept interfering. This reality thrust her into a world of fragmented objects which she experienced as annihilating. Aggression and projective identification were used here both as a defence against wishes of merger, and as a defence against acceptance of the separateness of the object.

As therapy proceeded, however, open warfare seemed to diminish and Sylvia began slowly to accept some interpretations not as attacks but as nourishment. At times she experienced guilt and shame at how she had treated me. She became more tearful and more desperate about her 'flawed' self, and became much more attached to me. At this point she began to miss approximately one session out of every three or four. In the transference she was, by now, a shy, vulnerable little girl, busy attacking herself rather than me. Her fear of wanting to merge with me was deeply hidden. The transference, meanwhile, was evolving towards a non-differentiated phase in which interpretations were neither rejected nor reflected upon, but simply taken in wholesale as food. She could not accept me as a separate, thinking person, but only as a source of comfort—a pre-breast, a placenta. This kind of passivity and non-differentiation was defended against in the way she tried to control my presence and absence by missing sessions, and by dismissing me completely during the time between sessions and during breaks. (She always 'forgot' the last session before a break, and often the first one afterwards.) In this way she maintained the illusion that she had created me and I was under her control. Only whilst under this delusion of omnipotence could Sylvia tolerate her need of me. A terrifying object could be fought with aggression, but a benign object was even more fearful to her because she could not employ aggression against it, or against her own wish to merge with it.

Wishes for merger—and for a pre-natal state of bliss, or a post-natal state of omnipotence—are not present only in female patients, but are universal wishes of humankind, as Grunberger has so eloquently argued (Grunberger 1989, 1990). What is evident in many female patients, however, especially when they are faced with a female therapist, is the degree to which merger can dominate the transference for substantial periods of time. I hope I have demonstrated some of the forms this can take, the reasons for this, and what this allows us to infer about the mother-daughter relationship, in both its conscious and unconscious aspects.

Chapter 12

The Search for an Alternative Space

It could be said that with human beings there can be no separation, only a threat of separation. (Winnicott 1971: 126)

The Paternal Space

Suddenly he remembered that the purse and the objects he had stolen from the old woman's chest were all of them still in his pockets, and had been there all the time! It had taken him until now to think of removing them and hiding them away! He had not even remembered about them just then, as he had been examining his clothes! What was wrong with him? In an instant he fell on them, taking them out and hurling them on to the table. When he had removed them all, even turning the pockets inside out, in order to make sure there was nothing left in them, he carried the whole pile to the corner of the room. There, right in the very corner, down at the bottom, the wallpaper was torn in one place where it had peeled away from the wall; he immediately began to cram everything into his hole, under the paper—in it went! 'All hidden from sight, the purse as well!' he thought with relief, getting up on his knees and looking stupidly at the corner, with its hole that was now bulging out more than ever. Suddenly he recoiled in horror. 'Good God!' he whispered in despair. 'What's the matter with me? Do you call that hidden? Are those things anywhere near being hidden?' '...My sanity really is deserting me! ...A certainty that everything, even his memory, even the simple faculty of reason, was deserting him had begun to torment him unendurably. 'What, is it really beginning now, is this the punishment beginning?' (Dostoyevsky 1991: 130-1)

This is Raskolnikov, hero of Dostoyevsky's *Crime and Punishment*. Raskolnikov is crazed. Having killed and robbed an old woman—a pawnbroker—and her sister, he returns home to find that he has all the stolen goods still on his person. He is in a state of panic and utter persecution—not unlike Orestes' after he has killed his mother. Raskolnikov, however, is trying to *hide*, to cover the evidence, and—eventually—to get rid of it. This entails disposing of all the items which belonged to the old woman; they must not be found on him or in his room. Even his own clothes have become incriminating evidence and must also be destroyed. Blood—as part of the dead women—has become persecutory evidence, like an accusatory, screaming Fury:

At that moment a ray of sunlight illuminated his left boot; on the sock that was peeping out through the crack at the front of the boot he thought he saw marks. He kicked off his boots: 'Yes, there are marks! The whole toe of the sock is saturated in blood... But what can I do about it? Where am I going to put this sock, the bits of my trouser-ends, the pocket lining? ...should hide them in the stove? But the stove's the first place they'll start rummaging about in. Burn them? But what with? I don't even have matches. No, I'd better take them somewhere outside and throw them away. Yes, the best thing to do is throw them away!' (Dostoyevsky 1991: 131)

Eventually he finds a spot quite a few miles away, a deserted, uninhabited yard, where he hides the stolen goods under a block of masonry. He then returns home, after a long detour, which includes a delirious visit to an old friend, with whom he fails to communicate. Nothing is the same anymore because Raskolnikov himself is not the same, and this is what he had not reckoned with. In his plan of the murder it was all clear: the old woman was a parasite, a useless creature, a 'louse' who sucked the blood of people in need. He needed money. He was far more important than this woman, and could easily kill her. He would then have proved to himself that he was one of the chosen, one of the winners rather than one of the victims.

What he could not plan for, however, were the reactions of his body and of his emotions—which play havoc upon him. In other words, he had not reckoned with the unconscious. Raskolnikov, like Orestes, seems to have been totally unprepared for what follows the murder of the woman. The invasion of himself by emotions and sensations which feel alien to him, the concrete reality of murdered women, mutilated bodies, and spilled blood, are not things for which his rationalist nihilism had prepared him.

We should not forget that Raskolnikov is fatherless, and feels that his mother and sister are his responsibility. The absence of a father signifies his lack of protection by a paternal super-ego, and its replacement by a grandiosity which is matched only by his contempt for all weakness and need. His mother's and sister's love for him—shrouded in weakness and need—fuel his resentment of his fate and his wish to rise above it by any means. His contempt for the old woman-'louse' is in actuality contempt for a parasitical mother, a mean, ungiving and draining mother—a vampire-mother split off from his real mother, not unlike Fairbairn's repressed bad object (Fairbairn 1943: 59-81). This split-off mother and his identification with her, this phantasied murder from his fatherless childhood, is repeated in reality, and his feelings towards her acted out in tragic and abominable circumstances.

Here we are not far from what Julia Kristeva has described as the 'abject'. For Kristeva, separation from mother depends upon mother becoming 'abjected'. Elaborating on Lacan's postulation that the symbolic emerges from the loss of the mother, Kristeva postulates the 'abject' as an experience of the anal mother. For Kristeva, the rejection and expulsion of the mother during the anal phase is the first step towards separation, which is then aided by the imposition of the symbolic. The abjected mother becomes the stuff of primal repression. In Western societies, Kristeva suggests, abjection becomes a support of the symbolic. She refers to corruption as the most common 'socialised appearance of the abject' (Kristeva 1990: 158-60).

Kristeva regards the abject as a necessary step towards the symbolic. However, unlike Klein, she never refers to any necessary working-through of this phase, or of its sadistic nature. In this sense, then, it would seem that her analysis of the abject is conspicuously incomplete. My own interpretation of Kristeva's 'abject mother' is that she is *the murdered mother*. Only the murder of the mother can be regarded as an explanation with sufficient strength to account for the regression to anal phenomena.

The subject can only rid itself of persecutory objects through projective identification. It seems to me that Raskolnikov's woman-'louse' is precisely such an object. The projection of this object onto the external world, and the acting-out of the sadism which corresponds to it, drag Raskolnikov into a world without love or compassion. Contempt for all morality and all kindness—which he sees as weakness—is what accompanies this act. This part of himself, cynical and cruel, promises Raskolnikov protection against need, and poverty. However, it is—in effect—a 'false father', an omnipotent part of the self which offers protection in the manner of—to use Rosenfeld's terminology—a 'gang' or 'mafia' (Rosenfeld 1987: 111-2), or of the Devil in Christian mythology. This part of Raskolnikov attempts to protect him from the weakness and impoverishment which the identification with the woman-'louse' evokes up in him. In the process the woman-'louse' loses all cohesion as an internal object, and becomes a 'bizarre object' instead.[49]

Even when persecutory anxiety is high this state of madness can be avoided through an identification with the idealised father, who acts as a protector against primitive anxieties, or— in more mature development—through identification with a good father, who is the custodian of the moral law. As has been mentioned, Raskolnikov himself has no such father; and it has been a recurring theme of this book that identification with a good parental *couple* seems almost totally lacking from Western culture. Such an identification would pre-suppose the working-through of the depressive position, and would form the source of a genuine morality, based on what Winnicott has described as 'concern for the object'—rather either fear or guilt, which currently tend to serve as the basis of our moral impulses. To ensure the Oedipus complex led to this outcome would imply a slow working-through of the anal phase and of the Oedipus complex, alongside the absence of a rigid power relationship between mother and father, in both the external and the internal world.

I have argued all along that the 'matricidal psyche' is regarded as the 'normal' way of separating from mother within Western culture, but that this implies a psyche which attains only a semblance of separation, by violent means. This state of affairs is reflected in *The Oresteia*, and—particularly—in Freud's description of the dissolution of the Oedipus complex. This 'normal' way is, in fact, a masculine way, since it utilises masculine anxieties—predominantly castration anxiety—and a masculine identification with father as the core of the super-ego, in order to create a rigid repression barrier. All the interactions explored in this book—between mother and daughter, father and daughter, mother and son, father and son—have been examined within this psychic structure. Although this masculine psychic structure is the 'norm' and, consequently, part of both the male and female unconscious, women—as we have seen—cannot, on the whole, attain the same radical separation from mother. They remain, to an extent, located between identification with mother and father, less split but more ambivalent, less schizoid but more melancholic, due to their identification with a damaged mother, and their idealisation of father.

In either case, however, the super-ego acts like a tyrant who has taken power after a period of chaos and passion, and restores peace by any means at his disposal, simply so that ordinary life can resume. The super-ego, by becoming idealised, reduces persecutory anxiety and opens up some possibility of a mental space. In this sense, then, the super-ego might be regarded more as an 'enlightened despot' than a tyrant.

Although there is a mental space which opens up after the dissolution of the Oedipus complex and the formation of the super-ego, in the sense that ambivalence is apparently reduced and powerful feelings suppressed, this is nevertheless a *limited space*, achieved at the expense of relations to the maternal, anal, sexual, and identificatory objects—which are thereby either repressed or transformed into 'bizarre objects'. This space is therefore a masculine space: the boy accepts it with relief, whereas the girl accepts it as only as a consequence of her relationship to her father, in order to allay his masculine anxieties, and her fears of an intrusive mother within the psyche.

The concept of 'potential space' was introduced by Winnicott, who regarded it as the location of cultural experience. He wrote:

> The place where cultural experience is located is in the 'potential space' between the individual and the environment (originally the object). The same can be said of playing. Cultural experience begins with creative living first manifested in play. (Winnicott 1971: 118)

For Winnicott, potential space is where mother and baby *meet*. Although potential space signals separation from mother, it also indicates unity with mother. It is a creative leap into the third dimension, the creation of a third term. 'This is the place that I have set out to examine', Winnicott stated, 'the separation that is not a separation but a form of union' (Winnicott 1971: 115). In a similar way, Bion uses the term 'contact barrier' to refer to a point of both contact and separation:

> The term 'contact-barrier' emphasises the establishment of contact between conscious and unconscious and the selective passage of elements from one to the other. On the nature of the contact-barrier will depend the change of elements from conscious to unconscious and vice versa. (Bion 1962: 17)

I think that these two concepts are, in fact, related. The creation of a 'potential space' between mother and baby is perhaps the same—or, at least, of the same order—as the creation of a 'contact-barrier' and of 'alpha-elements'. Bion coined the term 'alpha function' in order to describe the function of the psyche which enables the mother to act as a container of the baby's experience, and—by digesting and metabolising it—making it suitable for the baby to take back as his own. The baby is enabled to re-introject his experience because it has been made digestible to him through his mother's ability to metabolise it. By introjecting the experience, then, the baby also introjects the mother's alpha-function. Metabolised experiences become 'alpha-elements', which can be stored and which form the contact barrier. Alpha-function and alpha-elements are closely linked with the ability to think, dream, and to learn from experience.

As I see it, Bion's theory of thinking envisages a different relationship between conscious and unconscious from Freud's theory of repression. Freud saw the unconscious as barred from consciousness by a repression barrier which 'presses down' (so to speak) upon forbidden impulses and memories which attempt to push their way through. Bion's 'contact barrier', in contrast, envisages separation *and* contact between conscious and unconscious. This is an important difference from Freud, and reflects—I think—the changing structure of the Western individual, and the de-idealisation of the super-ego. 'This contact barrier', Bion writes, 'thus continuously in process of formation, marks the point of contact and separation between conscious and unconscious elements and originates the distinction between them' (Bion 1962: 17). It is its fluidity, then, which distinguishes the contact barrier from Freud's barrier of repression, as elements pass selectively from one side to the other. The dialectic of contact and separation between conscious and unconscious—and, by inference, between subject and object—as expressed in Bion's notion of the contact barrier, therefore precludes any rigid separation of conscious and unconscious, or any attempt to resolve the tension on either side. In this sense, then, the psyche is in a continuous state of digesting experience and translating it into conscious activity, through words or other symbolic means.

However, if there is a failure in the acquisition of alpha-function and alpha-elements, then the personality will be dominated instead by 'beta-elements'—undigested components of experience—which cannot be stored but are suitable only for projection. An individual in this state cannot think, dream, or use interpretations. Experience itself is persecutory. It is as if one were given exquisite food whilst lacking a stomach with which to digest it. The individual, however, does more than simply 'expel' experience whilst in this state. Through projective identification the individual attempts to find a 'container' and a meaning for his or her experience. In other words, by employing projective identification, the individual 'enters' another person, in an attempt to find a solution to his or her problems. However, this 'being inside the other' creates new problems of its own, including claustrophobia and persecution.

Hanna Segal, expanding Winnicott's concept of potential space, and linking it to Bion's theory of thinking, talks of a 'dream space'—a term she borrows from Masud Khan—in which dream-thoughts can be formed and symbolisation can take place. On the peculiar quality of the dreams of two patients, she writes:

> The dreams of both patients were characterised by very poor and crude symbolisation. I was struck both by the concreteness of the experience and the invasion of reality, as though there was no difference between their mind and the outside world. They had no internal mental sphere in which the dream could be contained. (Segal 1986: 92-3)

The development of this 'space' or 'container', in which transformation of beta-elements into alpha-elements takes place, announces the emergence of a third area, and thus puts an end to projective identification as the dominant mode of being and communicating. In the absence of such a space, projective identification dominates: the baby can only be either inside the mother, or the mother can be inside himself; or it can be outside mother, or mother can be outside himself. In the consulting-room a breakdown of the container in this way is experienced by the patient as the tyranny of the therapist and, by the therapist, as the tyranny of the patient. Alternatively it is experienced as utter abandonment and desolation. A space in which reflection might take place is lacking. Mutual devouring is the result. There is no symbolic reality, no 'as if' or optimal distance between the thinker and the thought, between the speaker and the listener. In more hopeful situations, however, the 'monad' might form, which is a regression to benign narcissistic relations (Grunberger 1989). Despite its defensive nature, it is a more hopeful sign.

The emergence of potential space is described by Winnicott as taking place between mother and baby in terms which are without gender. The roots of cultural experience, Winnicott argues, are situated long before the Oedipus complex and the emergence of sex difference, and have to do with the relationship between mother and baby. Some authors have argued otherwise. Lacan and Kristeva, for instance, assert that the symbolic order emerges only upon the entry of the father into the scene.[50] Similarly, Chasseguet-Smirgel attributes culture and civilisation to the functioning of the internal father. Her argument is quite compelling. In unambiguous terms she refers to Nazi ideology as a 'return to mother', a state of mind in which the ego-ideal (as a structure dominated by the internal mother) takes over and annihilates the super-ego, which is under the dominance of the internal father. She warns against the erosion of the Father and his Law; the alternative, she states, is barbarism and fascism (Chasseguet-Smirgel 1986).

In this model, then, we are presented with a cultural and psychic space which is created by the Father and his Law. Below this space there is only psychosis, perversion, or utopia. Since this space is defined by the paternal super-ego we are justified in calling it 'masculine'.

The Maternal Space

I have described the state of the psyche emerging from the Oedipus complex as an uneasy peace, based on the elimination of the early mother with all the passionate feelings, fears, and anxieties attached to her. This elimination of the mother is, for me, an act of psychical violence—the destruction of the object to save the self, or the boy's masculinity. In other words, it is a narcissistic defence. The result of this murder would be a very persecuted psyche, were it not for the formation of the super-ego, which functions as a moral defence. However, a psyche based on the murder of the early mother, and relying on the protection of the super-ego, is always in fear of persecution by the maternal, female object. A super-ego based on the castrating father would closely resemble Fairbairn's 'anti-libidinal ego', were it not that the idealisation entailed in the formation of the super-ego makes it also an ideal object. Its function is to maintain splitting, and to prevent confusion between the good and the bad object, with all the dangers of perversion, addiction, or psychosis which this would bring about (Meltzer 1964: 133).

However, at the end of the Oedipus complex the good and bad objects are reversed: mother becomes the 'bad' object, and the 'castrating' father becomes the protective, idealised super-ego.[51] The danger of confusion is great in this situation, and renders the psyche highly prone to perversion, unless a much more sophisticated synthesis of the good and bad objects takes place. The Oedipus complex must not been merely be 'dissolved', but worked-through, which entails—at the same time—the achievement of a synthesis of the good and bad objects. (This is, in essence, the depressive position.) My contention, however, is that the amount of persecutory anxiety involved, and the abruptness with which the Oedipus complex is dissolved, does *not* lead to such a working-through. I have also maintained that Freud, in describing the dissolution of the Oedipus complex, was actually describing only the Western psyche—a psyche which relies on splitting and repression for 'normal' functioning.

My exploration of *The Oresteia* was conducted in terms of its relation to the dissolution of the Oedipus complex. I disagree with the usual interpretation of *The Oresteia* as the passage from matriarchy to patriarchy. This has been viewed within psychoanalysis as a necessary step away from an omnipotent and engulfing mother towards a rational, reality-based father. Yet neither the events recounted in *The Oresteia*, nor the historical facts ascertained concerning the Mycenean civilisation, support this interpretation. There was never a matriarchy in Mycenae. The proud and cruel Clytemnestra came to power by killing an even more cruel and tyrannical male monarch. Agamemnon represents—I think—the 'old style patriarchy', based upon tyranny. What we are witnessing in *The Oresteia* is the transition from an old style of tyrannical patriarchy—through female revolution which establishes another tyranny—towards a democratic type of the rule of the Law of the Father. In the old type of patriarchy the father-king rules supreme over his people and over his family: wife, daughters, and sons. In fact, his daughters are treated as mere possessions—not only by him, but also by the gods, who demand the sacrifice of the daughter Iphigenia, in exchange for favourable winds that will take the Greek fleet to Troy. In this way, Agamemnon and his regime resembles Freud's 'primal father'—a figure which inspires dread and hate as well as admiration and submission.

When Clytemnestra kills Agamemnon she establishes another dictatorship, equally oppressive. This is an important fact which seems to have escaped recognition in psychoanalytic interpretations of *The Oresteia*. The power of the mother is indeed part of the baby's 'illusion', due to his state of fundamental helplessness, but this power is also a fact, because—due to their social position—women have been forced to defend their limited territory from any intruders. In other words, since motherhood has traditionally been the sole locus of power for women, but since it exists within an overall masculine culture, it has been used by women in a way that challenges the father's authority. This site of maternal power becomes a place from which the father is excluded. It is this exclusion which is portrayed in *The Oresteia*. The play places us within a circular process, a vicious circle which establishes the power of the mother by the very fact that it has been so violently crushed; the mother becomes a dangerous and persecutory object precisely because she has been murdered.

This psychical situation is brought about by the dissolution of the Oedipus complex, as described by Freud. The murdered mother returns to haunt the psyche, and exercises a firm grip on the whole of Western culture, as a persecutory object. Attempts by the culture to curb woman's power relate back to this aspect of the mother—the mother as a persecutory object. Meanwhile, woman—finding herself in a social situation of powerlessness—uses her child like a 'phallus' (as Freud put it, in characteristically male language) or as a 'weapon'. However, this triggers further attempts by the child and the father to eliminate her from the psyche. Each generation is forced to live out this drama, again and again. It is as if this vicious circle cannot be broken even by our contemporary 'egalitarian' society. If anything, motherhood is more than ever marginalised. In a culture based on the spirit of free enterprise and on technological omnipotence, motherhood seems almost an anachronism.

It is not my intention to idealise motherhood—far from it. Yet the splitting between the father and mother, on the one hand, and the idealised and persecutory mother, on the other, leaves the 'real' everyday mother stranded and excluded. On this schism Rozsika Parker writes:

> Definitions of femininity as a lived identity for women have, thanks to feminism, gained a certain flexibility over the past few decades, and we can observe that femininity is, at any one moment, both embraced and resisted. But the feminist ideal (by this I mean a historically changing concept of what a woman should be) in relation to motherhood has remained curiously static. In fact, the faster women's lives change, the more ossified and stereotyped become dominant representations of ideal motherhood... the representation of ideal motherhood is still almost exclusively made up of self-abnegation, unstinting love, intuitive knowledge and unalloyed pleasure in children. (Parker 1995: 21-22)

Parker describes the social taboo on maternal ambivalence. The self-negating mother—that is, the mother who denies her own subjectivity—follows, I think, from the matricidal premise. The taboo on maternal subjectivity is a protection against the dangerous, murdered, and undead mother.[52]

We are, then, once again, within the vicious circle. For if matricide is the only culturally acceptable way of dissolving the Oedipus complex, then the dead—or rather, the 'undead' mother—will come back to haunt the psyche with her persecutory presence. The cultural response to this has been the myth of the Virgin Mother, the infinitely loving and non-threatening mother who can control neither her fertility nor her (Divine) Son—a very re-assuring version of the mother. However, there is an ambiguity in the Christian myth which makes Mary a very enigmatic person, and which is—perhaps—a remnant from an older, more powerful virgin goddess whose generativity did not require a male contribution—namely: Mary's impregnation by God the Father *excludes the husband*. Mary becomes the receptacle of the Father's (*not* the husband's) son. Bearing the son of the Father makes Mary, in effect, the Father's bride or daughter, the Eternal Virgin, the non-sexual, passively receiving, powerless yet very powerful woman. This mixture of power and powerlessness, of omnipotence and impotence, is the traditional image of the mother in Western culture; both her power and her real submission derive from the father. However, this makes the husband uneasy. It is as if he were redundant and powerless. The splitting between the sexes, and between the generations, thus works to eliminate the possibility of a parental *couple*, and a shared male-female social authority.

Social reality becomes, then, the exact reverse of psychical reality, in an attempt to restore the balance of power as experienced by the child consciously and—most importantly—unconsciously. Mother becomes the idealised and powerless virgin in a manoeuvre which is akin to what Freud described as 'negation' (Freud 1925b). For Freud, negation is applied to a situation about to become conscious, but which is then verbally—or otherwise—reversed. The statement 'Mother is not dangerous' is a key instance of negation. Estella Welldon, in her very influential book *Mother, Madonna Whore* (1988), exposes the reality of maternal abuse, but also the reluctance of society to acknowledge that it exists. We enter the realm of negation as a defence against terror.

The phantasy of a dangerous mother becomes—with the dissolution of the Oedipus complex—the psychic reality of a dangerous mother, which is then transformed into the social reality of the ideal, self-negating mother. This ideal mother lacks flesh and bones, power and subjectivity. Also, importantly, she lacks pregnancy. Representations of pregnancy in Western art are very scarce. Although pictures of the Madonna and child are ubiquitous, the pregnant Mary, or even pregnant ordinary women, are conspicuously absent. Pregnancy brings us face to face with phantasies of female omnipotence. The male is truly redundant here; not only redundant, but also helpless. Envy and helplessness vis-à-vis the female are experiences which patriarchal culture attempts to obliterate in various ways, such as the non-representation or technocratisation of pregnancy. Pregnancy is shocking because it confronts us with our origin in the body of woman and nature, and reinstates the omnipotent mother as part of a natural law. It faces us with what Lacan called the Real, with what Kristeva called the 'abject'.

A culture which employs matricide and the paternal super-ego, as a means to achieve separation from mother, will find pregnancy a disturbing phenomenon. Fears and phantasies of a revengeful, archaic mother lead to the anaemic, fully sanitised view of pregnancy which pervades contemporary society. Humanity has always found it difficult to come to terms with our origins in the flesh, but this is a difficulty which confronts our culture in particular. From the perspective of masculinity, this concerns problems of differentiation and dis-identification. Patriarchal cultures all over the world have adopted different ways of working-through these issues. In Western culture, the attempt to regulate and technocratise pregnancy is one means of bringing under control the unmanageable feelings that it evokes, and turning it into a 'high tech experience'.

The conclusion of *The Oresteia* is full of references to the creation of 'a new space' in which to breathe and reflect—an Apollonian space of rationality, protected from primitive terrors by a paternal super-ego. This space is clearly masculine, created by the murder of Clytemnestra and the ruling of an Athenian court which declares the absolute right of the father. This space excludes the Real, our bodily origins, pregnancy, and the abject. Although writing from a slightly different perspective, Joan Raphael-Leff suggests:

Pressurised by a society which glorifies pregnancy, denying her ambivalence, the woman may feel compelled to

hide her negative feelings—even from herself—to maintain the idealised, blissful state she is meant to experience.
(Raphael-Leff 1993: 28)

The idealised, technocratic view of pregnancy denies not
only the woman's 'negative feelings', but also the terror and the
awe that pregnancy inspires. The miracle that unravels in front
of our eyes, the smallness of individual existence, and the sense
that we are lived by—used by—nature, is a reality which phallic, Western culture denies. Freud, however, realised these facts,
and discussed them with awe, rather than fear. He pointed out
that the individual

...is an appendage to his germ-plasm... He is the mortal
vehicle of a (possibly) immortal substance—like the
inheritor of an entailed property, who is only the temporary holder of an estate which survives him. (Freud 1914:
78)

Pregnancy as a 'quintessentially female experience'
(Raphael-Leff 1995) shares the fate of the omnipotent mother. Its
disturbing features are split off and denied, and an idealised,
sanitised version of pregnancy takes its place. Its ability to shake
us out of the routine and rationality of daily life is minimised.

The space which opens up for Electra and Orestes, after the
murder of Clytemnestra, is established not at the moment of
murder, but only after a long period of persecution and suffering, and the trial in Athens. The trial, in effect, is an attempt at
reparation. The violence involved in the murder of
Clytemnestra, however, involves far too much guilt, and ham-
pers any genuinely reparative work. Persecutory anxiety predominates, and Orestes is driven to use manic and moral
defences. Athene and Apollo finally step in to save the day with
their dictum that the murder of the mother was 'justified', or—
more fundamentally—that 'the mother is not the real parent of
the child' (Aeschylus 1986: 169). On this pronouncement, the
glorious and omnipotent father becomes the only parent. This is
by no means a genuine reparation, then, but instead a form of

absolution. The substitution of the murdered mother by the glorious father interrupts the work of mourning. The mother remains un-mourned, to haunt the son as a force from outside as well as from inside. A rigid repression barrier is, therefore, necessary to keep out this force.

The trial establishes the male principle—which rests on the law of the father—as the highest principle, yet at the same time it incorporates the female principle *at a lower level*. We should not forget that the Furies are invited by Athene to stay in Athens, and are given a cavern to inhabit (Aeschylus 1986: 174). This could be interpreted as a partial reinstatement of mother's world—which we also witness in the introduction of Mary into Christianity. This, to me, hints at the culminating point Western civilisation. We have advanced as far as becoming a culture which attains harmony between paternal and maternal principles, but which achieves this only by splitting. The maternal principle is split into a dangerous, murderous and murdered part, which is either relegated to the unconscious or projected outside; or else into an idealised, self-negating virgin, with both parts guarded and dominated by a paternal super-ego.

Perhaps it is possible to distinguish between the repression of the murdered mother, and more psychotic solutions. Repression of the murdered mother is a more mature solution to the problem. It allows the conscious part of the psyche to engage in the work of 'thinking', although it requires the maintenance of a rigid repression barrier. The more psychotic solution, on the other hand, involves excessive projective identification, and thus no repression and no capacity for thinking. The former solution is modern rationalism. The second, however, is increasingly manifesting itself within Western culture, as the paternal super-ego weakens and the terror of the murdered maternal object makes itself felt. Contemporary culture expresses itself through a state of hysteria, a return to a psychical violence which has been split off and denied, and can only be represented through monsters, aliens, or prehistoric beasts. The proliferation of these modern myths of evil, and of the male hero who fights against it, expresses the breakdown of the Western solution to basic human problems.

I have argued that 'normality' in Western culture is characterised by rigid repression. The mechanism of repression is—of course—central to Freud's theory of the unconscious. Repression, for Freud, operates as a ban on forbidden or intolerable impulses—that is, on 'infantile sexuality'. This is the rubric under which the early relationship to mother is conceptualised in Freud's libido theory. It is fair to say, however, that Freud's unconscious 'leaks'—so to speak—into consciousness, in all kinds of ways. It manages to bypass repression by forming substitutes for unconscious ideas (Freud 1915b: 154). Freud describes how an idea or group of ideas may be said to be repressed, whereas the affect attached to it is transferred to some other idea or thing. From this the formation of symptoms or the return of the repressed may follow (Freud 1915b: 154-8). This devious manner, in which the unconscious 'fools' repression does not, however, amount to a free exchange between conscious and unconscious, and contrasts markedly with Hanna Segal's notion of 'non-pathological repression' (Segal 1986: 78-9), and Bion's 'contact barrier'.

Segal envisaged 'non-pathological repression' as operating along a kind of 'permeable membrane', which permits communication between conscious and unconscious and allows symbolisation to take place:

> I want to suggest here that repression used by a healthy ego, well-integrated after working through of the depressive position, is not a pathological process and is not conducive to symptom formation. Indeed, under such normal conditions, the repressive barrier becomes a dynamic layer between the unconscious and the conscious, in which symbol formation occurs. Thus, the unconscious part is not cut off from the conscious but is in a state of constant communication and symbolic working through. This gives richness to our conscious life and leads to sublimation. Pathological repression responsible for symptom formation is qualitatively different. It is based on an earlier split, in which parts of the self are split off and never integrated with the rest. The 'return of the

repressed' described by Freud, is the return of the pathologically repressed. It is a breakthrough of the split off parts of the ego, objects and impulses, still under the sway of psychotic mechanisms, using psychotic concrete thinking and related to reality in a psychotic, magic, omnipotent way. The lifting of the pathological repression involves, therefore, the analysis of psychotic processes, even in the neurotic patient. (Segal 1986: 78-9)

As we have seen, Bion writes in similar vein about the 'contact barrier' which, at the same time, separates yet allows contact between conscious and unconscious, and which also—unlike Freud's repression barrier—allows communication between the two systems, leading to a creative way of responding to the world.

I do not know whether either Bion or Segal appreciated just how different their formulations were from those of Freud. This permeable membrane which both Segal and Bion describe is very different from repression. Freud was describing—first and foremost—that which he saw in his consulting room, and also what he had discovered through his own self-analysis. Consequently he concentrated on the Oedipal drama, and on post-Oedipal psychic structures. In this way, then, Freud, more than any other theorist, accounted for the *cultural* psyche—that is, the way in which culture is acquired through the structuration of the psyche. Freud therefore described a psychic structure which had *as its aim* the repression (rather than the integration) of the early relation to mother. This is a rigid form of suppression which allows—precisely—no 'constant communication'. In this sense, then, Freud was referring to a pathological structure (as Segal describes it), which, however, is regarded as 'normality' in Western culture. In his structural theory of the psyche, he described how the constitution of the Western, rational individual relies not on a gradual working-through of early anxieties, but on a violent elimination of the whole early constellation (cf. Freud 1924). He was describing the emergence of the 'rational' individual from the suppression of the 'creative' individual.

I have examined in previous chapters how Freud rejected the notion of a gradual 'working-through' of the Oedipus complex, but relied instead on the castration complex as a means of bringing about its 'dissolution'. Interestingly enough, however, when he writes about female development he begins to admit the possibility of the Oedipus complex coming to an end through the realisation of the impossibility of the wishes involved (Freud 1924: 178-9). Even so, he did not regard this as a model for a different type of development, but simply as an aberration of the male model, the male model being the cultural 'ideal'.

This 'ideal' relies on a collusion between men and women in order to slay the maternal monster. Prophecy Coles (1994) casts light on this through her interpretation of the myth of Andromeda, which she regards as a parable of the feminine denial of aggression and its projection onto men. The myth recounts Cassiopeia's boast that her daughter, Andromeda, was more beautiful than the daughters of Poseidon, the Nereids. Poseidon is incensed by these remarks, and condemns Andromeda to be tied to a rock and devoured by a sea monster. Perseus sees her plight, falls in love with her, and—using Medusa's head (a symbol of female castration)—succeeds in killing the monster. Coles argues that the destructiveness and hatred entailed within the mother-daughter relationship is projected onto a man, Poseidon, and onto the 'monster' he conjures up, which leaves Andromeda defenceless, passive, and in need of rescue. If it is indeed the case that hatred is here projected onto Poseidon, then it should also be noted how ready Perseus is to collude in this, to rescue the damsel in distress with whom he falls in love precisely because she is so defenceless and in need of a hero.

The collusion between man and woman to slay the maternal monster—and to substitute it with an innocuous, defenceless virgin—establishes a gender division and a psychic organisation based on severe splitting. What is conscious and rational has to be constantly protected from what is unconscious, murderous, and irrational. What is masculine has to be protected from devouring feminine forces, and what is 'acceptably' feminine has to be protected from the devouring maternal monster.

A Reverie of the Future

Is this all that woman can hope for? Indeed, we might ask: is this all that man or humankind can hope for? Can there be 'another space' which is not based on the murder of the mother? What I hope to have achieved here is a description of the reasons for the absence of this space, in the hope that by describing the problem we can approach a resolution.

I think that future generations will continue to struggle for a new mental space which is not predominantly masculine, nor based upon the murder of the mother. For this to happen, however, changes in external conditions are not enough. Today we are witnessing a flourishing of this masculine space, now inhabited by both men and women, and also a female revolution which seeks to abolish the father. Commenting on an article by Jerry Aline Flieger, Jane Temperley suggests that there are 'Father's Daughters', 'Mother's Daughters', and 'Prodigal Daughters'. 'What Flieger did not consider'—she writes—'was the possibility of a feminist who was the daughter of a mother *and* a father, a parental couple—a strange and telling omission' (Temperley 1993: 271).

A space created by the introjection of the parental couple can only arise with the working-through of the Oedipus complex. The current, patriarchal psyche and the masculine space created through the paternal super-ego, are both 'lopsided'. The question arises as to why no working-through of the Oedipus complex has been possible. Why is the Oedipus complex so abruptly and violently interrupted? In other words, how has the castration complex exercised such a strong hold on the psyche?

The very name 'castration complex' reveals its origins in masculine anxiety and defence. The transformation of a universal narcissistic trauma into 'castration complex' narrows down a vision of the human condition and transforms it into an issue concerning the survival of the male. This danger seems fundamental to the boy, who has come into the world out of female flesh, and must separate himself from mother. This is, of course, a universal male dilemma, but the solutions arrived at by different societies may vary considerably. Child rearing practices are thus closely connected with the way the Oedipus complex is—or is not—allowed to flourish, decline, and undergo a 'natural' death—or else, alternatively, allowed to evoke tremendous guilt, persecution, and to suffer a violent death. The terms used by Freud himself in describing the end of the Oedipus complex are in themselves telling: he refers to its 'destruction', and of how 'it is literally smashed to pieces by the shock of threatened castration' (Freud 1925a: 257).

In contrast to this violent death, Melanie Klein saw the outcome of the Oedipus complex as linked to the working-through of the depressive position.

The fact that the depressive position develops gradually explains why, usually, its effect on the infant does not appear in a sudden way. Also we have to keep in mind that while depressive feelings are experienced, the ego simultaneously develops methods of counteracting them. This, in my view, is one of the fundamental differences between the infant who is experiencing anxieties of a psychotic nature and the psychotic adult. (Klein 1952: 80)

The gradual nature of the development of the depressive position, and the simultaneous development of methods for coping with the anxieties it involves, contrasts vividly with the way Freud describes the end of the Oedipus complex. Klein emphasises the gradual working-through of anxiety, the slow work of mourning, and the interplay of progression and regression as aspects of normal development. Freud, on the other hand, seems to be pointing to a radical, violent rupture, to a moment of huge discontinuity due to an excess of persecutory anxiety.

Ronald Britton writes:

The acknowledgement by the child of the parents' relationship with each other unites his psychic world, limiting it to one world shared with his two parents in which different object relationships can exist. The closure of the

Oedipal triangle by the recognition of the link joining the parents provides a limiting boundary for the internal world. It creates what I call a 'triangular space'—i.e. a space bounded by the three persons of the Oedipal situation and all their potential relationships. It includes, therefore, the possibility of being a participant in a relationship and observed by a third person as well as being an observer of a relationship between two people. (Britton 1993: 84)

The creation of this triangular space is inhibited, I have argued, by the sudden and violent manner in which the Oedipus complex comes to an end—not with a whimper but with a bang—by the slaying of the maternal monster. However, there is also the question of early envy, and how this might interfere with the establishment and the working-through of the Oedipus complex. In a late formulation on envy, Klein regarded it a response to frustration:

But whenever he [the infant] is hungry or feels neglected, the child's frustration leads to the phantasy that the milk and love are deliberately withheld from him, or kept by the mother for her benefit. Such suspicions are the basis of envy. It is inherent in the feeling of envy not only that possession is desired, but that there is also a strong urge to spoil other people's enjoyment of the coveted object—an urge which tends to spoil the object itself. If envy is very strong, its spoiling quality results in a disturbed relation to the mother as well as later to other people; it also means that nothing can be fully enjoyed because the desired thing has already been spoiled by envy. (Klein 1959: 254)

The amount of frustration imposed on children in the course of child-rearing practices varies from culture to culture. Western culture has relied heavily on frustration as a pedagogic device, with all its consequent envy and attacks on the mother. Through the separation of work and home, Western culture has also contributed towards the creation of an 'absent father' which—in turn—has facilitated splitting between a frustrating, present mother, and an idealised absent father.

It would be easy to regard the technological era as a new development breaking away from traditional paternal authority, with all its certainties and its strict paternal-masculine morality, in favour of the establishment of the good mother. However, the matricidal psyche is the core of Western culture, and paternal authority is only one way of containing the terror it entails. Paternal authority has created a modicum of space for thinking—the Apollonian space of rationality—but at the expense of perpetuating a dark, repressed world of damaged, 'undead' objects. More importantly, paternal authority has been at the expense of female subjectivity. In this sense technological culture and the idealisation of technology is simply a logical development of a psyche which denies the origin of the individual in the parental couple.

I have argued that at the core of the life of the Western individual lie powerful narcissistic and phallic defences, which deny the parental couple as the source of that life. These defences favour a split in the psyche—between mother and father, masculine and feminine. This split has also been expressed as a breach between mind and body, or mind and matter. The ease with which the dominance of the mind over matter (operative in Western culture since the Ancient Greeks) has been reversed in the twentieth century supports my contention that bringing together these two parts of the psyche is not an easy matter for the Western individual. Although twentieth century physics has overcome the split, this has done very little to influence our culture as a whole. Narcissistic defences ensure that a relationship to God, or the machine, or to material goods is more important than a relationship to another human being.

The slaying of the maternal monster bypasses the experience of loss, and the mourning of the early mother and of early omnipotence. It also ensures the triumph of phallic narcissism. This traumatic loss, turned into a heroic feat, haunts the psyche forever after. It is expressed as a turning away from intimate relationships with people, or else—at times—as an orgy of destruction. I do not need to dwell on the unprecedented dereliction which the twentieth century Western world has unleashed upon the planet. The question I wish to pose, however, is how we might break out from this cycle of destructiveness. How can we mourn the loss of the good self if only the good self can mourn?

Dostoyevsky, in *Crime and Punishment*, poses exactly the same question. Raskolnikov sets out with the idea that killing the old woman is a heroic act. He imagines that he is a hero, a superman, above human morality and compassion. In his almost-delirious mind the old woman is a parasite, 'a louse', scum which he could eliminate just by an act of will. What he does not reckon with, however, is *the loss of himself* through this act—the killing of his good self. After he confesses his crime to Sonya he exclaims: 'Did I really kill the old woman? No, it was myself I killed, not the old woman! I bumped myself off, in one go, for ever!' (Dostoyevsky 1991: 488).

Raskolnikov realises in a flash that without the help of an external good object he is finished. It is in the person of Sonya, a young prostitute with a heart of gold—the 'Holy Sinner', one might say—that Dostoyevsky glimpses the essential goodness, a goodness beyond the morality of a paternal super-ego, which will act as a good external object. What Sonya understands intuitively is that Raskolnikov needed to mourn for his state of mind—his lost self—by acknowledging the devastating consequences his actions had upon his own person. After he has confessed the murder of the two women to Sonya she instructs him:

'Go immediately, this very moment, go and stand at the crossroads, bow down, first kiss the ground that you've desecrated, and then bow to the whole world, to all four points of the compass and tell everyone, out loud: "I have killed!" Then God will send you life again.' (Dostoyevsky 1991: 489)

What Sonya is asking of Raskolnikov is no empty, dramatic gesture. It is not simply asking forgiveness or exposing himself to the world. It is the introduction of a new mode of being, away from a paranoid-schizoid world, in a realm where an acceptance of the devastating consequences of one's own actions is possible, but only with the help of an external good object—in this case Sonya. In this way, a process of mourning—the mourning of the loss of one's own goodness—can take place, and through this a reparative state of mind may arise. We might also recollect, in this connection, Willie Brandt's historic and groundbreaking genuflection in front of the gates of Auschwitz. Through this act Willie Brandt did more for Germany's capacity to mourn and to accept responsibility for the holocaust than all the compensation the State provided to the victims.

Raskolnikov, however, does not understand:

> 'Is it penal servitude you mean, Sonya? Must I give myself up?', he asked blackly.
> 'You must accept suffering and redeem yourself by it, that's what.'
> 'No! I won't go to them, Sonya.'
> 'But how will you live, how will you live? What will keep you alive?' Sonya exclaimed. (Dostoyevsky 1991: 489)

Here Dostoyevsky goes beyond the paternal super-ego as a defence, towards something far more fundamental. He understands the need to face the consequences of one's actions through suffering and mourning. 'How will you live', Sonya asks when Raskolnikov resists, 'what will keep you alive?' Eventually, after considerable time has passed, Raskolnikov confesses his murders to the authorities, because—as Sonya predicted—he is unable to live with the hideous secret without disintegrating. On his way to the police station where he confesses, he remembers Sonya's original exhortation to kneel in the middle of the cross-roads: 'He kneeled in the middle of the square, bowed down to the earth and kissed that dirty earth, with pleasure and happiness. He got up and bowed down a second time' (Dostoyevsky 1991: 602). Passers-by poke fun at him, and this prevents him from uttering the fatal words 'I have committed murder'. But neither this act, nor the confession to the police, nor his ensuing exile to Siberia achieve the transformation of Raskolnikov, even though each is a necessary step. Ultimately it is his relationship with Sonya—a real relationship to an external object, as Klein would put it—which proves decisive. Through this relationship something inside him gradually changes— which he can neither predict nor control. A moment of acknowledgement, a moment of gratitude, and the ability to love is suddenly restored to Raskolnikov:

All of a sudden, Sonya was next to him. She had made her approach almost inaudibly, and had sat down beside him. It was still very early, the chill of morning had not yet relented... she gave him a pleased, friendly smile, but, following her habit, extended her hand to him timidly. This was the way she had always proffered her hand to him— timidly, sometimes not even proffering it at all, as though she were afraid he would refuse it. He had invariably taken her hand with a kind of revulsion, invariably greeted her with something akin to annoyance, on occasion remaining stubbornly silent throughout the entire duration of her visit. Sometimes she had feared him and had gone away in deep sorrow. But now their hands were not disjoined; he gave her a quick, fleeting glance, uttered no word and lowered his gaze to the ground. They were alone; no one could see them. At this moment the guard had his back turned.

How it came to pass he himself did not know, but suddenly it was as though something had snatched at him, and he was hurled to her feet. He wept, and hugged her knees. In that first split second she was afraid, and her whole face froze. She leapt up from where she was sitting and stared at him, trembling. But immediately, in that same instant, she understood everything. Her eyes began to shine with an infinite happiness; she had understood, and now she was in no doubt that he loved her, loved her infinitely, and that at last it had arrived, that moment... (Dostoyevsky 1991: 628-9)

Orestes and Raskolnikov present two very different solutions to the problem of destructiveness. Orestes' flight from the Furies ends in Athens, where the paternal gods—both male and female—pronounce him innocent and take him under their protection. This denial of guilt is not reparation. It is a manic defence and, as such, it does not help either to repair the object or to mourn its loss. It leaves Orestes stranded in the paranoid-schizoid world, whilst employing manic defences to deny this fact. Raskolnikov's journey through hell, on the other hand, ends in a kind of purgatory in Siberia, where we see him slowly working out his salvation, repairing his internal objects with his own suffering. The paranoid world of the creation and destruction of a monster in the shape of the old woman—an expression of his matricidal internal world—gives way, through the help of another woman, to an emergence of a depressive world of guilt, responsibility. Slowly, this leads to hope, and—most importantly—to the restoration of his own capacity to love. This is what Klein has described as the working-through of the depressive position.

We are, as a culture and as a planet, at a critical point in our history, since we now possess the means to destroy ourselves and our environment. More than ever we shall have to rely on our ability to recognise our own destructiveness, and on our ability to restore our own capacity for concern. However, a matricidal culture faces acute difficulties in working-through the depressive position. These difficulties, some of which have been explored in this book, must be recognised and reflected upon, if our faith in life is to be restored.

Notes

1 We must not forget that—for Fairbairn—the mother is the bad object *par excellence*, and is to be discovered under every other bad object, including the father.

2 The working-through of the trauma of the Oedipus complex can sometimes take place through the relationship to a daughter. The father-daughter relationship, so important for the daughter's road to femininity, is also vital for the father's working-through of his own persecutory anxiety. This theme is explored below, in Chapters 8 and 9.

3 In holding this opinion I diverge from the views of Bion (1967) and Hinshelwood (1997), who maintain a radical distinction between repression and projective identification.

4 In Francis Ford Coppola's cinematic re-interpretation, *Bram Stoker's Dracula* (1992), Count Dracula—like the infant—suffers a double trauma: firstly the loss (through suicide) of his beloved; and secondly, the refusal of the Church to lay her to rest with a Christian burial.

5 I am referring her to the version of the tale presented in Belá Bartók's opera *Duke Bluebeard's Castle*.

6 Klein refers to 'reparation' as the main mechanism by which the depressive position is worked through. Attacks on the object, which in the paranoid-schizoid position led to fears of retaliation by the object, have a different effect on the child once some integration between the good and bad object has been achieved. In the event of this (which signals the *beginning* of the depressive position) the child fears damage to and loss of the good object as a consequence of his own attacks. Making reparation to the object is, therefore, the basic route to restoring the object and also—through identification with it—to restoring the good self. However, if aggression and (therefore) guilt are too strong, the child finds it difficult to make reparation to the object. He might then follow one of several routes, 'manic reparation' being among them. Manic reparation refers to a particular kind of failure of reparation, which bypasses pain, mourning, and guilt, and magically restores the object.

7 In the first act of the opera Don Giovanni attempts to seduce Donna Anna, a respectable woman who refuses to succumb to his charm. When Donna Anna's father comes to her defence, Don Giovanni fights against him and kills him. In the final act of the play Don Giovanni accepts an invitation to dinner from the dead man, certain, in his delusion of omnipotence, that he can deal with him. Finally, however, Don Giovanni is dragged down into the underworld by Donna Anna's father.

8 Both, of course, finally find redemption, but this does not detract from my argument concerning the essentially *deathly* quality of the Western road to masculinity. It is a sign of Goethe's genius that he described this deathly quality, yet also attempted a final integration of the life and death instincts.

9 We can speculate here about Anette's parents' relationship with their own parents, and their sense of womanhood and manhood. Indeed there is some evidence that the mother's female line had 'ignored' men, pretending that women reproduced themselves from generation to generation. This 'elimination' of men, which promotes an illusion of parthenogenesis, creates above all an oppressive female world

in which the girl feels suffocated by mother. This can lead to matricide according to the model of Clytemnestra-Electra, as outlined in the Chapter 1.

[10] Freud stresses instead the girl's turning away from femininity and espousal of masculinity. I think, however, that from an object-relations perspective both amount to the same thing.

[11] Karen Horney regarded this attribution of 'castration' to the girl as a projection by the boy (Horney 1973). However, this interpretation avoids the question of the girl's own phantasy that she lacks any genitals, apart from what she regards as a minuscule penis, her clitoris.

[12] Klein agrees with Helene Deutsch's view that 'the vagina takes on the passive role of the sucking mouth' in a footnote to her paper, 'The Effects of Early Anxiety Situations on the Sexual Development of the Girl' (Klein 1932b: 196). In another part of the same paper, she refers to the girl's phantasy of the vagina as a mouth or anus (Klein 1932b: 210).

[13] When Klein introduced the term 'projective identification' in her paper 'Notes on Some Schizoid Mechanisms' (1946) she was referring to a particular object relation in which the subject expels unwanted parts of the self and projects them into the object—another person—with the dual intention of getting rid of the unwanted parts and of controlling the object.

[14] See Klein 1928, 1932a; Stoller 1968; Greenson 1993.

[15] The difficulty Freud had in relinquishing the role of the father and recognising the mother transference can be seen in his treatment of Dora (Freud 1905a).

[16] Indeed, the analogy with Minoan-Mycenean civilisation is doubly apt on this point, since it was a civilisation in which women were very prominent.

[17] See also Freud 1921: 101, n2; 1930: 113.

[18] This phenomenon had already been observed by Freud. In 'Female Sexuality' (1931) he found himself forced to admit that the positive Oedipus complex, which presupposes love for the parent of the opposite sex and hate for the parent of the same sex, 'applies with complete strictness to the male child only' (Freud 1931: 228-9). Freud rejected Jung's 'Electra complex', which postulated an exact parallelism between male and female development, precisely because he recognised that the little girl remained attached to mother well into the Oedipus complex.

[19] Lacan borrowed the term 'symbolic order' from the anthropologist Claude Lévi-Strauss. The 'symbolic' is one of three essential orders, the others being the 'imaginary' and the 'real', According to Laplanche and Pontalis: 'The Symbolic covers those phenomena with which psycho-analysis deals in so far as they are structured like a language. The terms also refers to the idea that the effectiveness of the cure is based on the constitutive nature of the Word' (Laplanche & Pontalis 1988: 439).

[20] 'Disillusionment' refers to the gradual ending of the baby's first relationship to mother, during which her near-perfect adaptation to the baby's needs creates the illusion that the breast belongs to him. The good enough mother gradually *disillusions* the baby by adapting appropriately to the growing baby's needs and introducing more frustrations. In Winnicott's model, the emphasis is on the mother's role. In Klein's theory—on the other hand—the emphasis is on the way the baby *mourns* the loss of the breast, as he begins to realise that the breast does not belong to him but to his mother, and that he has no control over it. Both theories refer to the same

psychical event—the relinquishment of omnipotence—but with the emphasis on different processes.

21 For Freud, the girl's equation in the unconscious of 'penis' and 'baby' is due to her frustrated wish to acquire a penis of her own. However, Freud himself made no distinction between the terms 'penis' and 'phallus'. The girl's narcissistic fulfilment is at issue, in which case the term 'phallus' seems more appropriate in this context. Later writers—most notably Jessica Benjamin—have interpreted the girl's wish for a phallus as an attempt to separate herself from her mother.

22 This version of the story—by the Brothers Grimm—is perhaps less well known, but nevertheless extremely interesting. It relates how Cinderella's father travels to a fair, after asking his three daughters what they would like him to bring back for them. The two elder daughters request beautiful clothes and pearls, whilst Cinderella asks for the first twig which brushes against his hat on his return trip. Her father does as she asks and Cinderella plants the twig on her mother's grave, where it grows into a large tree (Grimm 1982).

23 The theme of the girl's subjection to her father is explored below, in Chapter 9. At this point, however, I will simply remind the reader that Freud regarded the transfer of the girl's libido from mother to father as accompanied by a renunciation of the girl's active sexuality, and the espousal of a passive attitude towards him. The girl's identification with father is crucial, because it enables the girl to separate from mother yet prevents her from entering into a *totally* passive relationship to father.

24 This myth concerns the story of Persephone, the daughter of Demeter (who was the goddess of agriculture and fertility). Persephone was abducted by Pluto, King of the Underworld, and taken to Hades to become his wife and queen. Demeter's reaction was extreme mourning and rage. As a consequence the earth was plunged into eternal winter and became permanently infertile. Zeus, seeing the famine and misery to which humankind was subjected, implored Demeter to take pity. A compromise was reached whereby Persephone would spend some time with her mother on earth—during which the land would be productive and fertile—and some with Pluto in the Underworld, when winter would descend. This myth portrays beautifully the impossibility of the separation between mother and daughter. At best— with the intervention of the father (Zeus)—a compromise and partial separation may be attained. Here, unlike the myth of Clytemnestra and Electra, there is no hint of hatred.

25 The theme of father as a 'second chance' is explored below, in Chapter 8.

26 Kohut defines 'compensatory structures' as those psychic structures which have developed not merely as a defence, but as a way of compensating for some deficiency. He therefore differentiates these from what he calls 'defensive structures' He writes: 'I call a structure defensive when its sole or predominant function is the covering over of the primary defect in the self. I call a structure compensatory when, rather than merely covering a defect of the self, it compensates for this defect' (Kohut 1984: 3).

27 Kohut uses the term 'transmuting internalisation' to denote internalisation which leads to the formation of internal structure. Kohut sees this type of internalisation as happening early in life. It is related to the internalisation of *aspects* or *functions* of the idealised parent, rather than of the whole person—which is something that occurs at the later, Oedipal stage. The consequence of these internalisations is that the child itself comes to possess those qualities identified in the parent. However, this comes

about only if there are small 'failures' on the part of the parent with respect to these qualities—'failures' which are non-traumatic and phase-appropriate, so that the child can deal with them by internalising the functions of the parent which have 'failed'. 'Transmuting internalisation', then, leads to the formation of the very 'fabric of the ego', as Kohut put it, and creates structures which can control and regulate the drives, and provide a basic management of anxiety (Kohut 1971: 47-8).

28 For Winnicott the 'True Self' is the source of the 'spontaneous gesture' and of creativity and love of life (Winnicott 1960a).

29 Freud distinguished between two basic types of object choice, the narcissistic and the anaclitic. He wrote:

'A person may love:-
(1) According to the narcissistic type:
    (a) what he himself is (i.e. himself),
    (b) what he himself was,
    (c) what he himself would like to be,
    (d) someone who was once part of himself

(2) According to the anaclitic (attachment) type:
    (a) the woman who feeds him
    (b) the man who protects him...' (Freud 1914: 90)

30 The sons of Oedipus—Eteocles and Polynices—became embroiled in a deadly war against one another over the throne of Thebes. The elder son, Polynices, became king of Thebes after the fall of Oedipus, and had his father driven from the city. Eventually, however, Polynices was overthrown by his brother (with the help of Creon), and took refuge in Corinth, where he married and raised an army in order to attack Thebes and regain the throne. However, as Polynices was preparing to attack, the oracle prophesied that the side which Oedipus joined would win the war. Oedipus, who was—until this point—cursed and banned from Thebes by his sons and by Creon, was now wanted urgently by both sides. Firstly, Creon tried to win him over or take him by force, and then Polynices made the attempt. Oedipus, however, understood that their advances—despite appearances—had nothing to do with love or forgiveness, but everything to do with winning the war.

31 Sophocles' play Antigone (Sophocles 1982) is set after the battle between the sons of Oedipus. Both Eteocles and Polynices are dead, and Creon is the ruler of Thebes. Creon decrees that Eteocles is buried with full military honours, whereas Polynices is left for the vultures, unburied, unmourned, and without funeral rites. The penalty for disobeying Creon's decree is death. Antigone, obeying a higher moral law, rebels and attempts to bury her brother. She pays for this with her life. Antigone has since become a symbol of resistance against tyranny and tyrannical laws.

32 Marie's relationship to her mother should not be ignored, as this manner of defence is certain to have started there. Her relationship to her mother was fraught with difficulties and was wholly unsatisfactory (see chapter 7). There is no doubt that had her relationship to her mother been otherwise, the outcome of her relationship to her father would also have been different. Her primitive phantasies concerning masculinity and femininity might have had less of a hold upon her, and would not have led Marie to repress and deny her first identification with her mother. However, it is also true that had her relationship with father been different, some

of the anxieties and phantasies stemming from her relationship with her mother might have been worked-through.

[33] See, for instance, Chodorow 1978; Dinnerstein 1976; Rich 1979; Eichenbaum & Orbach 1982, 1983b; Herman 1989; Mens-Verlhulst et al. 1993, among many, many others.

[34] It should be noted that this quotation from Winnicott does not appear in a gender-specific context.

[35] I am aware that Winnicott did not use the term 'narcissism' but referred instead to 'the baby's omnipotence' and the 'subjective object' (cf. Winnicott 1971: 45, 102, 106, 108). The contrast is—therefore—between a subjective object, and an object that lies outside the baby's omnipotence.

[36] I am here accepting Klein's position, who regarded womb-envy and the 'femininity-phase' as fundamental in the development of the boy (Klein 1975a: 189-91).

[37] Luce Irigaray maintains that there is, in fact, no notion of difference in Western culture. She refers to this as 'the economy of the same', and describes how Freud expressed this in his theory of female sexuality: 'In fact, this sexuality is never defined with respect to any sex but the masculine. Freud does not see *two* sexes whose differences are articulated in the act of intercourse, and more generally speaking, in the imaginary and the symbolic processes that regulate the workings of a society and culture' (Irigaray 1985: 69).

[38] Freud's views on the convergence between masculinity and activity, femininity and passivity, are very complex. In *Three Essays on the Theory of Sexuality* (Freud 1905b: 219-20, n1) he distinguishes between three meanings of the terms 'masculinity' and 'femininity'. The first if these is the equation of masculinity with activity, and of femininity with passivity. The second and third meanings concern the biological and sociological significance of the terms. Freud concludes that the most useful of these definitions —from the perspective of psychoanalysis—is the first one, although he acknowledges that each individual possesses both trends within him or herself. In 'The Infantile Genital Organisation' (1923c) Freud unequivocally equates maleness with activity and femaleness with passivity, as regards the final stage of the development of sexuality (Freud 1923c: 145). However, in his later lecture 'Femininity' (1933) he appears to retract this, and expresses uncertainty as to whether this formulation is useful after all. He concludes: 'One might consider characterising femininity psychologically as giving preference to passive aims. This is not, of course, the same thing as passivity; to achieve a passive aim may call for a large amount of activity' (Freud 1933: 115). Winnicott adopts an altogether different formulation which equates maleness with 'doing', and femaleness with 'being'. Aggression—and activity in general—is, of course, a form of 'doing'.

[39] A crucial question here is whether the woman therapist has worked through her own destructive aggression, or whether—if not—a collusion is then established between therapist and female patient which leads to a denial of destructiveness. One might also wonder about the ability of male analysts to tolerate female destructiveness.

[40] The reason for this is discussed below, in Chapter 12.

[41] The question whether this perception is a projection of the patient's own dependency is an important issue, but one which I cannot enter into here. From the clinical point of view, however, it is *always* a projection.

[42] Klein regarded primary splitting as necessary for the structuration of the psyche (see Klein 1957: 191-2; 1958: 242)—as did Fairbairn (1944) and Meltzer (1964). Failure to achieve this may lead to psychotic illness.

[43] Occupation of this 'third space' facilitates the experience of being a subject observing an object; of being an object observed by another object; and of being outside the relationship between subject and object and observing the relationship itself. A 'pseudo third space', on the other hand, entails being only an observer of a dead interaction between two objects.

[44] I expand on this point in Chapter 12, below.

[45] The fable concerns some porcupines huddled together for warmth. The problem, however, is that if they get too close to each other, they prick one another. But, if they move too far apart then they freeze. The art lies in them finding an optimal position which is neither too painful nor too cold.

[46] See Chapter 7, above, in which Marie's relationship with her father is explored in more detail.

[47] Kohut regards the father as capable of offering a second chance to the child whose mother has failed him or her. A relationship with an 'idealised father', who compensates for maternal failure, can lead to the creation of what Kohut described as 'compensatory structures'. These often include the development of talents and skills, and should be differentiated from 'defensive structures' (see Kohut 1984: 10, 63, 105).

[48] In 'domination of the therapist' I include the idealisation of him or her, although I am aware that Kohut did not include idealisation as part of a merger transference.

[49] For Bion, 'bizarre objects' are the result of a minute fragmentation of the object so that it loses all cohesiveness and life. These fragments are then expelled into the outside world where they become persecutory. This is a psychotic defence aimed at freeing the individual of a hostile object inside him or herself, but it creates instead a bizarre and hostile external world (cf. Bion 1967: 50, 81-2).

[50] For instance, in *About Chinese Women*, Kristeva asserts: 'Through language, the Oedipal phase introduces the symbolic agency, the prohibition of auto-eroticism and the recognition of the paternal function' (Kristeva 1986: 148). On Lacan, Elizabeth Grosz writes: 'The "Law of the Father" as Lacan sees it, is the threshold between the "Kingdom of culture" and "that of nature abandoned to the law of copulation"' (Grosz 1991: 70).

[51] This is not Freud's conclusion, but my own.

[52] I am referring here to the social taboo on representing mother *as a subject and agent*. Instead, mother is represented from the point of view of the child's omnipotence, or from the point of view of the father's omnipotence. This is the Christian viewpoint of Virgin Mary, the only representation of motherhood which has been possible within the Christian culture. In this view of motherhood we see idealisation and the denial of maternal power at work, both deriving from the fear of mother.

Bibliography

Aeschylus (1986) *The Oresteian Trilogy*, Harmondsworth: Penguin.

Balint, M. (1979) *The Basic Fault: Therapeutic Aspects of Regression*, London: Routledge.

Benjamin, J. (1990a) *The Bonds of Love*, London: Virago.

Benjamin, J. (1990b) 'The Alienation of Desire: Women's Masochism and Ideal Love', in *Essential Papers on the Psychology of Women*, ed. C. Zanardi, New York & London: New York University Press.

Bettelheim, B. (1978) *The Uses of Enchantment*, Harmondsworth: Penguin.

Bion, W.R. (1962) *Learning from Experience*, London: Karnac.

Bion, W.R. (1967) *Second Thoughts*, London: Karnac.

Britton, R. (1993) 'The Missing Link: Parental Sexuality and the Oedipus Complex', in *The Gender Conundrum: Contemporary Psychoanalytic Perspectives on Femininity and Masculinity*, ed. D. Breen, London: Routledge.

Bronte, C. (1996) *Jane Eyre*, Harmondsworth: Penguin.

Brown, N. (1959) *Life Against Death*, Middletown CT: Wesleyan University Press.

Coles, P. (1994) 'The myth of Andromeda: an aspect of female sexuality', *Free Associations* 31.

Chasseguet-Smirgel, J. (1962) 'Feminine Guilt and the Oedipus Complex', in Chasseguet-Smirgel et al. 1985.

Chasseguet-Smirgel, J. et al., eds. (1985) *Female Sexuality*, London: Maresfield Reprints.

Chasseguet-Smirgel, J. (1986) *Sexuality and Mind*, New York & London: New York University Press.

Chodorow, N. (1978) *The Reproduction of Mothering*, California: University of California Press.

Dinnerstein, D. (1976) *The Rocking of the Cradle and the Ruling of the World*, London: The Women's Press.

Dostoyevsky, F. (1991) *Crime and Punishment*, Harmondsworth: Penguin.

Eichenbaum, L., & Orbach, S. (1982) *Outside In, Inside Out*, Harmondsworth: Penguin.

Eichenbaum, L., & Orbach, S. (1983a) *What Do Women Want?*, London: Fontana.

Eichenbaum, L., & Orbach, S. (1983b) *Understanding Women*, Harmondsworth: Penguin.

Fairbairn, W.R.D. (1943) 'The Repression and the Return of Bad Objects (With a Special Reference to the War Neuroses)', in Fairbairn 1952.

Fairbairn, W.R.D. (1944) 'Endopsychic Structure Considered in Terms of Object-Relationships', in Fairbairn 1952.

Fairbairn, W.R.D. (1952) *Psychoanalytic Studies of the Personality*, London: Routledge.

Figlio, K. (1995) 'Psychoanalysis and Freedom', paper presented at the Guildford Psychotherapy Centre, 1st April.

Freud, S. (1905a) 'Fragment of an Analysis of a Case of Hysteria', S.E. VII: 1-122.

Freud, S. (1905b) *Three Essays on the Theory of Sexuality*, S.E. VII: 123-245.

Freud, S. (1910a) 'A Special Type of Choice of Object Made by Men', S.E. XI: 163-175.

Freud, S. (1910b) *Leonardo da Vinci and a Memory of is Childhood*, S.E. XI: 57-137.

Freud, S. (1912) 'On the Universal Tendency to Debasement in the Sphere of Love', S.E. XI: 177-190.

Freud, S. (1913) *Totem and Taboo*, S.E. XIII: 1-161.

Freud, S. (1914) 'On Narcissism: an Introduction', S.E. XIV: 67-102.

Freud, S. (1915a) 'The Unconscious', S.E. XIV: 159-215.

Freud, S. (1915b) 'Repression', S.E. XIV: 141-158.

Freud, S. (1917) 'Mourning and Melancholia', S.E. XIV: 237-258.

Freud, S. (1918) 'The Taboo of Virginity', S.E. XI: 191-208.

Freud, S. (1919a) 'The "Uncanny"', S.E. XVII: 217-252.

Freud, S. (1919b) 'A Child is Being Beaten', S.E. XVII: 175-204.

Freud, S. (1921) *Group Psychology and the Analysis of the Ego*, S.E. XVIII: 65-143.

Freud, S. (1923a) 'A Seventeenth-Century Demonological Neurosis', S.E. XIX: 67-105.

Freud, S. (1923b) *The Ego and the Id*, S.E. XIX: 1-66.

Freud, S. (1923c) 'The Infantile Genital Organisation', S.E. XIX: 139-145.

Freud, S. (1924) 'The Dissolution of the Oedipus Complex', S.E. XIX: 171-179.

Freud, S. (1925a) 'Some Psychical Consequences of the Anatomical Distinction Between the Sexes', S.E. XIX: 241-258.

Freud, S. (1925b) 'Negation', S.E. XIX: 233-239.

Freud, S. (1930) *Civilization and its Discontents*, S.E. XXI: 57-145.

Freud, S. (1931) 'Female Sexuality', S.E. XXI: 221-243.

Freud, S. (1933) *New Introductory Lectures on Psychoanalysis*, S.E. XXII: 1-182.

Freud, S. (1937) 'Analysis Terminable and Interminable', S.E. XXIII: 211-253.

Goethe, J.W. (1949) *Faust—Part One*, trans. P. Wayne, Harmondsworth: Penguin.

Greenson, R. (1993) 'Dis-Identifying from Mother: Its Special Importance for the Boy', in *The Gender Conundrum*, ed. D. Breen, London & New York: Routledge.

Grosz, E. (1991) *Jacques Lacan: a Feminist Introduction*, London & New York: Routledge.

Grimm, J. & Grimm, W. (1982) *Fairy Tales*, trans. D. Luke, Harmondsworth: Penguin.

Grunberger, B. (1989) 'The Monad', in *New Papers on Narcissism*, ed. and trans. D. Macey, London: Free Associations.

Grunberger, B. (1990) *Narcissism*, trans. J.S. Dimanti, Madison CT: International Universities Press.

Herman, N. (1989) *Too Long a Child*, London: Free Association Books.

Hinshelwood, R. (1997) *Therapy or Coercion? Does Psychoanalysis Differ From Brainwashing*, London: Karnac Books.

Homer (1946) *The Odyssey*, trans. E.V. Rieu, Harmondsworth: Penguin.

Horney, K. (1973) *Feminine Psychology*, New York & London: Norton.

Irigaray, L. (1985) *This Sex Which is Not One*, trans. C. Potter with C. Burke, Ithaca NY: Cornell University Press.

Irigaray, L. (1991) *The Irigaray Reader*, ed. M. Whitford, Oxford: Blackwell.

Jones, E. (1948a) 'The Phallic Phase', in *Papers on Psycho-Analysis*, London: Maresfield.

Jones, E. (1948b) 'Early Female Sexuality', in *Papers on Psycho-Analysis*, London: Maresfield.

Jung, C.G. (1913) 'The Theory of Psychoanalysis', in *Collected Works*, vol. 4, London: Routledge & Kegan Paul.

Klein, M. (1928) 'Early Stages of the Oedipus Complex', in Klein 1975a.

Klein, M. (1932a) 'The Effects of Early Anxiety-Situations on the Sexual Development of the Boy', in Klein 1975b.

Klein, M. (1932b) 'The Effects of Early Anxiety Situations on the Sexual Development of the Girl', in 1975b.

Klein, M. (1946) 'Notes on Some Schizoid Mechanisms', in Klein 1975c.

Klein, M. (1948) 'On the Theory of Anxiety and Guilt', in Klein 1975c.

Klein, M. (1952) 'Some Theoretical Conclusions Regarding the Emotional Life of the Infant', in Klein 1975c.

Klein, M. (1955) 'On Identification', in Klein 1975c.

Klein, M. (1957) 'Envy and Gratitude', in Klein 1975c.

Klein, M. (1958) 'On the Development of Mental Functioning', in Klein 1975c.

Klein, M. (1959) 'Our Adult World and Its Roots in Infancy', in Klein 1975c.

Klein, M. (1975a) *Love, Guilt and Reparation, and Other Works*, London: Hogarth Press.

Klein, M. (1975b) *The Psycho-Analysis of Children*, London: Hogarth Press.

Klein, M. (1975c) *Envy and Gratitude and Other Works*, London: Hogarth Press.

Kohut, H. (1971) *The Analysis of the Self*, Maddison CT: International Universities Press.

Kohut, H. (1984) *The Restoration of the Self*, New York: International Universities Press.

Kristeva, J. (1986) *The Kristeva Reader*, ed. T. Moi, Oxford: Blackwell.

Kristeva, J. (1989) *Black Sun*, New York: Columbia University Press.

Kristeva, J. (1990) *The Kristeva Reader*, ed. J. Lechte, London & New York: Routledge.

Kundera, M. (1985) *The Unbearable Lightness of Being*, London: Faber and Faber.

Langs, R. (1988) *A Primer of Psychotherapy*, New York & London: Gardner Press.

Laplanche, J., & Pontalis, J.-B. (1988) *The Language of Psychoanalysis*, London: Karnac.

Lemoine-Luccione, E. (1976) The Dividing of Women or Woman's Lot, London: Free Association Books.

Lykke, N. (1993) 'Little Red Riding Hood, Antigone, and the Oedipus Complex', in *Daughtering and Mothering*, ed. J. van Mens-Verhulst et al., London & New York: Routledge.

Mahler, M., et al. (1975) *The Psychological Birth of the Human Infant*, London: Maresfield Library.

Meltzer, D. (1964) *Sexual States of Mind*, Perthshire: Clunie Press.

Mens-Verhulst, J. van, Schreurs, K., & Woertman, L., eds. (1993) *Daughtering and Mothering: Female Subjectivity Reanalysed*, London & New York: Routledge.

Mitchell, J. (1975) *Psychoanalysis and Feminism*, London: Pelican.

Parker, R. (1995) *Torn in Two*, London: Virago.

Perrault, C. (1970) *Fairy Tales*, London: Dover Publications.

Piontelli, A. (1992) *From Fetus to Child: an Observational and Psychoanalytic Study*, London & New York: Routledge.

Plato (1951) *The Symposium*, trans. W. Hamilton, Harmondsworth: Penguin.

Raphael-Leff, J. (1993) *Pregnancy: The Inside Story*, London: Sheldon Press.

Rich, A. (1979) *Of Woman Born*, London: Virago.

Rosenfeld, H. (1987) *Impasse and Interpretation*, London & New York: Routledge.

Searles, H. (1986) *Collected Papers on Schizophrenia and Related Subjects*, London: Maresfield Library.

Segal, H. (1986) *Delusion and Artistic Creativity and Other Psychoanalytic Essays*, London: Free Association Books.

Sophocles (1982), *The Three Theban Plays*, trans. R. Fagles, Harmondsworth: Penguin.

Steiner, J. (1993) *Psychic Retreats: Psychological Organisations in Psychotic, Neurotic and Borderline Patients*, London: Routledge.

Stoker, B. (1983) *Dracula*, Harmondsworth: Penguin.

Stoller, R. (1968) *Sex and Gender*, London: Maresfield.

Temperley, J. (1993) 'Is the Oedipus Complex bad news for women?', *Free Associations* 30.

Torok, M. (1964) 'The Significance of Penis Envy in Women', in Chasseguet-Smirgel 1985.

Welldon, E. (1988) *Mother, Madonna, Whore: The Idealisation and Denigration of Motherhood*, London: Free Association Books.

Wilde, O. (1949) 'The Ballad of Reading Gaol', in *The Works of Oscar Wilde*, London & Glasgow: Collins.

Winnicott, D.W. (1951) 'Transitional Objects and Transitional Phenomena', in Winnicott 1958.

Winnicott, D.W. (1958) *Through Paediatrics to Psycho-Analysis*, London: Hogarth Press.

Winnicott, D.W. (1960a) 'Ego Distortion in Terms of True and False Self', in Winnicott 1965.

Winnicott, D.W. (1960b) 'The Theory of the Parent-Infant Relationship', in Winnicott 1965.

Winnicott, D.W. (1965) *The Maturational Processes and the Facilitating Environment*, London: Hogarth Press.

Winnicott, D.W. (1971) *Playing and Reality*, Harmondsworth: Penguin.

Index

abject, the 208-9
absence 24
Aegisthus 37
Aeschylus 10
Agamemnon 36, 43, 85, 215, 216
aggression 65, 174, 179, 180, 181, 182, 187, 190
agoraphobia 81
alienation 11
aliens 98
alpha function 211-12
ambivalence 51, 107, 111, 136, 141, 185, 186
anal phase 34
Andromeda 224
anger 140
anti-libidinal ego 58
Antigone 63, 136, 160, 163, 166-7
anus 92
anxiety 100, 101, 124, 190
    castration 66
    infantile 48
    persecutory 56, 157, 209
    primitive 47-8
    repression 59
Apollo 37, 38, 39, 42, 220
Ariadne 114
Aristophanes 31, 33, 34, 41
Athene 28, 38, 39, 40, 85, 220, 221
Atreus 37

baby 25, 89, 117-18, 174-5, 180-81, 199
Balint, M. 189
Beauty and the Beast 63, 162-3
Benjamin, J. 77, 81, 94, 103, 121, 122, 123, 141-2, 156-7
beta-elements 24, 212-13
Bettelheim, B. 164
Bion, W.R. 24-6, 173, 211-12, 222, 223
bisexuality 53, 90
blindness 63, 167
Bluebeard's Castle 62-3, 159
boy
    adolescent 62
    love for parents 66
    psyche 66
    relationship to father 52, 56, 67, 77, 80, 123-4

    relationship to mother 51-2, 56, 90, 91, 106
Brandt, W. 230
breast 25, 33, 35, 100, 174
British School of Object Relations 48
Britton, R. 226-7
Bronte, Charlotte 63
Brown, N.O. 68, 74

Calypso 168
case histories
    Anette 197-201
    Danny 46-7, 77-80
    Jim 46
    Marie 82-3, 148-52, 169-71, 192-7, 198
    Marina 152-4
    Mary 127-31, 132-5
    Monica 144-7
    Sylvia 203-4
Cassandra 37
Cassiopeia 224
castration 33, 87, 178, 190
    symbolic 63-4
castration complex 50, 52-3, 56, 57, 59, 60, 92, 225
Charybdis 168
Chasseguet-Smirgel, J. 88, 139, 156, 190, 214
child
    and mother 34-5
    relation to parents 50-51
    separations 33
child rearing 226, 227
childlessness 96
children, doubts about having 136
Chodorow, N. 105-8, 112, 191
Christianity 17, 137, 176, 177
Cinderella 102, 103, 119, 121, 124
Circe 168
claustrophobia 81
clitoris 87, 88, 89, 90
Clytemnestra 85, 215
    Agamemnon 43, 216
    Electra 119
    murder of 10, 21, 27, 36-40, 220
Coles, P. 224
collusion 112, 141, 167, 176, 224